They Call Me Stein on Vine

By Gary Chen

THEY CALL ME STEIN ON VINE

Published by Gary Chen through CreateSpace

For further information please contact:
Gary Chen <gchen703@sbcglobal.net>

Or go to the website:
http://www.steinonvine.com

First published in 2014 by Gary Chen
Revised edition April 2015

Copyright © Gary Chen 2012

Copyright Registration Number TXu-1-861-738

Illustrations and photographs copyright © Gary Chen

Edited by Richard Ratner and Larry Rott

Cover by David Escobar

All Rights Reserved

Photographs courtesy of the author and by permission

ISBN 1495281418
ISBN-13: 978-1495281419

Table of Contents

INTRODUCTION 7
I: KID IN TAIWAN 9
   My First Guitar and Brother Charlie 19
   Learning English and Jazz Through Songs, Movies and TV Shows 22
II: COLLEGE 29
   Bull Camp In the "Victory Hills" 29
   NCSB (North Country Street Band) 33
   8/7 Water Disasters 37
III: COMING TO AMERICA 41
   BOSTON 42
IV: DETOUR FROM MY RETURN TO TAIWAN 49
V: STEIN ON VINE 53
   M. K. Stein 53
   Maury and Jule 55
   Lynn 63
   Early Days at Stein on Vine 71
   Maury Stein in the Studio 75
   A "Mensch" that Loved Animals 79
   Maury's cockatiels 80
   More M. K. Stein 82
VI: SOME OF MAURY'S FRIENDS 89
   Bill Berry 89
   Joe Bushkin 90
   Pete and Conte Candoli 90
   Al Cohn 95
   Benny Goodman 96
   Johnny Guerin 93
   Richie Kamuka 99
   Johnny Mandel 100
   Don Menza 102
   Red Mitchell 105

Gerry Mulligan 107
Chuck Piscatello 108
Nelson Riddle 109
Jimmy Rowles 110
George Mraz 111
Fred Selden 112
Bud Shank 113
Zoot Sims 114
Connie Stevens 116
Sonny Stitt 117
Sir Charles Thompson 119
Mel Tormé 120
The French horn players 122

VII: MAURY'S DEATH 125
Chinese fortuneteller 135

VIII: MEMORABLE STORIES FROM THE STORE 137
Stein on Vine logo 137
Keith Johnson 141
Old man's Shoe 144
Mike Milan 145
William Claxton and Herman Leonard 149
Frank Rosolino and Carl Fontana 150

IX: SOME OF MY DEAR FRIENDS AFTER THE MAURY ERA
.... 153
Chuck Berghofer 153
Ray Brown 155
Monty Budwig 165
Cachao 168
Pete Candoli 170
Benny Carter 174
John Clayton 176
John Collins 179
Eric Von Essen 180
Stan Getz 181
Eddie Harris 198
John Heard 201
Freddie Hubbard 203
Harold Land 206
James Leary 208
Jennifer Leitham 210

    Lou Levy (Label) 212
    Stan Levey 230
    Warne Marsh 231
    Al McKibbon 232
    Rudy Regalado 247
    Wayne Shorter 257
    Horace Silver 261
    Cedar Walton 264

X: MY FATHER 269

XI: MY FIRST VISIT HOME 275
    Stan Lai 281

XII: MY WIFE 285

XIII: MOM'S DEATH 290

XIV: CONCLUSION 296

Acknowledgements 297

INDEX 299

This is a picture of Maury Stein and me. It's the only picture we took together in 7 years. Maury was my so-called Jewish father who changed my life by giving me not only this most incredible ride, but also the opportunity to be who I am.

INTRODUCTION

Here's the story:

Today is December 11th, 2010. In a few weeks, this year will be history. For the past 30 odd years, this has been a joyful time for most of us. I am not a holiday kind of guy but I still enjoy seeing people happy and love the atmosphere that I normally feel in the air.

But this year is different! Everybody is struggling because of a brutal recession. The air is full of sadness. So many businesses went down; so many people lost their jobs and their homes. I'm sitting here in my store, the famous "Stein on Vine", wondering what the future holds for this so-called "Jazz Music Landmark", the only real old-time jazz music store left. Am I going to be just another once-upon-a-time memory? Is Jazz (the only true American art form that is recognized and respected by the rest of the world) always going to be just for the small percentage of people here in America?

Thinking about my life, what has happened for the last 50 some years, all the people that I have met, and all the things that I've experienced.

WOW!

Mom and Dad

Mom

1: KID IN TAIWAN

I was born in Taipei, Taiwan on June 30th, 1952, the Year of Dragon. Some people say that's "The Dragon", not the dragon head or dragon tail because June 30th is the center of the year (whatever that means). Dragon is supposedly "The Sign" that every parent wants their child to be, because Dragon symbolizes power, prosperity, and fortune. Plus, in the old days, only the Emperors could wear yellow silk robe with the golden dragon design embroidered on the chest (the prime ministers wore a deep purple robe with an Anaconda design). Personally, I was never a superstitious kind of guy - dragon or not, it's all bullshit to me!

My Dad was working for President Chiang Kai-shek when I was born. He was very busy and very seldom home. I remember that Mom told me she had to pack a little bag and walk by herself to The Grass Mountain Hospital around midnight to deliver me. My Mom is the most considerate, most kind-hearted, most wonderful human being you could ever imagine (I'm not saying that because she's my Mom), and even she said it was kind of sad! All of us brothers and sisters just love her to death and so does everyone else who knows her.

Dad was a very distinguished-looking man and a very sharp dresser. He also looked very serious. It probably had something to do with working for the "Pres". I remember this one old picture with my entire family in it. I was about 2 years old. We were standing by Sun-Moon Lake (one of the most famous scenic places in Taiwan). Mom was holding my baby sister Tina and me. Dad was in his uniform and had a pair of shades on and a revolver on his belt, looking real cool. I don't remember this but Mom told me that when I was very little, I was so afraid of Dad that I would hide underneath the table when I heard his car pulling into the driveway. Now that's sad!

Mom married Dad when she was 19. They were both from Beijing but Mom said she grew up in Shanghai. I never asked how or where they met or anything about their lives together prior to my existence. All I've heard was that life was wonderful before Mao took over China. Nobody had anticipated that Mao would put this great nation behind the so-called "Iron Curtain" for almost half a century.

Mom said it got to be very cold in wintertime in Beijing. She said when she was very little, she couldn't bear watching the maids with their hands all cracked open doing laundry with cold water, so she often bought hot water for them with her own allowance without letting her Mom know. Sometimes she would describe all kinds of foods they ate in different provinces. It just made my mouth water. I can hear her saying,

"We had this special kind of pear called honey pear. It was so big, so sweet and juicy. It takes two people to finish one."

My Grandfather Liu Rong-shen (Mom's father whom I regret to say I never met) was a Chinese Opera singer. Apparently he was very good and very famous since that's all I heard from Mom's old friends. Mom said Grandpa was a very good-looking man and he loved good food. Mom was his favorite child, so every night after Grandpa finished singing in the theater, he would always take Mom to all kinds of restaurants. Ironically, Mom's favorite restaurants were the ones that served Western food. I remember the name of one of the most famous of them "3 6 9" (It's only because we had one with the same name in Taiwan). Of course all the Western food they served in China had been modified for Eastern tastes.

I've seen some old pictures of Mom and Dad when they were very young, the way they dressed just like the Emperor Fu-yi in that movie "The Last Emperor". They both looked so good and slick.

In addition to being a famous opera singer, Grandpa was an opium addict. He must have made pretty good money so he could support his habit. Mom told me that Grandpa had to smoke opium everyday for at least a couple of hours in the afternoon otherwise he couldn't sing at night. At that young age, I really didn't know what it meant to be an opium addict, especially in Taiwan, since we didn't have any drugs. Even today, when you fly to Taiwan, the small print on the customs form says "Any narcotics, death penalty". They don't mess around over there!

Mom inherited Grandpa's talent - she was an excellent Opera singer but she quit right after marrying Dad. Mom is so cool she never shows off how good she is. She just kept it to herself.

Dad also loved to sing the opera. He actually studied with one of the best Opera singers in the country - Yang Shiao-lo when he was a youngster. Dad told us he had this rickshaw driver who was one of the fastest and smoothest in the country. Dad used to ride his rickshaw to take lessons from Yang every chance he got. Dad liked his driver so much, whenever he went to a great restaurant he always had the chef cook something for his driver first. I can just imagine Dad riding in the rickshaw, young, handsome – Chic! No wonder Mom fell for him.

Well, in order to really sing Chinese Opera correctly, you have to have very strict Chinese Kung Fu training, because unless you are physically trained, you can't move gracefully when you sing, and that's a big part of the Chinese Opera singing. Kind of like Jazz, since most of the great Jazz musicians were classically trained. You just can't say what you want to say fluently unless you have the dexterity and the total control of your instrument, and classical training definitely gives you that.

Ask Jackie Chan; he'll tell you how hard he was trained when he was just a little boy in the group called "7 Little Lucky Stars". There were 7 boys in that group, and their ages were from around 6 to 17. They put on a great show. My Dad was a very close friend of Jackie's master Yu Tsan-yuan, who had a very beautiful and famous movie star daughter Yu Sue-chio. The star of the "7 Little Lucky Stars" was the youngest at 6 years old, and he was outstanding. I don't think that was Jackie. Jackie was kind of in the middle if I remember correctly. Master Yu actually brought the whole team to our house once. My Dad knew Master Yu loved peanuts; so he prepared several different kinds of peanuts for him to try. I remember watching Master Yu nodding his head as he told Dad those were the best peanuts he'd ever had.

The problem with Dad's singing was - he wasn't that good and he didn't know it. He worked very hard on the Kung Fu part but the singing part wasn't too hip. He always had an Erhu player accompany him at home. Usually there were a lot of people hanging out in the house and Dad always had Mom cook for everybody.

I remember one day I came home from grade school, the house was full of people and Dad was singing. I told Mom,

"Dad's out of tune".

Mom told me to hush.

Well, China was considered one of the 5 strongest countries in the world right after World War II – China, United States, Great Britain, France and the Soviet Union. The Chinese civil war started from 1927 to 1950. It was the war of difference in thinking between the Nationalist Kuomintang (KMT) led by Chiang Kai-shek and the Chinese Communist Party (CCP) led by Mao Tse-tung fighting for the legitimacy as the government of China. The war started and stopped several times before the Second Sino-Japanese war. And, after Japanese lost the war, two parties started the war again in 1946. Many factors had attributed to Chiang's defeat – Internal corruption (as Chiang mentioned in his diary), initial strong support from the U.S. diminished and stopped… Chiang started losing the war and finally he had to retreat to Taiwan.

Dad flew his whole family (except for his father) to Taiwan in 1949 with Chiang. Dad had an older brother and a younger sister, and they were both married with children. So there were a whole lot of people coming with Dad. Dad was a high ranking official in the Air Force, so the family never suffered on the trip, unlike other people's horror stories of taking boats (kind of like the retreat from Vietnam).

Mom said, her mother, whom I didn't know nor did I hear much about was a very serious woman and that she used to beat the shit out of Mom. I can see that from the very few pictures that I'd seen. None of Mom's family left China with her when Dad took her to Taiwan. They all stayed, hoping nothing's gonna change after Mao took over. SUPLISE!!!

When Chiang Kai-shek first retreated to Taiwan, there were quite a few bloody battles between Chiang's so called "Mainlanders" and the Taiwanese natives. For the local Taiwanese, Chiang's people were considered intruders. Even now, there's still some hostility between Mainlanders and Taiwanese. I remember in the old days, if a Taiwanese wanted to marry a Mainlander, Oy Veh, it's like a Catholic marrying a Jew.

I don't know anything about when my parents arrived in Taiwan, where they first stayed, where they moved to; I wasn't around yet. I just remember we lived in Grass Mountain close to where President Chiang lived for a while and later on we moved right next to a dentist, Dr. Chen, in the city of Shi-Ling.

Dad's father was a banker in Nan King so I was told. Funny, nobody ever talked about him. It's like he never existed. I sometimes wonder if he died in the Nan King Massacre in December 1937.

Dad's mom was a highly educated woman, which was very unusual especially for that time. Grandma was a trip! She hated me! Yes, she hated me. Up to this day I still don't know why she hated me so much. She often told people that both my sister Tina and I were unnecessary. What a horrible thing to say about your own grandchildren. Mom used to get real upset and cried every time she heard Grandma cussing me out.

Grandma spoke a little English and she was very well read. I think she was a teacher of some sort in China. She used to read the newspaper from the top to bottom every morning (actually I should say from right to left). Mom used to do Grandma's hair every morning. I remember - One day when Mom was doing her hair, Grandma was cussing Nixon out when Nixon went to visit China for the first time. It was funny to watch a Chinese old lady bitching about Nixon.

Grandma used to get up every day at 4 in the morning to exercise. I was a senior in middle school and I used to study very hard every night (to prepare for the joint exam for high school) until I heard Grandma exercising in the yard, then I would turn off the lights and go to sleep, so she wouldn't bitch about me wasting electricity. Every night, while studying, I always had the radio tuned in to American Armed Forces Radio Station listening to all the American pop songs.

Grandma finally moved out of the house when Mom and Dad divorced. I knew she really wanted to stay with Mom but she had no choice but to move out with her son. Mom said there were two things she did in her life that made her feel bad. Not letting Grandma stay was one of them, and I can't remember the other one. Can you imagine, only two things?

Grandma lived to 97 like Chiang Kai-shek. Last time I saw her it was right before I left Taiwan for the States. She almost didn't recognize me. Grandma had always been hard of hearing and I suspect that's probably one of the reasons why she lived so long.

*****

From L to R: Me, sisters Tina and Grace, nephew Howard and his wife Lily; seated my wife Michelle and Mom

I have 2 brothers and 2 sisters - Grace, Charlie, Steve and Tina. I am number 4. I have to say they are the nicest people you could ever wish for as your siblings. I don't think I have ever met any nicer people. They are all like Mom, always thinking of others first. They are kind, considerate, and generous (sometimes too generous). I took them all for granted. I just thought every family was like that. Man, was I wrong!

Dad's boss didn't get along with Chiang Kai-shek's son Chiang Jing-ko who eventually became the president of Taiwan. Dad knew his military career was over, so he quit. I didn't know this until years later from Mom that when Dad decided to call it quits, they offered him the position of Police Chief of the 3rd division, which was the most "profitable" police station. The district included all the best hotels, bars, restaurants and all kinds of underground activities. Dad refused it because he said it was a dirty job. So, I guess he was a man with some principles. (What a dumb ass!)

So, instead of being a filthy rich police chief, he decided to go into the clothing business, which he knew nothing about. Of course he lost everything. So, for the first time, the family started to have a taste of poverty. I'm glad I was too little to know exactly how hard it was. I vaguely remember Mom was crying over not being able to come up with the money to buy my grade school uniform. She had to borrow from her friend.

I don't remember that I ever had a toy to play with. Neither did any of my brothers and sisters, at least not that I could remember. But, somehow we boys managed to make our own toys - bows and arrows, the Ninja flying cross, cards, and marbles. I remember I had a couple of friends working at a machine shop, and they helped me make my first Ninja flying cross. My brothers and I, we won a lot of cards and marbles because we were so good at it. Boys will be boys.

Another one of my favorite things to do was to hang out at the newsstands, squatting down reading all the comic books for free. I actually learned how to play baseball from reading the comic books.

I never envied the kids that seemed to have everything, nice toys, fancy clothes -------. I guess even at that young age, the material things just didn't thrill me that much.

When I was in grade school, we were living in a village in which all the people worked at the President's office. It's kind of like the White house except the President doesn't live there.

We had a neighbor who was in college. He started telling stories to all the kids every night after dinner at the playground. We sat around and listened to him telling Alexander Dumas' "The Count of Monte Cristo". That was my first introduction to foreign writers. We kids were just fascinated by the story. The guy, whose name I can't even remember, was such a great storyteller. All the kids were staring at him the whole time wouldn't even acknowledge the calling and yelling from all the Moms.

I loved to read. Ever since I was very little, I started to read all the stories about Chinese history, all the fairy tales from dynasty to dynasty, especially the stories about the end of the Ching Dynasty and the beginning of Republic of China - the secret double agents from WWII who worked against the Japanese invasion, and all the novels about Kung Fu fighting. Later on I got into Greek mythology and other translated foreign fairy tales. I loved to read so much sometimes I would hide in bed underneath the cover using a flashlight to read at night so Mom wouldn't scold me. But I really screwed up my eyes. I'd been wearing glasses since I was 9. Then I tried hard lenses, soft lenses, and then laser correction which I'd had four times already for various problems.

When we were growing up, all we had for entertainment was an old radio. Every night, all of us (except for Dad) would sit around the radio after dinner and listen to the soaps. The stories were fascinating. Most of them were about families, wars and young lovers. It was such a trip that eventually I found out whom those voices belonged to. I have to say that was one of the biggest disappointments. When you listened to all those voices, you automatically imagined the faces to match the different voices. But eventually when you found out that sweet voice you've been listening to actually belonged to a big fat woman and you pictured a handsome young guy turned out to be a raggedy looking old fart, that's disappointing! I guess in a way I started to understand life is not always the way you imagine.

Dad borrowed money from some bad dudes. They came to the house to collect interest every day. Finally Mom had to sell all her jewelry to get rid of them.

Although life was hard and we didn't have much, but we never starved. Mom was such a great cook she always came up with some delicious food with whatever she had. Since the government was providing rice, salt, flour, peanut oil, and coal for people working for the government, military, and the schools, we always had food to eat. I remember the black bean sauce with dried diced tofu and shredded pork wrapped in thick flour pancakes was so delicious. Every once in a while I would mention those pancakes to Mom and told her how wonderful they were and how much I missed them, she always sighed and said how hard those days were and she didn't even know how we got through it.

I don't know why I was so afraid of Dad. I always thought he was so unapproachable. I remember one night we kids were all asleep when Dad came home. I was actually awake but when Dad asked,

"I've got some raisins here. Does anybody want any raisins?"

I love raisins, and I was dying to have some, but I pretended that I was asleep. Why? I had no idea. But up to this day, raisins are still one of my favorite foods.

Now, my Dad wasn't really a bad guy, he was just a natural big pain in the ass. He had way too much ego and way too many women. I think he still had that old bullshit value that men can have extramarital relationships. Plus, he was never there for his children like most fathers were. "Selfish" is probably the best word to describe him. Maybe it was because he was with the "Pres" all the time; he kind of played that role at home. Although, I do remember he told me once,

"I'd much rather leave you a skill than leave you a lot of money."

He didn't leave me shit!!

Dad sent me to learn Tai Chi from this guy Dad called him master Yao, and Chinese brush writing from a real master, Master Liu when I was about 6. I wasn't so sure about that Yao guy, but Master Liu was a real bad motherfucker. Some of his writings look just like they were carved by a sharp knife; they were breathtaking if you know anything about Chinese calligraphy. Master Liu even looked like a bad motherfucker. He had long white hair and long white beard. As a matter of fact, he kind of looked like that Chinese Kung Fu master in that movie "Kill Bill 2" by Tarantino. Sometimes when Master Liu was very pleased with my work, he would use his brush dip in red ink and double circle the words that he liked, and his wife would give me some Chinese desserts as a reward. I guess that really motivated me to work even harder. I had never seen Master Liu smile the whole time I studied with him.

They had no children, so they treated me like their own child. I actually won second prize in the brush writing competition.

Eventually we moved away from that neighborhood. I never heard from Master Liu until years later, Mom told me that he had died, and I had no idea what happened to his wife.

*****

My First Guitar and Brother Charlie

I think I was around 10 when I first noticed a guitar in the house. Sister Grace was kind of taking guitar lessons. So I started to fool around with it. I don't really know exactly what happened, things just started to make sense to my ears little by little as far as how to finger all the chords on the fingerboard. I actually became obsessed with the guitar. I played all the time, I mean ALL THE TIME - trying to figure out how to play everything I heard on the radio and all the songs I liked from the albums I'd collected. The interesting thing was that most of the songs I liked they were all blues.

In those days there was no sheet music available where I was growing up and the truth is I couldn't read music anyway. So I just had to figure everything out by ear.

At home we had a small record player that looked like a little suitcase. It's one of those that started to turn when you pick up the needle. I spent so much time having my ears right next to that tiny little speaker trying to figure out the tunes I wanted to learn. That's all I ever wanted to do. I remember Mom used to ask me how come I was always home playing the guitar and listening to records or visiting the record store down the street, not like other kids always out playing. I told her,

"I am playing; this is what I like to do".

Sometimes I tried so hard to work on a passage I couldn't figure out, I would even dream about it, figuring it out in my dreams and remembering it after I woke up. I remember the first time I figured out the major 7th chords, I couldn't stop playing them. I learned a lot about 4-note chords from figuring out all those Burt Bacharach songs: "The Look Of Love", "Alfie", "This Guy's in Love With You"... I like Dionne Warwick. What happened? They don't write songs like that any more. Forget about Cole Porter!

My oldest brother Charlie was in the Air Force Junior Academy when I was in grade school. The first time he came home on a short break, I was so impressed watching him salute Dad, who was of much higher rank. It was so cool. But Charlie was even more impressed by the song that I played for him. He gave me a buck.

So I started to play for him every chance I got. By the time I was 13, I was actually asked to play for a party. I joined my brother Steve's band when I was in high school. We even made a TV appearance. We were actually pretty good.

Dad and brother Steve

Brother Charlie, he has been such a wonderful and successful human being. He joined the Air Force when he was only 15. He was so young to endure all that tough physical and mental training and he was always #1 in his class. He was the first student they allowed to fly solo. I still remember how he got thrown into the swimming pool (a tradition) after he safely landed. We were all so proud of him. He became one of the youngest Generals in the Air Force. He actually got elected as one of the national heroes. The jets in Taiwan in those days were very old. The Air Force purchased them from the U.S. I think they were F-104's. Once Charlie risked his life by landing instead of ejecting when he had some serious mechanical problems. He saved the government millions of dollars.

*****

Learning English and Jazz Through Songs, Movies and TV Shows

I learned English from listening to songs. The very first song I ever learned was Paul Anka's "Diana", and the second was "Love You More Than I Can Say". I've always had good ears, I could hear exactly how they pronounced each word even though I had no idea what the hell they were saying.

By the time I was in junior high, I already spoke better English than all my English teachers. In the old days most of the LPs didn't come with lyrics so I had to figure them out. Words like "penny arcade" or "sycamore" were very hard for this little guy to understand, but I got them all figured out. How? I have no idea! Eventually many thought I was born and raised here in the States.

I've always been fascinated by languages. I'm glad I was born Chinese because if I had to learn Chinese, man, that would have been a bitch. I really think Chinese is one of the hardest languages, especially when it comes to writing. We have 35 different dialects. A few of them are similar, but most of them sound totally different from one another. Often, you can't even communicate with your fellow Chinaman if you don't speak the same dialect. But when you write them down, they are all the same. Pretty wild!

I watched a lot of American TV shows when I was growing up. My favorite shows were: "77 Sunset Strip", "The Saint", "Mission Impossible", "Ironside", "Gunsmoke", "Twilight Zone" ------ but I think "The Fugitive" was my all time favorite. Dr. Kimble traveled around, kind of giving me a free tour of the U.S. It's funny, I've been living in the States for over thirty years, and I have never felt any culture shock. It seems like I've learned about this country through songs, movies and TV shows.

I particularly loved "The Ed Sullivan Show". I remember so well when the Beatles were on, the government blacked out the whole performance. When Ed Sullivan announced,

"Ladies and Gentlemen, the Beatles!"

And then - nothing! That's right, just Nothing!!! I was so upset. Same thing happened with the Tom Jones Show when he had "Blood, Sweat and Tears" as guests. The government cut that too because of the band's long hair. Incidentally, "Blood Sweat and Tears" was one of my favorite bands. I really think they had great musicianship and wrote great charts. David Clayton Thomas is hell of a singer. But for some reason they never made it as big as "Chicago".

Thankfully, the government did not black out Johnny Mercer on The Andy Williams Show. Now, that was a treat! I'm not a big fan of Andy Williams but on this particular show, I remember Mercer and Williams were sitting on the steps of the stage, singing a medley of many songs titled from A to Z without missing a beat. I was impressed. Johnny Mercer is my all time favorite lyricist but I had no idea that he sang and played piano so well. Not too long ago, I happened to catch PBS's Johnny Mercer special. Boy, what a show that was, and what a career, what talent!!! . It was such a shame to see that when that era was gone, his career was gone too.

Duke Ellington was in town for a short visit when I was about 13. I caught him on TV. I wasn't at all hip to jazz at the time. The closest thing that I'd heard was some boogie-woogie piano playing from The Lawrence Welk Show. I liked the big band sound and all those well-harmonized vocals. The songs were kind of corny but still nice.

When I saw Duke, I didn't know what to make of it and certainly didn't understand what the hell they were doing but I was so impressed by that old black man with a ponytail conducting the band the way only Duke knew how and the sound coming out of those horns. It was breathtaking. I remember sitting right in front of the TV set with my mouth open trying to understand what I was hearing.

Man, was Duke slick!

*****

I listened to a lot of singers. As a matter of fact, Ella Fitzgerald was the one who really turned me on to Jazz because, when you don't know anything about Jazz, you can always get an idea by listening to the songs you're familiar with. After you hear the song, then you listen to different musicians play the same song - that's when you can really appreciate their interpretation. That's what Jazz really is - to recreate music on the spot in accordance with the original melodies and chord progressions. I love all those songbooks she did with different arrangers. Actually both Ella and Satchmo (Louie Armstrong) really opened up my ears to jazz. I really think Ella and Satchmo should be included in music appreciation classes in America, so at least kids can learn something about their own music.

I like Sinatra, especially his earlier stuff and all the records with "Capitol". What a performer! I like his confidence and the way he tells the story. Sinatra was a very interesting singer. He didn't have as much facility and range as some other singers but he can sure make you listen to every word he sings. I believe firmly that good singers are good actors. Sinatra was definitely a perfect example of that. No wonder he won an Academy Award.

The album, "Sinatra and Basie at the Sands" is a favorite of mine. The band sounded so good they made Sinatra an even better singer.

I like Bobby Darin's cockiness, and the way he swings. I love Nat Cole's piano playing and of course his smooth, beautiful baritone voice. But sometimes he exaggerated the pronunciation a bit too much. Like,
"MONA LEESAAAA -----".

But ELLA, now that's my all time favorite. I just love everything she did. She's got the most incredible ears, and her time was impeccable. I think Ray Brown really made her "the first lady of song" by introducing her to Be-bop. She's a jazz musician! And that's why she can interpret all the songs the way only jazz musicians can. When she scats, she really sings the changes. The way she sang "How High the Moon", forget it!

The other singer that I know of who can do that almost as well is Mel Tormé and I bet you Mel must have studied the shit out of ELLA. Sarah Vaughan, Carmen McRae are terrific also, as is Peggy Lee, who for me is the sexiest female vocalist. These people were the Real Deals.

I can't stand listening to most singers scat because they have no idea what the hell they're doing. They don't even know that, for starters, it requires a high level of musicianship and a perfect ear to scat, and then you must have something to say. In other words you almost have to be a real jazz musician to be able to scat and have it mean something.

I'd learned quite a few standards (American popular songs) from watching all the old movies, especially the ones with Fred Astaire and Gene Kelly. I was fascinated by the way they danced and the orchestra and big band accompaniments. Gotta give Sinatra a lot of credit for all those movies he was in with Gene Kelly. He danced his ass off. I guess when you're young and hungry enough, you can do anything they want you to do.

Through the movies, little by little I got hip to all the great songwriters – Irving Berlin, Cole Porter, Jerome Kern, Rogers and Hart, George and Ira Gershwin, Oscar Levant, Harold Arlen, Johnny Mercer, Jule Styne ----.

*****

The marching band that I joined in high school was the very first and only musical training that I've ever had. I learned how to read music, and I also learned about all the other instruments. I was playing baritone horn because nobody else wanted to. But I really enjoyed it and worked real hard at it. I remember I was practicing the fingerings even when I was riding on the bus holding on to the bar and tapping my fingers as if I was playing the horn in my head.

Well, we were very lucky because every kid in the marching band just loved to play and we all took pride in it. We tried to find as many music charts as we could. The whole band was taking it very seriously; we practiced and rehearsed all the time. The school was built when the Japanese ruled Taiwan (The Japanese occupied Taiwan for over 50 years until they lost WWII and that's why the older generation of Taiwanese all speak Japanese). It was an old concrete building. Right at the entrance of the school, there's a hall that had the best acoustics. Whenever we practiced there, the whole building was shaking. I can't tell you how thrilling that was. We did so well we actually won the National Marching Band Competition. What surprised me the most was my Dad showed up at the competition with a camera, and he took quite a few pictures of me.

Amazing! I thought he didn't give a shit.

I can't really remember when my parents were divorced. I think I was in junior high. I just remember one day I came home from school and found Mom crying. She finally told me that she and Dad were divorced. In those days, you just don't hear about people getting divorced in Taiwan. I wasn't quite sure how to react to that except I wasn't upset. As a matter of fact, I even made a joke about we should celebrate.

I made Mom laugh.

*****

The education system in Taiwan was very different from what it is today. Grade school was only up to 6th grade and that was mandatory. After that, you could choose whether or not to continue. Some kids from farming families had to quit and worked on the farm instead. A couple of kids in my class were brilliant, but they had to give up school to work for the family. What a shame! I remember when they first came to school, they didn't even have shoes to wear.

After grade school, we had to take a joint exam to middle school (junior high), and then, 3 years later another joint exam to high school, and yet another one (the one) to go to college.

There weren't enough colleges in the country to accommodate so many high school graduates. I remember the year I took the exam, only 20% of all the high school grads passed. And they sent you to different colleges according to how well you did on the exams. To make things worse, for all the boys, if you don't pass, they would send you to the military.

How nice!

*****

When I was in high school, 4 kids aged 17 to 21, committed a robbery and accidentally killed an old woman. They were all captured. Taiwan was still under martial law at the time when President Chiang Kai-shek was still alive. All four of them were sentenced to death. I happened to catch the late night news on TV one night. It was a live broadcast from jail titled "The Last Supper!" The reporter was interviewing the kids in jail. I remember one of the kids was crying and told the reporter,

"Please tell my Mom I'm sorry!"

The next day, all 4 of them got shot!

For the longest time, we didn't have any serious crime after that.

*****

The joint exam to college took two days, 3 subjects each day -- Chinese literature, English, Math, History, Geography and Chinese Democracy. When I took the exams, I was so nervous; I couldn't sleep worth a shit the night before. The next day I was so tired, I didn't know how the hell I got through the day, but I made it somehow. After I got home, I was exhausted and thirsty, so I ate a big mango and went to sleep. Not too smart, since a few hours later I got up in the middle of the night with serious diarrhea. That was just great.

Luckily, the second day as soon as the test started, I was cool.

Mom asked me how I did right after I finished all the tests. I told her, "Probably Fu Jen University."

I was right. Fu Jen it was!

II: COLLEGE

Bull Camp In the "Victory Hills"

Fu Jen is a Catholic university. But it has nothing to do with religion. It's just owned by Catholics.

What a colorful 4 years. I had so much fun I don't know how the hell I got my business degree.

After freshman year every boy had to go to the "Victory Hills" to take 3 months military training in the summer. Chiang Kai-shek was still trying to get everybody ready for taking China back.

Now, the Victory Hills are in the city of Tai Chong, which is on top of a mountain that was made of red clay. It was so damn hot and humid you can't even imagine. Most of the sergeants were mean and nasty (at least that's what they wanted us to think). They were all professional soldiers, and they were not too thrilled about us college kids. To most of them, we were just a bunch of spoiled brats. Which is true - we were. To make a soldier out of every one of us, they tried to get us every chance they got. Most of them never graduated from junior high, so they hardly knew any English.

They had this routine worked out to get us, and it goes like this:

If you are laughing at the wrong time and the wrong place and you were caught, they would call your number, (in the bull camp, everybody was identified by numbers. Mine was #23)

"Number so and so, what are you laughing about? You think your teeth are whiter than the rest of us? What kind of toothpaste you use?" (everybody was using Hay-zen toothpaste in those days)

"Hay-zen toothpaste? Get out of there and give me 20 pushups!"

One day I got caught. The Sergeant screamed at me,

"Number 23, what are you laughing about? Get out of there! You think your teeth are whiter than ours? What kind of tooth paste you use?"

"Colgate!"

The Sergeant didn't expect a different answer and he certainly didn't know how to repeat Colgate, so he hesitated for a second, and said,

"Ah----, Ok, … go back!"

One afternoon, as we were practicing Tae Kuan Do in front of the company courtyard under the blazing sun; the Captain came out of his room from the second floor and blew the whistle as loud as he could to stop the practice. He said,

"I just heard the radio, Bruce Lee died."

And he just walked away back to his room. We were left standing there, looking at each other, didn't know what to think.

We got our rifles on the 3rd day. What an experience! First time I touched a real weapon. It was an M1 Garand. The excitement wore off in no time because we didn't expect it to be so heavy and plus we had to clean the damn thing every day. It was the rifle they used in WWII. I remember watching one of my favorite old TV shows "Combat" starring Vic Morrow and Rick Jason. Vic Morrow was carrying a Thompson automatic machine gun and

Rick Jason carried an M1 carbine and the rest of the guys were all using M1 Garand. I couldn't believe how well it shot in spite of the heaviness and the beat-up look.

I was ok with all that hardcore physical training, although sometimes it got to be very hard. But one thing I hated the most was that 3-minute shower. The 3-minute shower including undressing, soap, rinse, dry, get dressed and ran back to the group. If you weren't ready in the group by the time the whistle was blown, it's your ass. And, sometimes, right after we finally finished cleaning up the whole day's dirt and sweat, they would make us run 3 laps around the courtyard until we got soaking wet again, then they released us to go to bed. Can you imagine? All 40 some people cramped in one little room, soaking wet from running, no AC, hot and stinking like hell, and then tried to go to sleep. I don't know how the hell I managed to sleep every night.

I started to count the days since the very first day I got in the camp. And the first thing they taught us to do was how to sew our own blankets. It was so funny to watch all the boys trying to sew for the first time.

I was always the first one getting up every day around 4 in the morning. I couldn't stand fighting for the bathroom. We only had 15 minutes to make the bed (like a square tofu), wash up, get dressed, and line up in the group. Again, if you were not ready by the time the whistle was blown, it's your ass.

Sometimes, when we were out in the field, our shirts and pants were totally drenched by sweat in the heat. I remember I used to tell myself,

"Man, if you can get through this, you can get through anything!"

Before graduation, we had to pass a couple of serious tests. One of them was to march about 40 miles fully loaded in one day. We started around 5 o'clock in the morning. Thank God I was a sharp shooter so they picked me to be the scout who walked between two companies. So I was able to walk by myself and not get cramped in the crowd and I was able to check out the scenery even thought there was pretty much nothing to see but still… One time it was so hot, I actually dashed into a small food joint and poured down a whole plate of shaved ice. My head was hurting so bad from the freeze burn. It was pretty funny now to think about how I dashed into the joint with a rifle on my shoulders, helmet, backpack and all.

Another test was we had to crawl along a white line about 30 yards in the mined area. The mines were going off left and right, and the machine gun was spraying on top of our heads to keep us from getting up. It was quite a crawl. Both my elbows and knees were torn and bled. But I couldn't help feeling proud and had this big old smile on my face after I finally reached the other end.

3 months finally crawled by and it was like a nightmare. They really made a soldier out of almost everybody. I was buffed! I remember looking out the window on the train coming home, I felt like I just got out of a different world. But you know what? I really think every boy should have that kind of discipline training once in his lifetime. We all had it way too easy. We take too many things for granted. Freedom for one, you don't know how precious it is until you lose it.

After we went back to college, for the whole semester all we talked about was what was happening on the Victory Hills. I remember one of the girls in our class used to tell us, "Jesus, don't you guys have anything else to talk about?"

****

NCSB (North Country Street Band)

From L to R: Keith Lin, Me, Stan Lai

College was a fun time. I met Stan Lai and Keith Lin, two of the most talented musicians I could ever find as my partners. We met at a concert. I was invited to play for Taiwan University's freshman welcome party. Both Stan and Keith were invited to play too. I didn't think much of it at the concert except I thought both of them were pretty good. Little did I know the next day Keith would come to my classroom and tell me that Stan and he were thinking about putting a band together and they wanted me to join them. And there you have it, we played together ever since.

From L to R: Stan Lai (bending down), Me, Keith Lin

We were all self-taught, couldn't read music worth a shit, but we liked the same kind of music and we all could figure out tunes. It was really meant to be that we ended up playing together. We were going to the same college and we're about the same age, and we became great friends and played together for over 4 years.

From L To R; Stan Lai, Keith Lin and Me

The little club that we played at since freshman year was called "The Idea House". We actually bought the club from David (a college alumnus) when he decided to give it up. So we were the bosses. We were able to play whatever kind of music we liked to play. We got to be quite famous. Often times, musicians coming from different parts of the world would come down and jam with us. We had different bands playing every night, but we were always the main act. The club was doing very well and we got to be quite famous that it became a trendy thing for all the college kids. They loved to come see us play if they could afford it. We were the only club that opened from 7pm to 11pm every night and made money.

There was a small noodle cart right behind the club. Sometimes I would go there to have a bowl of sesame paste noodle if I didn't have time to eat dinner. It was so good and it only cost about 20 cents. Unbelievable!

We called ourselves NCSB (North Country Street Band), because we played all kinds of music like a street band. And we're all from Taipei, which is on the north side of Taiwan. Actually Stan Lai came up with the name and we all agreed. We played a wide range of music, basically everything – a lot of blues, country, folk and southern rock since it was in the early 70's. Every once in a while, we'd learn some old songs and have a showcase like "Oldies night" or "Beatles night". That was a lot of fun. Eventually we started to play some Jazz standards. Tunes like "Paper Moon", "The Girl From Ipanema", "Polka Dots and Moon beans", "Scotch and Soda"... It was kind of a natural progression that after you play for a while, you start to have the need to hear something harmonically more interesting and complicated. And Jazz is it. That's why I always thought BB King is one of the luckiest musicians because he can play the same kind of music forever and still have fun. God bless him!

I found an old issue of DownBeat at a newsstand where they were selling a lot of the old magazines that were left by all the GIs based in Taiwan in those days. Inside, there was a section that had Jazz critics reviewing all the new releases, one of which was Miles Davis's "Kind of Blue" and it had a 5 star rating. I had no idea at the time who Miles was or any other guys who were mentioned in that magazine. Later on, I finally got myself a copy of that amazing record. Bill Evans said in the liner notes, "All the tracks were recorded in one take and the musicians didn't see the music prior to the session." That's incredible! The musicianship of every one was unbelievable. I never heard anything like it. I just loved to listen to that album over and over. I was totally taken by all the tunes and every solo played. Trane (John Coltrane, tenor sax) pretty much kicked everybody's ass. I never heard Cannonball (Adderley on alto sax) play better. I listened to that album so much I know all the solos. Up to this day, that is still one of my very favorites.

I've been listening to Miles forever. What an unusual individual. Nobody plays the trumpet like Miles. Every decade, he would come up with a record that just shook the whole world, "Birth of the Cool", "Kind of Blue" and "Bitches Brew". Although Miles' music style was constantly changing, Miles had always been the same. His sound remained the same, his technique remained the same. He just found different ways of expressing himself. What a master.

Stan Lai had a chance to buy quite a few great Jazz albums and he taped them all for me. So I got hip to almost everybody. Listening to all those tapes, other than Bird (Charlie Parker), Miles, Trane and Getz, I was most impressed by Ella's "Live in Berlin". That was the first time I ever heard a human voice that could improvise just like an instrument. I didn't know what to think after that. I played all those tapes every night until I fell asleep. Since I was a guitar player, Wes Montgomery and Jim Hall very easily became my favorites and they still are. I can't say enough about Wes Montgomery's playing. He made all those commercial pop songs sound so hip. His phrasing, his comping and his time still knock me out whenever I listen to him.

I heard somebody asked Andres Segovia what he thought about Wes Montgomery, he said, "I wish I had his thumb."

*****

8/7 Water Disasters

We have typhoon every year in Taiwan usually around August and it always comes with a lot of rain. I remember that we had this serious typhoon in the early 60's called 8/7 Water Disasters, because it happened on August 7th. It rained so hard the whole village was covered by water. We had to retreat to a higher place. It was in the middle of the night when Mom woke us up. She and Dad rolled up all the sheets and blankets, carried them walking in the water to take the government bus to a local school, which was on much higher ground. Somehow I got separated from my family in the dark and I was alone in this bus with all the strangers. The bus stopped at a nearby temple for a minute to pick up more people. We all got out of the bus to check out the water. From where the temple was, I could actually see our house since it was the first house on the block. But all I could see was the roof, all the houses were under water and it was still raining.

I followed everybody back into the bus and we drove to this Gym of a local high school. That's when I finally saw my Mom and Dad and the rest of the family. Mom was worried to death about me. Well, for us kids, it was kind of fun and adventurous to see so many people sleeping on the floor in this big old hall and waiting in line to pick up food and water. This all came back to me when I saw on TV about hurricane Katrina hitting New Orleans. How about that! I had the same experience 50 years ago.

One time it rained so hard, our club was flooded. I got a call from Keith around midnight and he told me that the whole block was covered by water according to the janitor; you couldn't even see the street. We decided to go check out the club on my motorcycle. We had to stop about two blocks away from the club because water was way too deep. I had to literally swim to the door and dive into the basement to rescue all the instruments and equipments. We got there early enough so all the stuff was still floating around almost touching the top of the basement not soaked in water. But Stan's

Martin D-35 acoustic guitar was damaged. It was Sooo fucked up, totally warped and soft. I don't remember this but Stan reminded me that I was the one actually brought that guitar back to life. He said,

"You were the one went to some place behind the train station to buy these blue drying pellets that turned red when saturated with water, and you kept filling the inside of the Martin every day with a new batch of the dehumidifying agent. Since it was expensive to get the pellets, even though you were getting them wholesale, we found that by using a heater on the red ones, they would turn blue again, so we can reuse them, and we did. And voila, it was its old self. I couldn't believe it."

Stan said he was stunned when he saw the damage and unbelieving that it came back to life.

I don't remember how long it took us to clean up the whole place. I had this picture of me standing in front of the club with my jeans rolled up to my knees holding a guitar totally destroyed by water. That was some scene.

*****

We (Keith and I) used to go play snooker together almost every night after the gig on our way home. I was riding a motorcycle and Keith rode with me with both of our guitars. We lived in the same direction so usually I dropped him off first and then went home. There was this one pool house right across the street from Taiwan University that we always went to. One night when I was aiming for a shot, I heard the American Armed Forces Radio Station announcing, "Jazz musician Paul Desmond died of lung cancer at age 53..." I was in shock because we just learned how to play "Take 5".

From San Francisco, Paul Desmond is one of the few alto sax players I like, a melodic player with beautiful sound. I heard somebody talked about Desmond's playing:

"They should give him an award for not trying to sound like 'Bird'".

I have always been different from the kids I grew up with. I somehow learned to be different mostly by keeping my mouth shut. The music I was listening to and the movies I loved, I hardly had anyone to share with before I met Stan and Keith.

III: COMING TO AMERICA

It was a last minute decision for me to come to the U.S. I never thought about leaving Taiwan even though most college graduates would do almost anything to come to The States. I had no reason to leave Taiwan. I got good gigs. In addition to playing at our own club and the TV show "Pop's", after I got my business degree, I was also working for a garment exporting company, which was doing very well. In those days the garment business was big in Taiwan. So I was cool. Plus, I had many private students taking guitar lessons from me.

But life doesn't really always work so simply. It has its own way of complicating the hell out of everything. Out of the blue, I suddenly felt empty and lost. I began to wonder about what's the real meaning of life --- my life.

"Is this it?"

I kept asking myself.

I didn't enjoy playing the same old shit over and over every night, I certainly didn't like the bullshit I had to deal with day in and day out with the so-called business people. It was OK for a while because I was so busy that I didn't have time to think or feel until the 6-day break for Chinese New Year. That was the first time I had some time for myself. At the end of the 6th day, I just didn't want to go back to that same routine anymore. Not quite understanding exactly why I felt the way I did, and why I was not happy, I started to ask myself - what I'd choose if I could do anything I wanted for the rest of my life?

Answer: Play jazz!

That didn't take long.

So I started to ask myself again if there's any reason why I couldn't go and learn how to play jazz? I simply could not come up with any. But the only thing I worried about was my Mom. So I told Mom that I was thinking about going to the United States to learn jazz. Not even knowing what jazz is, Mom simply said,

"Well, it is your life, if that's what you want to do then go for it!"

Just like that, I quit my day gig but kept playing and teaching, tried to save up as much money as I could and applied to Berklee School of Music in Boston at the same time. A few months later, I left the club to the guys and hopped on an airplane to the United States of America.

****

BOSTON

Boston! What a great introduction to the history of the US for a foreigner. Harvard, MIT, BU, BC, Symphony Hall, Boston Pops, Fenway Park, Boston Garden, Haymarket, even Logan Airport has its own charm, and of course, Berklee School of Music.

That was probably the happiest 3 years that I've ever lived in my whole life.

There was a funny little story that happened when I first got to Boston:

> I was walking down Boylston St. and I was hungry when I smelled charbroil. So I looked around and I saw Burger King. I had no idea what Burger King was. We had no fast food joints in Taiwan back then. I walked inside and just watched how people got their food. I waited in line and checked out the menu on the board. Hamburger - that I

know, Cheeseburger - I know that too. But "Whopper", what the hell is a Whopper? So I ordered a hamburger.

I'd been playing by ear for so many years my knowledge about music was limited. It was so great to finally learn the correct terms and names for everything I'd been playing. The theory and harmony with both jazz and classical were fascinating to me. Never in my wildest dreams did I ever think that I would have the chance to learn how to write for big band and study Bach's 4 Part Fugue. I'd never been so excited about learning.

I remember my first day at Berklee, there was a placement test for all the new students. They had to figure out where we were at so they'd know which ensemble to put us in. The teacher put a sheet of music in front of me and asked me to play it in second position on the guitar. I told him I don't even know the first position. So I started from the very bottom, level one, which was totally cool because I didn't want to miss anything.

I was really working hard because this was the first time in my life that I was learning everything that I always wanted to learn. I was so excited about absorbing everything. I studied and practiced till 2 or 3 o'clock in the morning every night.

Berklee is a great school but tough. They let anybody in but they flunk the shit out of you if you don't work. Well, at least it was like that 30 years ago. I was doing very well, as a matter of fact, my GPA was 3.9 three years in a row. One of the girls who worked in the financial aid office told me that I could have gotten a scholarship, but I didn't even know there was such a thing. Too bad! That was 500 bucks per semester I missed out on.

It was hard. Every teacher treated us like they were the only teacher. I was taking at least 18 units per semester and that was a lot of work, especially courses like Arranging and Composition. It could take forever just to write just a few bars that I was happy with. I remember one time during the finals, in the elevator; this one kid was asking how the other kid was doing. The other kid said,

"Man, I haven't slept for 2 days, trying to finish that god damn big band chart".

That's exactly how busy everybody was.

My first big band chart took forever for me to finish and then you have to copy all the parts. But it sounded so good I couldn't believe my ears when I heard the rehearsal band playing my chart. Even the teacher applauded. I guess if you'd listened to enough Duke and Basie, you would come up with something halfway decent. That's one thing great about Berklee; you can always have your charts played by the student rehearsal bands and some of them were excellent. I really took advantage of it.

Ear training was the easiest course for me due to years of using my ears listening to everything. I developed keen ears so that I can hear just about anything. That was the only subject that I didn't have to spend time to prepare when it comes to midterms and finals. The teacher would play a chord on the piano and we had to identify the chord. It was sad to see a lot of kids who just couldn't hear at all. Somehow the teacher knew I had good ears so instead of playing one chord, he would played a 4 or 8 bar progression, and I nailed them every time. One final exam, we were asked to write out the bass drum part off of the drum solo from that famous original recording "Take 5". They kept playing the drum solo over and over. I got it perfectly.

I found a little attic in Jamaica Plain not too far from the school. The rent was only 90 bucks a month. It had a small bedroom, a good size living room and a very small kitchen and bath. Not bad for 90 bucks. It was cheap even then. The attic was on the 3rd floor of this hunter and fisherman's house and it had its own entrance. The owner had a home in Maine and he stayed there most of the time. So, basically I had the whole place to myself.

There was a little skylight on the ceiling in my bedroom. One night in the middle of the night, I woke up because it was so bright outside. I looked out the window, it was snowing, and it looked just like a picture on a Christmas card with all the New England style homes. It was sooooo beautiful!!! I had to get out of the house and walked in the snow for a while. Mind you I'm from Taiwan, I'd never seen snow before. You can imagine how thrilled I was.

Boston is such a charming city. Can't tell you how much I liked it there, and when I found out about Chinatown, I was home free. I remember the first time I went to this little Chinese market in downtown Boston, seeing all those familiar jars and cans of Chinese food and all the ingredients, I was in heaven. I never cooked in Taiwan, but I started to try to remember a few simple dishes that Mom used to cook. I was writing to Mom regularly and asking her how to cook certain dishes from time to time. A phone call to Taiwan was so expensive in those days and the connection wasn't the greatest. I remember - It cost about six dollars for just the first 3 minutes, and then a dollar for each extra minute. So every time before I called I would list all the things I wanted to say. Today it costs nothing and it sounds like you are talking to somebody next door. Eventually I was able to cook some pretty damn good Chinese home cooking. I invited one of the guys in the class who lived just around the corner from the house for lunch one Sunday, and he was totally knocked out by my cooking. In those days, the cost of living was not nearly as high as today. I remember when I went grocery shopping, for 20 bucks; I could fill up two big bags of grocery including steaks that I almost couldn't carry. Today, 20 bucks you get a bag you can lift with one finger.

I got myself a roommate after the first semester. Alan was a guitar player also and he actually served in Vietnam. He had a Gibson cherry red ES-335, which I loved (eventually I got myself one). We got along very well. One night he had me try some smoke. We were supposed to play afterwards. But that was my very first time getting stoned. I was so out of it, I couldn't even tune the guitar. I kept turning the wrong tuning machines. So that was the end of that jam session. I guess if you want to be able to play high, you got to practice high.

There was a little jazz club on Boylston Street called "The Jazz Workshop". Later on it was shut down because it didn't meet the fire code. First time I went there I saw Kenny Burrell. He had a trio with Sherman Ferguson on drums (can't remember the bass player). What a guitar player Kenny is. I first learned about Kenny was from that album he recorded with Trane. He was only 25 and he sounded great then. Now he's right in front of me playing that big Gibson Super-400. Kenny's got big hands and it was so great being able to watch him in person playing up and down the fingerboard effortlessly. His tone was full and the lines were tasty and bluesy, totally my cup of tea. That was the first time I ever saw great jazz musicians live and I was so close to them. I was in heaven. They sounded so good I ended up staying for both sets. I sat there stunned and watched them packing up. Kenny came down and sat with me and asked me how I was doing. I told him that he made me realize I got a long way to go. He said,

"So what, I'm still learning."

I saw a lot of my favorite players in Boston. Bill Evans, Dexter Gordon, Sonny Rollins, Art Blakey, Slam Stewart, Gary Burton, Ray Brown, Mike Stern...

I saw Sonny Rollins at Symphony Hall with McCoy Tyner and Ron Carter. They did an album with that trio. That was some concert. McCoy's left hand voicings in fourths (intervals) were impressive and distinctive. Ron Carter's time and his bass lines made it so easy for Sonny. And Sonny, man, he blew me away! I have never thought that was possible for a human being to play the way Sonny played. That raw, edgy, and full sound that he gets out of that horn, the energy, the length of each solo, the humor and seriousness of his ideas, he was just incredible. I have to say I was dead tired after listening to him play. What an awesome emotional ride that was.

When Dexter Gordon was playing at Berklee Performance Center, I happened to work backstage. He was so drunk they had to make coffee for him. I didn't think he was able to play. Little did I know, he got on stage and played his ass off. I really like the early Dexter, his harmony was way ahead of his time. He influenced almost everybody You can hear Dexter in a lot of great players. Trane was one of them, and Sonny was another. But that concert was my first experience witnessing how somebody could be so fucked up and still manage to play so well. It must have taken a lot of practice.

I was so impressed by Bill Evans. The whole concert he didn't say a word. He got on stage and just started to play. He looked terrible, very pale, face puffy, fingers swollen. But he sounded gorgeous. Bill Evans' got the most beautiful touch, and his voicings are mysteriously beautiful. What a treat to watch Bill Evans play live. He played tune after tune without even looking up. After he finished the set, he got up pointed his hand to the drummer then the bass player and left.

This is what Miles said about Bill Evans in his autobiography:

"Bill had this quiet fire that I loved on piano. The way he approached, the sound he got, was like crystal notes or sparkling water cascading down from some clear waterfall."

And he said,

"I've sure learned a lot from Bill Evans. He plays the piano the way it should be played."

I've heard this story from Lou Levy (one of my favorite piano players) about Bill Evans:

> One time Bill was playing at the Vanguard in New York, he had an accident right before the gig, and his right arm went paralyzed. He couldn't even lift it. But somehow he managed to finish the set with his left hand and middle

pedal. Most people don't even know what the middle pedal is for, needless to say how to use it for the whole gig. That's crazy!

Every once in a while I would be asked, "Who is your favorite Jazz musician?"

I really think that's the dumbest question because there is no such thing in Jazz that you can name one as your favorite. There are just way too many great ones and they're all different. I can name several favorites for each instrument.

But I can always listen to Bill Evans.

Anytime!

IV: DETOUR FROM MY RETURN TO TAIWAN

Three years passed by in the blink of an eye. It was time to go home. Enough education, now it's time to put it to use, plus I can make some serious money over there. I had a good taste of life. There's no way I can live like a young jazz musician here struggling through life not knowing where the next rent check is coming from. It just don't work that way for me, but that's how it is here in the U.S.. Sad!

Well, there's no direct flight from Boston to Taiwan, you either layover in San Francisco or LA. I had a few friends in LA, so, LA it was. I took a train from Boston to New York with my friend Hovic (excellent guitar player from Iran). I always like trains. Boy, what a ride! I was looking out the window watching all the trees, houses, cars, and people passing by, for a minute I thought I was in Taiwan.

It was Christmas Eve, the airfare was only 99 bucks. I think we flew TWA. I remember- Hovic was bitching about them feeding us only apples and crackers.

My Chinese old buddies Leo Wang and Ernest Guan came to pick me up from LAX. I was in a tee shirt and they both had sweaters on. I guess that's how much people can adapt from the tropical weather like Taiwan to snowy cold winter like Boston.

Leo was my classmate in Fu Jen University. We hit it off right away along with a few other so called "hip Chinamen". Leo turned out to be my very best friend. After Ernest moved back to Taiwan, Leo was pretty much my only Chinese friend in the U.S. We used to hang out every chance we got. He was the one that hip me to all the great Chinese restaurants. Some of them are real holes in the wall, but they are so good. A few of them I'm still going to after all these years.

Me and Leo Wang at Hollywood Bowl

I decided to stay and enjoy the Southern California sun for a while since I was really not in a great hurry to go home. Having spent all my money in Boston, I thought I'd better find a part time job, so at least I could put some food in the fridge or pay some rent. That's how I was brought up, never took advantage of nobody.

Music store seemed to be a logical place for me to work for a while. So I opened up the yellow pages and looked into the music section. (30 some years ago, no google yet) The first thing that caught my eyes was "Stein on Vine" with a picture of a guy playing a soprano saxophone.

I called.

An old voice answered the phone,

"Music shop!"

I asked if they needed any help.

The old man said, "Well, come over let me take a look at you."

And he hung up on me.

So, I looked it up on the map (again, no google) and tried to find out where the store was. I drove all the way to Hollywood. Jim was working in the store at the time. He asked me if he could help me with anything.

"I guess I'm here to see Mr. Stein." I said.

He picked up this white intercom hanging on the wall (that thing actually worked in those days) and said, "Maury, there's an oriental fellow here to see you".

Then he hung up the phone and said, "He'll be right up".

So, I looked around the store, checking out some books and all the pictures on the wall. There were quite a few pictures with a lot of naked women standing in line waiting for something. What appeared to be very funny was that there were a couple of pictures with bunch of musicians holding their instruments with no clothes on either, playing for the party. I thought that was kind of unusual. Later on I found out it was a nudist camp beauty contest and the owner of the store, Maury Stein, somehow got the gig as the bandleader. I guess in order to play the gig; all the guys had to be nude too. And of course Maury and all the cats had no problem taking their clothes off.

(Those pictures are still on the wall in the store today. Too bad, most of them turned yellow and faded.)

Well, in no time the back door opened and an old man walked in. He was followed by a whole bunch of people. The first guy I recognized was Ray Brown, and there was Freddie Hubbard, Lou Levy, John Heard and some other people I didn't recognize.

The old man reached his hand out and said, "What's your name?"

I shook his hand and said, "My name is Gary."

The old man said, "Come back tomorrow ten o'clock"

That was it. He never asked me anything else. So I left.

I went home and told my guys, "You know what? I think I might have a job. I couldn't understand that old man very well."

Just like that, the next day, I started my journey with "Stein on Vine".

V: STEIN ON VINE

*****

M. K. Stein

If I can use only one word to describe Maury Stein, it has to be "fantastic". He was a fantastic human being; he had such a unique personality and he had lived the most fantastic full life imaginable.

Maurice Kerwin Stein was born on Nov.25th, 1910 in Chicago, Illinois. His wife Viola came from a very well-off family in Chicago too. Viola told me that her father was in the steel business and she actually dated Boxing Champ Barney Ross. Maury told me that he was once one of the ring men for Barney Ross.

I have no idea how them two met and how long they had been married (Maury's line – my wife's been married for 50 years). I just remember Maury told me on their honeymoon night, Maury took Viola to a local night club in Chicago, the beautiful sister singer came over to their table and sang to Maury something like "Oh, baby, baby, baby", Viola got pissed off and slapped Maury in the face right there.

Some honeymoon!

Maury studied clarinet with Buck Wells (also Benny Goodman's teacher) from age 12 to 16. Benny Goodman and Stein were Chicago neighborhood friends. Maury played clarinet with the WGN Symphony Orchestra and won the 1938 Paul Whiteman clarinet award. Maury also played the first alto saxophone with the Jack Teagarden band. The second chair was his 16-year-old student and protégé, genius Stan Getz.

Mike Stein (Maury's son) once told me the story that one time Maury got the gig playing at the Ambassador Hotel on Wilshire for the Academy Awards and he took Stan Getz along. In the lobby, Maury saw Mike. He called,

"Hey, Mike! Come here, come here. I want you to meet this kid Stan Getz. He's playing better than I now."

Stan said, "No! I'm not".

Maury had the biggest heart, he always took care of people. He was a father figure to most jazz musicians in town and everybody loved him. I've never met anybody like Maury who was so well loved by so many people. Every day he had visitors from all over the world and most of them were Jazz greats. I've met almost all my heroes at Stein on Vine. So many that it would be much easier for me to name the ones I didn't meet.

Maury never refused anybody whenever he was asked for help. Guys would come to Maury with all kinds of problems and Maury always bailed them out. And not just for musicians only, for instance, this painter Rico told me he came to the store one day and asked Maury if he could paint the outside wall for him, and Maury just told him, "Go paint it!"

I'd seen Maury let guys stay at the guest-house in his Beverly Hills home for months at a time when they were having problem paying rent. I'd seen Maury bail one of the guys out of jail when he couldn't pay alimony. I'd seen Maury asking me to take a ride with him to his carpenter's house to check up on him because he hadn't come around for days and didn't answer Maury's phone call. I'd even seen Maury loan a guy four saxophones to play a session and the next day we found out the guy was in Mexico. But that's Maury, always looking out for people.

Maury was a sucker for talent even though he was an excellent musician himself. If you can play, you immediately won his friendship and you could get away with a lot of shit.

****

Maury and Jule

Maury was the youngest of three. He had an older brother Jule Styne and an older sister Claire. Jule was a British-born American songwriter especially famous for a series of Broadway musicals. He had numerous hit songs and standards such as " Three Coins In The Fountain", "It's Been a Long Long Time", "The Party's Over", "Just In Time", "Time After Time", "People", "Diamonds Are A Girl's Best Friend", "I Guess I'll Hang My Tears Out to Dry", "Let It Snow, Let It Snow, Let It Snow" (it's so ironic that many famous Christmas songs were written by Jews) -------If you read Jule's bio, you wouldn't believe how many songs he'd written and how many hits he had. He was one of Sinatra's favorite songwriters.

Maury told me Jule was playing with the Chicago Symphony as a piano soloist at the age of 8, and he wrote his first hit "Sunday" at age 20.

The second day that I worked at Steins, I answered a phone call. I said, "Stein Music!"

The guy on the phone said, "Is Maury there?"

"Yes, who's calling?" and after a pause, he said, "Frank"

"Frank who?"

And after a longer pause, he said, "Tell him Sinatra is calling".

I was shocked and rushed to the back to get Maury.

So, I talked to Frank Sinatra on the phone.

I had no idea at the time that Maury was Jule Styne's brother and Jule had written so many great hits for Sinatra. Funny, when I was in Taiwan the first time I saw the name Jule Styne, I was wondering whether that was a woman or man. Jule changed his spelling from Stein to Styne for whatever reasons. But I think one of the reasons must have been there's a Jules Stein Eye Institute in UCLA. Jule probably didn't want people to confuse him with a different Stein. And, Jule made so much money from the royalties of all his hits. It would have been a shame if the checks went to the wrong Styne.

One time Maury took me to Sinatra's party at Chasen's in Beverly Hills. The minute we walked in, Milton Berle saw us, and he yelled from across the room,

"Hey, Maury, is Jule still your brother?"

I guess Uncle Milty knew the family. Lou Levy was playing piano for the party that night (he always played for Sinatra's private parties). I was standing right next to Lou so I could watch him play. I remember Maury told me to be careful with my drink, don't put it on top of the piano (which I wasn't about to do). Within minutes, he knocked over his own drink and spilt the whole drink right into the piano. You should have seen the look on Lou's face.

I'd met Sinatra a couple of times at his parties but I never spoke to him. Same thing with Miles Davis. A few times I was in his dressing room at the Hollywood Bowl and I just left him alone.

Both Sinatra and Miles almost had the same effect on people. I can't explain what that is. They had such charisma, you just don't want to piss them off.

Maury took me to Lalo Schifrin's (wrote the theme to "Mission Impossible") house once; Clint Eastwood was at the party and he came over to introduce himself to me, "Hi, my name is Clint."

I laughed and told him, "I know who you are. My name is Gary."

I thought that that was very nice of him.

But at that party, there were 10 piano players and they took turns to play the blues in C. I can't remember them all, Lou Levy, Mike Lang, Hank Mancini, Lalo Schifrin, Pete Jolly, ... That was a lot of fun watching composers like Hank and Lalo playing the blues.

Monty Budwig (bass player for the party) and I played a game of pool together and I beat the shit out of him.

****

Maury also told me the story that when Jule wrote that song "People", he actually wrote it for Sinatra, but Sinatra didn't like the song (I can see why, that's not really Sinatra's song), so he called Maury up and told Maury,

"Hey Maury, did you hear the new song Jule wrote for me? What kind of shit is that? I can't sing that song!"

So Jule gave it to Barbara Streisand.

After Streisand made that song a hit, Sinatra called Maury again,

"Hey Maury, you didn't tell Jule what I said about his song, did you?"

"No!"

"Well, keep your mouth shut!"

Maury had his own late night live music show in Chicago at the world famous Chez Paree where he was the leader of the jazz band. He said that gangster brothers owned the club and they liked him. Jule was an impulsive gambler so says Maury and he told me once,

"My brother Jule is not only a great musician, he's also a chemist."

"Really?! I didn't know that."

"Yeah, he takes money and makes shit out of it."

****

One time Jule was playing cards at the club and he was losing his ass. Maury got very worried so he went to one of the owners and told him Jule was losing too much money. "He can afford it." *The brother said.*

"No! He can't! The government just took all of his money."

The brother looked at him and yelled at the dealer, "Hey Charlie, how are you doing over there?"

Charlie said, "I'm doing fine, Boss."

"Charlie, who are you playing with?"

"Jule Styne, Boss."

"How is he doing?"

"I'm killing him!"

"Unkill him"

"Yes, Boss."

A few moments later, the Boss asked again, "Charlie, how's Jule doing?"

"He's about breaking even."

"Send him home!"

Maury had a very interesting relationship with Jule. Well, people like Jule Styne, they are geniuses. They have such concentration on one thing, they usually don't pay that much attention to anything else. Maury said sometimes he'd walk by Jule and say hello to him, "Hi, Jule!"

Jule wouldn't even acknowledge him.

I think it was Claire (Maury's sister) who told me that when Jule was 16 years old in high school, he was already famous for his musical talent. He was trying to put together a big band for one of his musicals, and he needed one extra clarinet player. Maury had just started taking clarinet lessons at the time, so Jule told Maury to sit in the band just hold the clarinet pretending that he was playing. Jule specifically told Maury, "Don't play! Just sit there and hold the clarinet." And of course, Maury played!

Claire said that was the last gig that Jule ever gave Maury.

Claire also told me Maury had always been a troublemaker as a child. When they were in grade school, one day her woman teacher asked her,

"Is Maury Stein your brother?"

Claire said, "Yes!"

And the teacher started to cry.

Maury said he had two heart attacks in 1953, and he wasn't working much so he called Jule for some help. He said,

> "Jule, this is Moish... this is your brother Moisha... your brother Maury...it's your brother...Jule... Remember Mom? ... Jule? Jule?"

Maury moved to California in 1943. He actually got a gig raising turkeys for the US Navy. I remember he was telling the story about how sometimes he would lose all the turkeys because of some kind of disease that would just wipe them out. He was trying to remember the name of that disease, before he could come up with anything, Jake Hanna said,

"Thanksgiving!"

Jake Hanna - one of the Greatest drummers of all time, from Boston, worked with Toshiko Akiyoshi, Maynard Ferguson, Woody Herman ----.

Maury loved Jake. He told me more than once that Jake played drums like a great tap dancer.

Even though Maury had made a name for himself by his unique character, he had always been living under Jule's shadow all his life. Maury became very quiet whenever Jule was around. Jule came to the store a couple of times, and Maury was like a little kid following his big brother around. He never said a word. That was so un-Maury-like.

One time Jule was visiting us in the back room, sitting by the piano, and he asked Lou Levy and me,

"You guys want to hear a great song?"

"Oh, sure!"

So he started to play this beautiful tune. Both Lou and I were totally impressed. Jule had very small hands but that didn't stop him from playing all those gorgeous voicings. Lou said,

"Wow! That's beautiful! Who wrote this?"

"I did!!!" Jule shouted.

What ego! Well, then again when you have that kind of talent you deserve to have such ego.

Somebody asked Jule about how he writes his music. Jule said,

"Simple melody with charming harmony."

*****

Maury Stein in the Studio

Lynn

Me and Lynn

Lynn had been with Maury for a long time. She told me when she first owned the musical instrument wholesale company on Washington Blvd in downtown LA, Maury would go there every so often to pick up a few things. One day, Lynn was helping Maury. When she was bending down to reach for something; Maury gave her a kiss on the back of her neck. That was it. They'd been together ever since. Now, dig this, Lynn was a multimillionaire, and she was not only beautiful, she'd also never been married. She was willing to be with Maury for 35 years in spite of the fact that Maury was married. That tells you something about the old man. I actually asked Lynn once why they didn't get married, she said,

"I don't want to marry him. He's dirty, he's sloppy, and he's always drunk, but he's a lot of fun."

What a hip lady.

First time I met Lynn was at Carmelo's (jazz club in the Valley). Maury took Lynn to see Ira Sullivan and Red Rodney. We planned to meet at the club.

Ira and Red had a showcase going from 1980-82. Ira was born in Washington DC. He is one of the very few musicians who can play brass and woodwinds equally well.

Red was born in Philadelphia. He started his career playing trumpet at age 15. Inspired by Dizzy Gillespie and Charlie Parker, he changed his style to Be-bop. He joined the Charlie Parker Quintet in 1949.

Monty Budwig was on bass. Monty's got great time and always played beautiful solos.

Joe Diorio was on guitar and Joe sure is a one of a kind guitar player. He was born in Waterbury, Connecticut, a true Charlie Parker disciple. I love Joe's harmony.

Even though it was kind of a pick-up band, they sounded real tight together. They played some very nice arrangements.

I was already in the club when Maury and Lynn showed up. Lynn grabbed my hand and said to me,

"I want to get to know you, sweetheart, Maury had told me so much about you."

I was very quiet in those days. I hardly said anything. Sometimes Maury would make fun of my quietness by saying, "Shut up, Gary!"

Lynn asked me, "Tell me sweetheart, what is your secret of selling? Maury told me you could sell anything."

I didn't know what to say because I never thought I had any secrets or methods that I use to sell. So I told her,

"I never try to sell. I just ask people what they want and what kind of money they want to spend and see what I can do."

Every year, Maury and Lynn would take a week vacation and usually they would go to Hawaii. Three months after I started working for Maury, he gave me the keys and wanted me to take care of the store while he was gone with Lynn. I was very surprised that he would trust me with the store since I was basically still pretty new at it.

Lynn pulled a fast one on Maury. She told me, as soon as they arrived at the hotel on the big island, Lynn sent a telegram to Maury, which read,

"Don Ho is in LA, where the fuck are you?"

Apparently Maury told Viola that every year he had to go to Hawaii to work for Don Ho for a week.
Lynn said, "You should have seen the look on his face when he read that telegram."

Another time in Hawaii, Lynn told me she couldn't find Maury in the hotel room early in the morning when she woke up. The hotel was right on the beach. You open the sliding door you can walk right into the ocean. It was raining pretty hard that morning, and Lynn finally saw Maury walking along the beach, soaking wet, looking down, and trying to find something in the sand with his feet. Lynn burst out laughing because she remembered a year ago, they stayed at the same hotel and Maury lost a jar on the beach.

Since Lynn had her own business in Orange County, she stayed down there on the weekdays and came up to LA to spend the weekends with us. But she and Maury talked everyday, sometimes 2, 3 times a day. Maury usually got pretty juiced in the afternoon especially when he had visitors from out of town. His tongue started to get bigger and a lot of times Lynn would get upset with him. Sometimes I happened to be in the back room while Maury was on the phone with Lynn and he would say something like,

"Listen honey, I only had one drink so far, I swear to God, this is the first drink I had all day. Ask Gary, he's right here."

And then he handed me the phone and winked at me. I answered the phone, before I said anything, Lynn said,

"Isn't he terrible? Put you on the spot. That fool, like I can't tell he's drunk! Alright sweet-heart, love you and I'll see you on the weekend."

I never had to say anything!

My 30th birthday! I was with Maury and Lynn. I remember we had dinner at the "Cock and Bull" right across the street from Lynn's. Oh, by the way, Lynn bought a condo just a few blocks from Maury's years ago.

I proposed a toast at dinner,

"Wish me happy birthday you two. Today is my 30th birthday. I never celebrated my birthday because I feel everybody's got one every year, there's really no need to make a big deal out of it. But I'm so glad I have you two here with me on my birthday."

They were so surprised and happy for me. I also said,

"You know, I feel so fortunate that I can say if I die tomorrow, it's ok. I had a ball."

Not too many 30-year olds can say that.

Lynn had a surprise party for Maury on Valentine's Day in 1982. We called it "Happy Valen-Stein". It was on the 6th floor at the Sunset Tower where Lynn lived. Lynn asked everybody to dress in tux. She told Maury they were invited to a horse show and he had to wear tux and boots. As they were going down in the elevator, Maury heard music coming out of the 6th floor so he asked Lynn to stop the elevator because he wanted to check out what was going on in there, which was exactly what Lynn expected Maury would do. You can imagine how surprised Maury was when he opened the door and saw everybody cheering,

"Happy Valen-Stein, Maury!"

Everybody showed! All the guys dressed in tuxes. Stan Getz flew in from up north. I guess Lynn forgot to tell him about the tux. So when Stan showed up, he was wearing a white butcher jacket, (don't know where the hell he got that) no shirt, just a bow tie around his neck. When Maury saw him they were just staring at each other for a minute then they hugged. I had to take a picture with Stan with that white butcher jacket just to make sure that I have some proof that it really happened.

Stan invited Lynn and me to this concert at which they honored all the famous composers - Johnny Mandel, Alan Bergman, Henry Mancini, Burt Bacharach, Paul Williams and whole lot of other famous composers at the Shrine Auditorium in down town LA. I saw Joe Williams (jazz singer from Georgia) backstage. He was performing that night too. He said to me, "I saw you last night on TV."

I said, "No, you didn't."

God knows who he thought I was.

But anyway, I had no idea what great seats Stan had given us. We're at dead center front row. On my right was Antonio Carlos Jobim. And the guy sitting right behind me was Sammy Kahn. They must have been wondering who the hell this Chinaman was.

Stan loved Lynn. I remember one time Stan was playing at the Universal Amphitheater. This was right after Maury died. Stan wanted to visit Lynn so he called me and asked me if I could arranged to see Lynn after the concert. I picked him up from the Universal Hilton and took him and his grandson Chris to Lynn's. Lynn cooked pork roast for us. She could cook a few dishes well and pork roast was definitely one of them. Stan kept telling his grandson, "You see, grandpa's got some great friends! Don't I?"

Lynn had a hell of a time adjusting her life after Maury's death. She told me that she had the same dream every night for God knows how long. She always dreamed about Maury walking away from her and she couldn't catch up. There wasn't much I could do to make it easier for her except spending time having breakfast with her every Sunday. Lynn was so worried that she was taking too much time from me. I kept telling her I enjoyed being with her talking about Maury, and that made me feel better too. We did that for a long time. Her family tried to hook her up with different men, so she started dating again. It was so hard for her because how do you find a guy to replace Maury?

But she did - Skip, a country singer and bass player in a small country western band in Orange County. (Which reminds me of this funny story that somebody told me about Buddy Rich. When Buddy was very sick in the hospital, the nurse asked him if he was allergic to anything, Buddy said, "Yeah, country western.")

There was quite an age difference between Lynn and Skip. I think Lynn was at least 10 years older. But somehow they got along very well. I remember Lynn called me up one day and told me she was marrying Skip and there was no party, just her family and Skip's. They rented out the condo in Beverly Hills and moved to the desert. They invited me over and I spent quite a few weekends with them in Palm Springs. I could tell Skip was very good to Lynn. She seemed to be very happy. Skip and I got along fine. As a matter of fact he was my best shooting buddy. We did a lot of target shooting in the desert.

Both Lynn and Skip flew to Vegas to attend my wedding. I'm so glad my wife finally got to meet Lynn because she really was like a mother to me.

Lynn had asthma ever since I knew her and it was getting worse and worse at the end. Finally Skip called me one morning and told me Lynn died.

*****

Maury Stein – a mensch who loved animals

Young Maury Stein

Early Days at Stein on Vine

Well, Maury and I didn't start out getting along and having a great relationship. In fact, it was pretty hard for me in the beginning. He was not an easy person to work for. You'd never know what kind of mood he'd be in. He had very little patience and he mumbled. I was having a hell of a time trying to understand him at first. He didn't know I never worked in retail before and half of the time I couldn't understand a fucking word he said. But a few months later I was the one doing all the translation for him whenever customers couldn't understand him.

Speaking of mumbling, Stan Fishelson was probably the worst of all. Stan was one of the trumpet players in Woody's 2nd Herd (when Woody had the most famous 4 brothers), and he was the contractor for the Schubert Theater. Often times he would be in the store first thing in the morning to see Maury. He would be sitting right in front of Maury and yakking away,
"Moish, this guy………."

I couldn't understand a word he said, and neither could Maury. Finally, Stan stopped talking, Maury raised his head, pulled down his glasses and looked at Stan right in the eyes and said,

"No shit!"

*****

I sold a student alto saxophone a few weeks after I first started working for Maury. The price tag on the horn said $350. So I sold it for $350 plus tax. It was simple enough I never thought much of it. But right after I finished the deal, Maury walked in from the back room. As soon as he found out what was going on, suddenly he got very upset. He opened up the case and took the horn out, shoved it right in my face and screamed at me,

"Look at this horn, it's been completely overhauled. It cost me $300 just to put it in shape, I lost money on this deal."

He totally embarrassed me right in front of the customer and I could tell the customer was feeling pretty uncomfortable too. I didn't know what to do. I just stood there feeling awful. The last thing I wanted to do is to make the old man lose money. But he never stopped. He just kept going at it by saying shit like: "Goddamn it, it's my fault, it's all my fault! I should have changed the price. Goddamn it…!"

He was trying to put that old Jewish guilt trip on me and it was working. I was so hurt and embarrassed and totally didn't know what to do. But he still wouldn't let go, kept bitching and bitching. I finally got pissed off. I held my fist tight and banged it on the glass counter and screamed at him, "Goddamn! Maury, how the fuck do I know the price was wrong. Do you want me to leave?"

He was in shock!

He looked at me with a look of disbelief and said, "Calm down now, calm down."

And, without saying anther word, he got up and said, "Come, come with me".

He took me to his famous back room for the very first time, and poured me a drink, and that was it. From then on, we started that father and son relationship.

He was the father I never had and I was the son he always wanted.

Later on I found out why he was so pissed off. See, Maury had this unwritten routine worked out. Every time when somebody wanted to buy a horn, he would come up from the back to demonstrate – (clarinet, flute or saxophone), and he might even give them a quick lesson, kind of like putting on an act. That was his thing. He enjoyed that. But here I am, didn't know what the hell was going on. I just went ahead and sold a saxophone without consulting him. That pissed him off.

Oh, by the way, that alto sax I sold didn't cost Maury $300 to fix and he didn't lose any money on that deal.

He was full of shit!

*****

When I first started working for Maury, there was a white Japanese Stratocaster copy electric guitar hanging on the wall that I liked very much, but I couldn't afford it. So I finally gathered enough courage to talk to Maury that maybe he could let me pay it off. Without even thinking Maury just said, "Take it home".

I said, "Maury, you didn't hear me, I can't afford it. I have to make payments."

Maury said, "I heard you, Gary, I heard you alright. I want to give you that guitar as a gift, so take it home."

I didn't know what to say except "thank you" and took the guitar home.

Next morning, I got up early and went to the bank took out $250 cash from my savings and went to the liquor store. I bought 5 bottles of Chivas (Maury's favorite Scotch) and 5 cartons of Sherman's cigarettes (Maury's favorite cigarettes) and brought them to Maury's back room. When Maury opened the back room door and saw me with all the stuff, he was totally in shock. Maury was so used to helping people, doing things for people, taking care of people, he was not used to people being nice to him. He didn't know what to say.

It took him a minute and finally he said, "Uh...that's not the idea. I...all right, I...I'll take care of you."

*****

One day this older rock guitar player came in the store, and he wanted to see some violins. I didn't know who he was. So, I showed him all the violins we had in the cabinet. He started to play one after another. He had a very unique style of playing. He must have been self-taught. He played with a lot of soul and he sounded very good. He finally asked me how much was that old beat up looking violin which I thought had the best sound of all. Warm, dark and full, and I think that was exactly what he was looking for. I told him I had to check with my boss. So I brought the violin to the back room showed it to Maury and asked him how much did he want for that old looking thing. Maury took a look at it and said, "Get me $500."

So I went back to the front and sold the violin for $3000. Yes! I did. Why? Because I knew I could. Plus, if worse came to worst, I just didn't make the sale, that's all. Well, the truth is, I could tell that was a very well made old hand-made instrument. Maury had a lot of knowledge about old violins and bows but not when he was drunk and having a good time with his friends. And I also could tell how much the guy liked that violin from the way he played. You just can't hide your feelings through music. If you like the instrument you sound different. This ugly thing really had the most gorgeous sound, even better than some of those 5, 6 thousand dollar violins he tried. And I knew he could hear it too. So there!

Later on Maury came up and sat behind his desk checking out all the sales (which he did everyday), and when he saw that $3000 receipt, he was stunned and he turned around with his eyes wide open, looking at me and said,

"Jesus, what happened? What did you do? You devil you!"

And immediately he took out his wallet and pulled out a couple of hundred dollar bills and said, "Take it. This is for you."

I told him, "No, Maury, I can't take this money. Business has been so slow, we've been losing money every day, now I finally made some money for you, I can't take this money."

He couldn't believe it. He called Lynn right away, "Lynn, you wouldn't believe this kid..."

*****

Maury Stein in the Studio

Maury loved to play. He loved to play tenor sax but he doubled on all single reed instruments - Clarinet, bass clarinet, contra bass clarinet, tenor, alto, soprano sax and flute. He could play some decent violin too. (That generation of musicians, most horn players could play some violin) Maury could play. He was definitely a good musician.

He played the Red Skelton Show (an American variety show that was a television staple for almost two decades). Maury told me that he hated this violin player on the show. So one time during the break, he rubbed some soap on that violin player's bow, and when that guy tried to play a solo (Live on air), he couldn't get any sound out of his violin. Brutal!

Maury was doing a lot of studio work like everybody else was in those good old days. He was the favorite of a lot of composers and arrangers. David Rose was one of them. David Rose was a British-born American songwriter, composer, arranger, pianist and orchestra leader. He wrote music for many television series, including "It's a Great life", "Little House on the Prairie", "Highway to Heaven", "Bonanza" and "Highway Patrol". He was the music director for "The Red Skelton Show" too. How funny, I never would have thought I would get to know the man who orchestrated the "Bonanza" theme and one of the guys played on that recording when I watched that show in Taiwan as a little kid.

Maury was on almost every one of those TV series. Which reminds me: One time when Maury was sick in the hospital, I happened to be with him when David Rose came in to see him early in the morning. David was in tux with a bow tie hanging on the neck looking real cool and he looked at Maury and asked, "Are you OK?" Maury said, "Yeah, I'm fine."

I could tell they were very close.

David turned around and said to me, "Take care of him, will you?" Then he just left.

One of Maury's cousins Bob Danziger wrote a book titled "A Funny Thing Happened on the way to Energy Independence". He mentioned Maury in his book. This is what he wrote:

> "When Maury went to the cardiac care unit at Cedars-Sinai hospital near Beverly Hills, notices were posted at the Musicians' Union, word got around, and within twenty-four hours the unit was full of musicians. Drinks were being mixed in the bedpans while vodka bottles hung from the IV. A pungent smoky odor spilled out of the unit's door. Pills and powders lay on the pizza boxes, which I'm sure didn't come from the pharmacy or the nutritionist. Into all this—and I swear this is true—walked one of the greatest saxophone players of all time, Stan Getz, who got off the freight elevator naked except for a patient smock and his tenor sax and marched into the unit playing "Oh, When the Saints Go Marching In."

In those days, the store was right across the street from where we're at now and it was inside the Musicians' Union. Maury showed me some of the ads that he placed in the Musicians' Union paper. Things like,

"On Sale - Famous Batons for left-handed conductors"

I wish I had saved all the ads just for laughs. They really show how naughty Maury was.

Maury also told me he taught Warren Beatty how to fake playing soprano sax in that movie "Heaven Can Wait", and he never got paid!

Maury came from the swing era. He had a beautiful sound on his tenor and he played good ballads. But when he tried to play "Giant Steps", after the head (melody), he would play those licks that Lou Levy had written out for him, and that was funny. Just the idea of watching this old Jew trying to solo over Bebop changes with that corny swing. It was precious! I remember seeing both Freddie Hubbard and John Heard looking at each other not knowing what to say. It was cute!

That reminds me of another story:

One time this old Jazz musician came in to have his flute repaired. We were having a nice chat while he waited. He said, "Gary, I was born in '97----"

> I said, "Wait a minute, when were you born again?"
>
> "1897!"
>
> "Oh, ok, I thought I heard wrong. That makes you 91 years old. Man, you sure don't look it!"
>
> "Well, I am, and I'm feeling good! But let me tell you something Gary, one thing I can't stand are those horn players play with that horrible, corny, short vibrato. It sounded so bad it makes my dick soft."

I was laughing so hard!

I did a session with Maury. It was one of the Blake Edwards movies and Bill Berry was the contractor. It was so funny to see all the guys cheering when they saw Maury walking in and how everybody followed him to the bathroom on the break.

I think it was Ray Brown, who told me that when they were in Japan playing a big concert, somebody was joking around and said, "Hey, there's Maury Stein." And the whole band jumped up, "Where?"

Another time one of the guys came back from a Japan tour with a big band. He said, right after they finished the first half of the concert, this little Japanese lady came down to the bandstand and shouted at the top of her lungs with that Japanese accent, "Do you know Maulee Stein?" And the whole band answered, "Course we know Maury Stein!"

Maury was a terrible driver. He always drove on the centerline of a two-lane street. I don't know how he managed to avoid accidents, especially considering that most of the time he had Bengie (his white poodle) on his lap. You should have seen him driving with Bengie on his lap and trying to take a snort.

There was one time he came home from sitting in at Donte's playing with the Candoli brothers. He hit a fire hydrant on his way home around two o'clock in the morning. Since I wasn't with him that night, I had no idea what happened. He came to work next morning, didn't tell me anything about the accident. I guess he was embarrassed. But he did call to report the accident. I overheard him say,

"Listen, honey, how the hell do I know whom that fucking fire hydrant belongs to?"

Maury lost his favorite set of Selmer clarinets (both A and Bb) by leaving them on the ground in the Musicians' Union parking lot and driving away. By the time he came back for them, of course they were long gone! He'd been playing a Buffet ever since and he was never completely happy with it. So often he would call me up from the back room and say,

"Listen to this, Gary…" and he'd play his clarinet over the phone for me. He said, "I finally found the right mouthpiece for this fucking clarinet."

But the next day he'd call again and say, "Ah, shit! That's not it."

He always used the word "heart" to describe horns. He said, "Those two clarinets I've lost had such heart. This Buffet plays very well but it's a real cold mother".

I knew exactly what he meant.

*****

A "Mensch" that Loved Animals

Maury loved animals. He had an amazing connection with them. He fed all the Hollywood pigeons in the store's parking lot. Those pigeons would shit on everybody's car except Maury's. Maury had a two-seater convertible blue Cadillac that never got shat on. Once he tried to show me a brown pigeon named "Charlie" while he was tossing the seeds. He looked around for a long time and finally said,

"He's not here today."

Stan Getz told me that when Maury went to visit him, his dog "James" would follow Maury around. Stan said, "James was my dog but when Maury was here he'd be by Maury's side all day long, and the strangest thing was James died the very next day Maury died. Ain't that something?"

*****

Maury's Cockatiels

I don't know how long Maury had those two cockatiels. They were already there when I first came to the store. Maury loved them so. He covered them every night with towels and left them with a light. Every morning as soon as he came in he would go straight to the back checking out those two birds - fed them and played with them. Those two birds were a trip! I don't know how but Maury actually taught them to sing "In A Little Spanish Town". I'm not kidding. Those two birds could sing the melody perfectly. And the amazing thing was every morning they would start singing as soon as Maury's truck pulled into the corner. They actually recognized the engine sound of Maury's truck. So, when those two birds started singing in the morning, everybody knew Maury was in and started to work.

Maury sometimes loved to play games with the guys in front. He would walk all the way around the building and sneak in the front door, trying to catch what everybody was doing. Sometimes he would say something to the guys like,

"Why can't you pretend that you're working?"

I have a picture of Maury playing a fiddle, and one of the little cockatiels was resting on the tip of his violin bow dancing with every stroke that Maury played.

Incredible!

One night I was following Maury home from Carmelo's. It was around 2 o'clock in the morning and it was raining pretty hard. We took Laurel Canyon (a winding road) back to Beverly Hills. Maury suddenly stopped right in the middle of the road (that's how he drove), and got out of the truck. I had no idea what was going on so I got out of my car and ran up to him only to find him trying to feed a coyote with the leftover from the restaurant that we had dinner at earlier. There he was, soaking wet, "Come here… sweetheart… come on… come here, come on ……there you go…"

And the amazing thing was that coyote slowly came over, grabbed the food from Maury's hand and ran away.

Maury was such a good-looking guy, handsome and charming. I have quite a few pictures of him when he was much younger, that blue-eyed, blonde Jew, he looked so good. He loved women and women loved him. Viola told me that one of her girlfriends once said,

"When Maury walks in the room, the wall starts to dance."

He sure had that kind of effect on people.

I don't know how many people had told me that Maury was the first one to give them credit when they couldn't afford to buy. I'm sure that he got burnt a few times but that never stopped him from helping guys out.

A "Mensch", that's what Maury was!

*****

More M. K. Stein

I sold a cello to this young Korean couple. The wife was the cello player, not very good but good enough for the husband to buy her a better cello for her birthday. It was a 100 year-old German cello and it had a beautiful sound. I sold it for $1000 because there was a crack near the sound post, but the crack was well repaired. It was really a great deal because the cello was worth at least $3000 even with the crack.

Well, the next day the couple came back and wanted to return the cello because of that crack. I figured Maury would just give them their money back and forget about it. A cello like that I could always sell to somebody who would really appreciate the instrument and even pay more for it. In other words these people didn't know they got a great deal. But Maury refused to give them the money back. As a matter of fact, he simply said, "No, I can't give you your money back."

And just turned around and walked away.

The guy stood there for a minute, and after Maury disappeared he suddenly picked up the cello and wanted to smash it against the wall. I was right next to him, I caught his arm and grabbed the cello from him and I yelled at him,

"Are you out of your fucking mind? You guys got yourself a great deal. This cello's worth a lot more than what you paid, and you know it has a beautiful sound. You should be very happy. You are not being taken. Please trust me. You are doing fine."

The guy finally calmed down and his wife said something in Korean to him. He stood there in silence for a minute and then he reached his hand out, shook my hand and said, "Thank you!"

And they left.

*****

Maury and I went down to Orange County to see Lou Levy play one night. It was at a restaurant called Bob Burns at Newport Beach. Both Chuck Findley (trumpet player from Pennsylvania, worked with Jimmy Dorsey, Buddy Rich, Tonight Show Band...) and Bobby Shew (trumpet player worked with Tommy Dorsey, Woody Herman, Buddy Rich...) were on the gig. Bob Magnusson (from New York) was on bass, Sherman Ferguson (from Philly) on drums, and Lou.

The night before, Maury and Lou played a private party in Beverly Hills. After the party Lou was supposed to follow us back to Maury's to grab a bite. But he never showed. He got pulled over by the cops for 502 (DUI).

Around 2 o'clock in the morning, Lou called. The minute Maury picked up the phone, he said, "Which police station are you in?"

Lou said, "How do you know?"

"Well, you should have been here two hours ago."

Anyway, Maury had to bail him out of the Beverly Hills Police Station at 3 in the morning.

Now, a day later we were in Orange County watching Lou playing his ass off. Chuck and Bobby really sounded good together. Bobby is a true Clifford Brown School Bebopper. (Clifford Brown---aka "Brownie", one of the most influential Jazz trumpeters from Wilmington, Delaware. Died at age 25), and Chuck's got so much facility that he can play anything. They have a different sound but they harmonized well.

Bob Magnusson and Sherman were totally locked in. The band was smoking. Everybody was on. The whole night Maury was sitting right in front of Lou, singing,
"502, eyes are blue..."

Maury was terrible and Lou was so embarrassed.

On our way back, guess what? The police pulled us over. Of course Maury was driving. If you saw the way Maury drove, you would have pulled him over too. I remember saying to myself, "Oh, shit!"

Cops asked Maury for his driver's license, and then they asked him to get out of the truck to walk a straight line. Maury got pissed off, he said, "Bull shit! You walk this way when you are 76." I said to myself again, "Oh, shit!"

But, cops let us go.

*****

Maury was a great storyteller. Every day he would be telling some stories to whoever was in the backroom. Even though he'd been telling the same stories for God knows how many times (because he was so good at it and so into it) it was still funny and interesting.

Larry Gelbart (wrote the TV show M.A.S.H.) was hanging out with Maury one time. Larry loved Maury and he loved Maury's stories, so he asked, "Maury, tell me a story."

Maury was about to tell the story but instead he said, "Well, you've probably heard this one already."

Larry said, "Maury, whatever the story is, I never heard it. So, tell me the story."

We tried to record Maury telling all the stories once, but as soon as we'd put a microphone in front of him, he'd just freeze. I mean, he couldn't do a thing. He was not funny at all. Ain't that a bitch?

I never met anybody as ballsy as Maury. He was fearless. He almost had a fistfight with a 20 year old in the parking lot because the kid was driving too fast and Maury hated people driving fast into the lot because of those two dogs and all them pigeons.

*****

There was a Chinese restaurant "Shanghai Diamond Garden" on Pico that Maury and I often went to. One time Maury and I were sitting at the bar having a drink waiting for a table. This beautiful tall blonde walked in and she sat right next to Maury. Maury took a good look at her and turned around said to me,

"She's ham, but I'll eat it."

Some people called Maury, Lynn, and me "The Trio" - an old Jew, a gentile, and a Chinaman. We used to go out almost every Saturday night. Maury loved to use the name "Dr. White" to make all the restaurant reservations. One time we were in a steak house, and somebody was choking on a piece of meat. The hostess screamed that there's a doctor in the house, and when they came to our table, Maury immediately said, "I'm an animal doctor."

I hooked up Lynn's brand new VCR, which had been sitting in her living room for weeks. The three of us watched Mel Brooks' "High Anxiety" and "Blazing Saddles". I don't know what's with the old Jews and farts. Both Maury and Lou just love all the stupid fart jokes. Maury was on the floor when he saw the cowboys in Blazing Saddles farting away after they ate all them beans. Lynn and I were just looking at him and asked, "Are you ok?"

Maury was laughing so hard he couldn't even breathe. But come to think of it, it was quite a picture with an old Jew, a gentile, and a Chinaman watching Mel Brook's movies drinking and laughing.

*****

Maury was really a Jewish father to me. He only paid me $2.65 an hour (that was the minimum wage) for over 2 years. But when I had that serious toothache he sent me to a Beverly Hills dentist. Cost him over $2000!

When my rent went up, I couldn't make it anymore. I was so pissed at Maury. I spent all my time taking care of him I didn't even have time to find a 2nd job. So I told him I was very upset and I needed to talk to him. He got nervous and waited all day for me in the back room. I finally finished up the shop and went to his room. He was waiting and looked worried. I said,

"Maury, you never had to ask me for anything. I just went ahead and did everything for you. Now they raised my rent. I can't make it anymore. You took care those losers way better than you take care of me. I am so disappointed that I have to ask you for money. I don't ever ask for money, but I earned it."

I embarrassed the shit out of him. He gave me a raise and that was the end of that. I remember- years later when I told Lynn the story she kept telling me, "Good for you! Gary. Good for you."

Mom came to visit me one time and I had a chance to introduce her to both Maury and Lynn. They had been dying to meet Mom. At the dinner table in Beverly Bistro, Mom told both of them how grateful she was that they took care of me and she told Lynn that she was my American Mom. Lynn was so touched.

Maury loved Mom. Every time he talked about Mom, he always said, "Your mother is so beautiful. She's got the most beautiful white hair."

What I miss the most were the times when Maury and I spent alone in the back room. Like I said, there were always a lot of people in the back. So whenever we were alone, Maury would ask me to play a couple of tunes with him. We had a lot of fun. Too bad we didn't do that very often because usually Maury was too busy entertaining people. I miss him walking over, giving me a hug, saying,

"Good, Garala, Good."

Sometimes I can't figure Maury out regarding music. As much as he loved music and as much as he loved to play, I never saw him listen to any records or tapes (no cd's or iPods then), and he never went to see any movies. In those days we didn't have cable. It's not like today where you can pretty much stay home and watch any movie you want.

I remember the first time I played him the tape of Coltrane's ballads album. He was totally blown away. He kept picking up his horn and tried to play what Trane played, and he kept saying,

"Wow...! Wow...! That's incredible."

Every year on Thanksgiving, Maury always cooked a big turkey just for the two of us. Viola never joined us. I usually arrived at Maury's around 2 o'clock in the afternoon and watched him finish cooking the bird with stuffing and all. We pigged out with his two dogs. I always ended up taking at least half a turkey home.

Viola was very different when it came to food. She had the same home-made hamburger and either baked or mashed potato everyday for as long as I had known her. That's all she ate, hamburgers and potato. Can you imagine? Same food every day and every night for all those years? But she looked great!

Well, the relationship between Maury and I had some very interesting changes through the years. At the beginning, Maury was definitely the father figure. Later on, we're like the closest friends. At the end, Maury was the kid, and I became the father. He was trying to hide things from me from time to time.

I remember - he finally had a physical. He told me the doctor told him to cool it. I was the only one that he told that to because he didn't want anybody to nag him about his health.

A few days later, I happened to be in his back room. I knew he wasn't supposed to do anything, but I saw this big old line on his glass desk. I looked at him and he looked at me, neither one of us said anything. I turned around and started to look for things. Suddenly, I heard this big old loud snorting sound and I turned around and looked at him with my eyes wide open. Before I said anything, he said, "Oh my god, what have I done?"

*****

There was another time when I went to the back room and saw this long straw laying on Maury's desk (the kind of long straw you see in those Polynesian restaurants when you order one of those big Mai Tais that everybody shares the drink with their own long straw). So I asked him,

"Maury, what the hell are you doing with that long straw?"
Without even thinking, Maury said,

"Ah… my doctor told me to stay away from coke."

VI: SOME OF MAURY'S FRIENDS

There were always a lot of people hanging out in the back room. You don't know who you're gonna run into. A lot of times guys could pick up a gig or two just by hanging out at Stein-on-Vine. So many great musicians played together here, only here and nowhere else. Jam sessions every day with big name travelers as well as local guys. Stan Getz and Zoot Sims. Stan and Al Cohn, they never played together after Woody Herman ----. Too bad we never recorded any of those jam sessions. We all took it for granted and thought it would never end. Too bad! I could have been rich!

*****

Bill Berry

Cornet player and big band leader, Bill's from Benton Harbor, Michigan. He had played with Woody Herman and Maynard Ferguson before joining Duke Ellington in 1961. Bill played with Thad Jones-Mel Lewis orchestra in New York. Later on led his own big band. Moved to LA and re-formed his group as LA Big Band in 1971.

Bill was not only a great cornet player. To me he was probably one of the best casual bandleaders. He worked with Maury for so many years. Maury always got the best gigs, especially those Beverly Hills party gigs. When you have Bill Berry on the gig, you'll never have to worry about what tunes to play. Bill would just start out a perfect tune for the occasion without even thinking about it. I hate when you have bunch of professional musicians trying to figure out on the bandstand what tunes to play.

One time we were at a Beverly Hills party. The band was cooking but there was nobody listening, dancing or even enjoying themselves. Bill turned to me and said, "These people, they got all the money in the world but they don't even know how to have a good time. Pretty sad! Ain't it?"

I talked to Bill about Duke Ellington's Taiwan visit when I was just a kid and he told me the story that when the band was in Taiwan, Duke was so pissed off at Paul Gonzalves (Duke's tenor sax player, best known for playing 27 chorus solos on Duke's "Diminuendo and Crescendo in Blue" at the 1956 Newport Jazz Festival) for being late for the rehearsal again.

Duke said to him, "Paul, you're just a slow boat to China".

And Paul answered, "Yeah… but Duke, we're already in China."

Bill told me this story about one of his friend's two sons, David and Danny. Both of them are good musicians. David plays trumpet and Danny plays alto sax. David decided to become a doctor. Danny stayed with the sax. When Danny got the gig with Count Basie, David called his dad.

> **"Dad, Danny's playing with Basie now, and I'm just a fucking Doctor."**

*****

Joe Bushkin

From New York City, Joe had been one of Maury's oldest friends.

In his over 70-year career as a pianist, trumpeter, arranger and composer, he worked for Benny Goodman, Tommy Dorsey, Bing Crosby, Satchmo, … - a "musician's musician" is what Joe was called. He had written a few hits. "Oh Look At Me Now" is probably one of the most famous ones. He lived in Santa Barbara, 40 acres right along the coast. It must be nice.

Joe was always nice to me. I remember one night I was sleeping with the TV on. Suddenly I heard this familiar voice, and I said to myself half awake,

"I know this voice."

So I looked up, it was Joe, playing a jazz musician in that old movie "The Rat Race" with Tony Curtis. Joe was natural. It was funny to see him play himself in the movie. He was good.

I have this old faded picture that Joe sent Maury quite some time ago hanging in the store. The picture was Joe and Bing Crosby standing at a train station looked like somewhere in Europe. Joe was playing a Dizzy Gillespie model trumpet with a bent bell. Bing was smiling looking at Joe. In the back of the photo, Joe wrote,

"Dear Maury, these are the most beautiful people. —Too bad. But Bing & myself decided to show them what a real invasion feels like. It was too much. --- Tell you all about it when I get back around Sept. 10th. --- Love you and miss you, Joe."

You can tell how close they were and how much Joe loved Maury.

I don't know when this happened but I do have a copy of this audiotape titled "Maury Stein at Cedars-Sinai with Dr. Bushkin". Apparently when Maury was sick in the hospital one time, Joe went to visit him at Cedars', and according to Maury, Joe got in the hospital with a suitcase full of shit including a tape recorder. They got so fucked up and recorded this tape of two of them playing around. It started out with Maury saying,

"Well today, we have Dr. Bushkin here to examine my belly button which is in very fine condition. Wouldn't you say so? Doc?"

Joe said, "Yes, Maury, your belly button is fine." And then Joe asked, "Now Maury, who was that young couple that was just here?"

Maury said, "Oh, that was Tom and Louise."

"So what were they doing here, Maury?"

"Well, they just wanted to know if I had any pain and I told them Yes, I do. Would you like some?"

Then they went on pretending they were the hosts of The Tonight Show and had George Benson playing one of his hits "Breezin'" (just a fragment) and then they kept on going and quoting some silly quotes.

I can just picture those two guys totally fucked up and having a good old time in the hospital room like two little kids.

Anyway, Joe was a one of a kind musician. He told me he was self-taught. I remember one time Lou Levy asked him if he ever practiced any scales. Joe said, "Hell no! I write my own scales."

Joe told me that he always left the piano lid open in his house. He said, "Pops, there's nothing like whenever you walk in the room, there's somebody smiling at you."

*****

Pete and Conte Candoli

Both brothers were trumpet players born in Mishawaka, Indiana. Pete was 4 years older. He told me when Conte first joined Woody's band at age 16, he had to fly home from wherever they were, back to his high school to take the midterms and finals.

Somebody told me once that when Dizzy was asked who was his favorite white trumpet player?

Dizzy said, "Conte Candoli is the best white trumpet player."

"Who else?" "…Conte Candoli is the best white trumpet player."

When you think about it, the way Dizzy played and the way Conte played, it makes total sense!

One day Pete and Conte dropped in the store at the same time. They were so surprised to see each other. Those two brothers were special. They were the nicest people and they truly loved each other. Pete told me that he and Conte never had a fight with each other. I believe him.

Just so happened there was a little kid in the store with his father to buy a trumpet. Conte started to talk to the kid and gave him a few pointers about how to play the horn. I couldn't help but telling the kid how lucky he was to have two legendary trumpet players to show him how to play the horn and the father was totally knocked out by meeting the Candoli brothers.

Years later when Conte died, the next day I was driving with my wife to get some breakfast and we were listening to KLON (jazz radio station out of Long Beach, CA). Somebody called in and shared the story about when he took his son to buy a trumpet at Stein on Vine, there were two gentlemen at the store, and they were kind enough to show his kid how to play the trumpet.

He said, "I had no idea who those two gentlemen were until Gary Chen the owner of Stein on Vine told my son how lucky he was. That's when I found out those two were the famous Candoli brothers. I thought I needed to call in and share the story."

*****

Al Cohn

Al's from Brooklyn, New York, and he was considered one of the most lyrical tenor saxophone improvisers. He was best known as one of the 4 brothers in the Woody Herman band. He also wrote arrangements for the band. Incredibly talented musician, I love his playing, his compositions and arrangements.

One day Al came in and asked me to show him some metal tenor mouthpieces. I gave him a Dukoff no.7 to try. He put it on and played just one fast line for about 3 seconds and said, "OK, I'll take it."

I asked, "That's it, Al?"

"Yeah, I get confused if I played more."

There's a famous story about how quick minded Al was. One time he was playing in a club in Europe, some fan offered to buy him a Danish beer called "Elephant". Al thought for a second and said,

"No! I drink to forget."

Al was a well-read, well-informed, most intelligent musician. He was one of those guys can finish a crossword puzzle in 5 minutes.

Al did a few duo gigs with Lou Levy. I loved it. He played so well and so did Lou. It's very hard to play with just saxophone and piano. Especially for piano players, you have to play all the time but not play too much. Lou was an expert at that.

I remember one time Lou and Al were playing at the top floor of the Hyatt Hotel by the airport. Just so happened my friend Bobby Lai (Stan's brother) was visiting me from Taiwan, so I took him to check them out. Bobby is one of the very few of my old Chinese friends who truly love jazz. He was totally impressed by both Al and Lou. Al played just like his reputation as a lyrical flowing soloist. He had endless ideas and Lou was right there with him. When you only have two guys in the band, you play exactly how much you know, there's no place to hide.

Al didn't come to LA that often. Last time he played at Alfonse's with Lou, Chuck Berghofer (bass) and Nick Martinas (drums), the club was jam-packed. Everybody wanted to hear Al. So every time when Lou played at Alfonse's, the owner Charlie would always ask Lou,

"Any more Al Cohns?"

I miss Al and Lou's big smile every time they saw me at their gigs.

*****

Benny Goodman

According to Mike Stein (Maury's son), Maury and Benny were neighborhood friends in Chicago. What a neighborhood with Benny Goodman, Jule Styne and of course Maury.

Benny used the back room to rehearse with Lou Levy one time when he was in town playing for the Merv Griffin show. I remember Benny needed some reeds. So, Maury told me to bring all the Vandoren #1 ½ and #2 clarinet reeds to Benny. And Maury told Benny, "All right Benny, I'll let you try as many reeds as you want, and only pay me for the ones you like."
So Benny started to open up box after box of reeds. He didn't even put the ligature on, just held the reed with his thumb and blew a couple of notes and then threw the reed on the floor. I don't know how many boxes he went through.

He finally said, "Ah ha! Finally found one."

Maury said, "Pay me for that reed."

Benny said, "This is my own reed."

On that same day, Benny wanted to have his clarinet adjusted. So Maury had Manny (our horn repairman) take a look at Benny's horn. I happened to go to the back for something and I saw Benny pull up a chair, sit right in front of Manny, and stare at him working on his horn. I sensed the uptight tension right away. So I said to myself "let me get the hell out of here." Can you imagine? Having Benny Goodman sitting right in front of you watching you fixing his clarinet? Thank God, Manny did a great job.

In Taiwan I saw the movie "The Benny Goodman Story" with Steve Allen and Donna Reed. I liked it. Years later I saw it again. But this time it was so different because I actually knew a few guys in the movie. I loved those old big band movies. They used all the real musicians.

We have this old picture hanging on the wall with Benny and Stan Getz. Benny looked so happy and Stan looked so young. I think Stan was only 17, and he was playing a white Brilhardt mouthpiece.

*****

Johnny Guerin

JOHN GUERIN
DW DRUM ARTIST

Johnny was born in Hawaii but grew up in San Diego. He played drums with Buddy DeFranco (Be-bop jazz clarinetist) in 1960. Moved to Los Angeles where he started to work with big names like Frank Sinatra, George Harrison, Frank Zappa, Joni Mitchell, Peggy Lee, Ella Fitzgerald, Nelson Riddle…

Johnny Guerin was another one of the guys always came to see Maury. What a drummer. He told me he was totally self-taught. He said,

"Gary, I never took any lessons. I just played. When I was 16, I thought I was good enough to play with anybody, so I went to see Trane at the Light House. After they finished the first set, I went up to Trane and asked him if I could play with him. Trane was very nice. He said, "Ah ... thank you very much, but I have Elvin and we had a few things worked out, maybe some other time". But you know what, Gary? I wasn't ready! Same thing with Miles. When he played at the Light House, I asked him if I could sit in, Miles said, 'Go fuck yourself!'"

Later on Johnny decided to fool around with alto sax. He had a Martin and I overhauled it for him. He was getting pretty good. Last time he played for me, he actually had a sound.

Somebody brought me a few pictures of this concert taken somewhere in LA with Johnny on drums, Victor Feldman on piano and congas, Chuck DeMonico on bass and Tom Scott on sax and flute. Everybody looked so young. Johnny looked like he was only 15. How sad! In that picture, Tom is the only one still around. Last time I saw Tom in the store, we were both laughing about how we've put on quite a few pounds.

*****

Richie Kamuka

A tenor saxophone player, born in Philadelphia, PA, Richie played with Stan Kenton, Woody Herman, Chet Baker, Maynard Ferguson, then Lighthouse All-Stars, later on with Shorty Rogers and Shelly Manne.

Maury told me this story about Richie:

Richie came in one day and he wanted to try out all the tenor mouthpieces. He finally found one that he liked the most, and he said,

"I want to buy this mouthpiece and don't give me any discount, charge me full price. Just do it, don't ask me why!"

After he paid for the mouthpiece, he brought it to Maury and said to him,

"There you go Maury. This is the right mouthpiece for you. You'll like it."

Well, like I always said, some people just got class. And, you can tell how much Maury was loved by the guys

*****

Johnny Mandel

From New York City, Johnny is not only an excellent trombone and bass trumpet player, he is also one of the most renowned composers and arrangers today, if not the best in my opinion.

Johnny came to visit Maury from time to time. Like everyone else, Johnny loved Maury. Sometimes he would even stay over at Maury's. We used to call Johnny, "Mendel", and Johnny calls me "Chen-Stein".

I was really thrilled the first time I met Johnny because I've been a big fan of his ever since "The Shadow of Your Smile". I was only 13 when Johnny wrote that song. I remember spending quite a few nights trying to figure out all the changes. Never in my wildest dreams did I think that I would have the opportunity to have a drink and hang out with the guy who wrote "The Shadow of Your Smile".

Every time after I closed up the shop and saw Johnny's Saab parked in the lot, I would have a big smile on my face.

What talent!!! Some of Johnny's most famous compositions include: "Suicide is Painless" (theme for M*A*S*H*), "Close Enough for Love", "Emily", "A Time for Love", and of course "The Shadow of Your Smile".

Johnny wrote a book "The Johnny Mandel Songbook". It has most of his hits. If you really spend some time playing all the songs as written, you'll find out just how hip and gorgeous Johnny's arrangements are. You can't add anything to it. They're just perfect. As a matter of fact, if you analyze and study Johnny's harmony, you'll realize that's what Jazz is really all about.

We spent quite a few nights in the back room hanging out talking about everything. Johnny played baritone horn one night after he played a few tunes on piano. I knew he was a good trombone player so I wasn't surprised that he sounded pretty good on the baritone horn.

Johnny told me when Miles was recording "Birth of the Cool" he wanted to use Johnny on trombone. But unfortunately Johnny was in LA, so he missed it. I can tell how much Johnny wished that he could have been on that gig.

We were hanging out together at Herb Alpert's "Charlie Chaplin Studio" in A&M records when Herb was hosting Stan Getz's Memorial. I was the first one got up and gave a little speech about Stan. Afterwards Johnny and I were standing in the back having a drink and listening to Stan's music. Johnny told me that certain musicians have the sound that could touch people right away regardless whether the listeners have any knowledge about music, and Stan is definitely one of them. Billie Holiday is another one.

I couldn't agree with him more.

*****

Don Menza

Don Menza, Photo by Donald Dean

Menza was born and raised in Buffalo, New York, a tenor sax player, arranger, composer, and Jazz educator. He had worked with Maynard Ferguson and Stan Kenton. Later on he spent a few years in Germany with his own quintet. Joined Buddy Rich in 1968, and then moved to LA and played in the bands of Elvin Jones and Louie Bellson.

Don built a whole entertainment center (including a TV set) for Maury. We had a lot of fun watching all the ball games in the back room. That's when that stupid joke was going around,

"What's the score?"

"2 to nothing."

"Who's winning?"

"2!"

Don's big band played Frank Rosolino's memorial (Rosolino - a great trombone player from Detroit, Michigan, committed suicide after shooting his two sons in 1978). It was hard to see Frank's son (who was losing his vision) survive that terrible tragedy.

The band was really swinging hard. Menza wrote some mean charts. That tune "Estate" (Italian--means "summer" written by Bruno Martino and Bruno Brighetti), has one of the most beautiful melodies. Don's arrangement was so perfect you can almost feel the heat. I remember Shelly Manne was on drums. Shelly had an accident earlier and he broke his foot so he was on crutches. He played the whole set with one foot. You can't even tell there's anything missing. Both trumpet players Bill Berry and Jack Sheldon were trading 4's (taking 4-bar solo's back and forth) and they were awesome! I like Don's arrangements. Don is a hell of a flute player as well.

Maury and I used to go to Menza's house all the time. Maury loved Don and Rose. Don is one of the very few people who never took advantage of Maury's generosity and Rose cooks the best linguini with white clam sauce. I even got the recipe from her.

Every year the couple invited everybody to come to their house for Christmas. It was like an open house. Rose would cook up a storm to feed all the guests. Probably half of the LA jazz musicians would be there. It was a great hang. I really miss going there with Maury, watching Menza's mini train going around the living room and listening to Pavarotti. What a couple and what great times!!!

Don's son Nicky had been taking drum lessons from almost everybody since he was a little boy. He later on became quite a drummer himself. He ended up joining "Megadeth" and became a heavy metal star. I remember Maury and I actually went to "The Troubadour" to see Nicky play one night. They were SOOO LOUD! It was funny to see Maury hanging out with all the metal heads. That's another great thing about Maury. He could fit in anywhere, with anybody, young, old, didn't matter. But the next day I overheard him talking to Lynn on the phone,

"…Well, I went to see the deaf brothers last night…"

*****

Red Mitchell

RED MITCHELL

PHOTOGRAPH
JAMES GUDEMAN

Born in NY City, Red played bass and piano. But he played piano and alto sax in the Army band, later switched back to bass. He played with Chubby Jackson's big band at Bop City 1949, then Woody Herman from '49 to late '51.

Red was another one of Maury's oldest friends. He came to see Maury whenever he was in town. The first time I saw Red play was at Alfonse's. He played duo with Herb Mickman on piano, and then they switched since they both play both instruments. That was interesting. I remember I was sitting in the club and saying to myself,

"There's something wrong. Red's fingering doesn't match the sound coming out of that bass."

I was drinking but I certainly wasn't drunk. I didn't find out until later that Red tuned his bass in fifths like a cello instead of fourths.

I like Red's version of "I Get a Kick out Of You". He called it "I'll Kick the Shit out Of You".

Red told me that he bought a bass from Maury in the late 50's and he actually told Scott LaFaro to check out Maury's Prescott bass (Abraham Prescott born in Deerfield, New Hampshire 1789. One of the earliest American violinmakers and mainly made double basses and cellos) and Scotty ended up buying that bass from Maury and played it until the day he died in a car accident. That bass was totally damaged. Samuel and Barrie Kolstein of New York completely restored it (beautiful job) and brought it to the bass convention at UCLA in 1988.

Red and I played that bass at the convention and we were both amazed how good the bass sounded, especially on the G and D string. All the notes just jump right out at thumb position. No wonder Scotty played the way he played.

Incidentally, that car accident happened only 2 days after Scotty played with Stan Getz at the Newport Jazz Festival, 10 days after he recorded those two live classic albums with Bill Evans and Paul Motian "Sunday at the Village Vanguard" and "Waltz for Debby" at age 25.

Like my friend Stan Lai said, "Those two live albums were so beautiful, you want to cry."

*****

Gerry Mulligan

Mulligan was born in Queens Village, Long Island, New York, but the family moved around a lot because of his father's job. Moved to Reading, PA at age 14 where he started to study clarinet and saxophone. He also explored his interest in arranging and later played saxophone professionally in Philadelphia. Came back to New York, joined Gene Krupa 1947, played and recorded with Miles Davis's nine-piece band in 1948. He played baritone sax and arranged several tunes on Miles Davis' classic recording "Birth of the Cool", probably the most famous jazz baritone saxophone player of all time.

Mulligan was in the store one day. We had a nice long chat. I told him how much I've been enjoying his music ever since I was a kid.

He said, "Gary, you are a fine gentleman with great taste!"

Well, Mulligan was another one of the bandleaders like Art Blakey and Horace Silver, who always managed to find young talented musicians. Geoff Keezer (piano player) is definitely one of them. First time I heard Geoff play with Mulligan, I was impressed!! Years later when Geoff was playing with the Ray Brown trio, I went to see them at Catalina's. The next day Geoff came to visit. I told him that he sounded so good that I'd like to hear him in a different set up. He told me that that was his last gig with Ray. Evidently, he felt it was time for him to move on doing his own thing. I actually heard that in his playing that night.

*****

Chuck Piscatello

Chuck had been running Carmelo's. As a matter of fact, he built the whole club with his own two hands. Chuck played drums and he was the kind of guy that everybody loved. I saw so many great players at Carmelo's including Stan Getz. But the band that I was most impressed by was Clare Fischer's Salsa Picante and his 2+2 singers. I always love Clare Fischer, his playing, his harmony and arrangements. But that vocal group really blew me away. All four voices came in perfectly harmonized in a DIFFERENT key after the intro. I got goose bumps when I heard that. They were fantastic. Chuck was doing a great job getting all the great players. He was like an in-house drummer, played with almost everybody.

Chuck loved Maury!!!

I remember one night some asshole shot and shattered the storefront glass door. I got a phone call from ADT in the middle of the night and ended up staying in the store for the rest of the night because there was no alarm and no front door. I didn't bother to call Maury. The next day I waited till Maury came in then told him what happened. The next thing I knew Chuck came in and gave me a big hug thanking me for taking care of the old man.

After Chuck's brother (Carmelo) died, the family decided not to let Chuck run the club anymore. That's when all the guys stopped going there and the club started going down.

Chuck built a chair for Maury and brought it to him a couple of days before he had a heart attack and died at home at age 43. That was the first and only time I saw Maury cry.

I remember pulling into the parking lot that morning and saw Maury's truck. So I went in the back room to give him a hug but I saw Maury standing there, crying. I said, "Jesus! Maury, what's wrong?" He said, "Chuck died!"

I was in total shock! I just saw him two days ago with that chair.

Sad! After Chuck died, that was the end of Carmelo's.

*****

Nelson Riddle

Nelson was born June 1st, 1921 in Oradell, New Jersey. He was a trombone player, arranger, composer, bandleader, and orchestrator. His career had a long stretch from the late 40's to the mid 80's.

He started piano lessons at age 8 and trombone at 14. After graduating from high school, Nelson started playing trombone and writing arrangements for various local dance bands. Moved to New York in 1943 working for the Charlie Spivak orchestra and studied orchestration under composer Alan Shulman. He joined the Tommy Dorsey orchestra in 1944 and came to Hollywood in 1946. His sound and arrangements made him one of the major arrangers for Capitol Records. He had worked with singers like Ella Fitzgerald, Frank Sinatra, Dean Martin, Nat Cole, Judy Garland, Peggy Lee, Rosemary Clooney, Johnny Mathis, Keely Smith and Linda Ronstadt.

Nelson had always been one of my all time favorite arrangers.

First time I met Nelson, he came to the store to buy some bandstands for his big band. He was kind of grumpy. I told him I've been a big fan of his for many, many years, especially all those songbooks that he arranged for Ella.

He said, "I stole everything from Mozart and Debussy".

It must have something to do with that particular instrument, all the great arrangers that I know of, they're all trombone players: Nelson Riddle, Johnny Mandel, Billy Byers, J. J. Johnson, Tommy Dorsey, Glenn Miller…. maybe it's because where they sit in the band, they can hear everything better.

I watched quite a few of Sinatra's live TV shows. Nelson was the conductor for most of them. What great shows they were. When Sinatra had Ella on the show, Lou Levy was the piano player. The trio worked perfectly with Nelson's orchestra.

*****

Jimmy Rowles

Jimmy was from Spokane, Washington and I heard he studied piano privately. He got started with Ben Webster, and later worked with Lester Young and Billie Holiday in the early 40's, then with Benny Goodman, Woody Herman, Les Brown, and Tommy Dorsey. He moved to California in 1951 and freelanced ever since.

What a piano player and composer Jimmy was. He loved coming to the store to visit Maury. He actually did a recording with Maury in the back room. Jimmy had always been one of my favorite west coast piano players. Stacy, his daughter, was an excellent musician too. It was so sad. After her car accident, she pretty much drank herself to death. She never got the recognition that she deserved as a trumpeter and singer.

I had a chance to hang with Jimmy one night in the back room, just the two of us. He told me quite a few stories. He talked with that raspy voice,

"You know, Gary, the first time I played with "Lady" (Billie Holiday), I went to her hotel room, I knocked on the door and waited for a while. Suddenly the door just slammed opened. There she was, buck naked!!"

He also told me that his son was a bass player too. He said, "Too bad, my son did not want to be a musician. He could have been as good as George Mraz".

Well, that's quite a statement because George Mraz is one of my favorite bass players.

Anyway, Jimmy started to play and sing all night long. Tune after tune. He kept asking me, "You know this one? Good!"

We hung till 4 in the morning. He was so drunk. I insisted on getting him a cab. He left his Volkswagen Bug in the lot and came back next day to get it. I'll never forget that night.

*****

George Mraz

Every time Maury and I went to see Stan Getz play, Mraz would be on bass.

I asked Stan once, "You like George Mraz, don't you?"

Stan said, "Oh, sure! He made some of the bass players I worked with sounded like they got 5 thumbs."

To me, Mraz is a perfect bass player. He's got great time, great feel, perfect intonation and he bows like a mother. When he plays he really spells out the changes, no bullshit just good music. Last time I saw George was at Catalina's with Hank Jones. What a duo! Everything was so effortless. I love Hank Jones. What a master piano player - such class, such taste. Mraz played some gorgeous arco solos, perfectly in tune and melodic, just like a horn player.

Out of tune arco bass solo is a bitch to tolerate. I heard Mraz was a violin virtuoso when he was a kid. That didn't surprise me. He's from Czech Republic, so they call him "Bad Czech".

How appropriate!

*****

Fred Selden

From Los Angeles, Fred's one of the busiest studio musicians. He had been nominated for a Grammy as conductor, arranger and composer. He plays all reeds and a variety of different ethnic flutes. He is also one of the first guys to play an EWI (electronic wind instrument). He played EWI on "Star Trek" for 18 years, a great musician and a great friend. It's always nice to see his warm, smiling face coming into the store.

Fred told me he bought his first Selmer cigar cutter alto sax from Maury when he was about 7, 8 years old. He said Maury came to his house with a few horns for him to choose, and his brother actually dropped one of them and dented the bell. Maury even volunteered to go to his house to give him some free lessons.

Fred told me he actually bought Bud Shank's horn. As a musician, it's got to be a big thrill that you get to play one of your mentors' horn. I bet you Fred must feel honored and privileged that he has Bud's horn. When I told Fred how Bud got that gig bag from Maury, he said that just made that horn even more special to him.

Incidentally, Fred played all the flute parts in that movie "The Last Samurai".

Great job!

*****

Bud Shank

Bud was born in Dayton, Ohio. He started with clarinet, later on switched to saxophone, worked with Charlie Barnet before hitting the West Coast jazz scene.

Bud came in one day to visit Maury. I have this old picture of these 5 guys, Maury and Bud holding an alto sax, both Dave Pell and Bob Cooper with tenor sax and Buddy Bregman (arranger, also Maury's nephew) standing in the middle. The picture was probably taken at least 50 years ago. Maury had a baby face so he actually looked like the youngest of all. There's a little grease spot on Bud's head in that picture. So when I showed Bud the picture, he said, "Who shit on my head?"

The day after, Bud called me, "Gary? Bud Shank! Listen man, yesterday when I was in the shop, I told Maury I needed a leather gig bag for my horn, and Maury just gave me one. I think he really took the friendship a bit too far. I can't just take the bag from him for nothing. If he keeps doing that, we won't have a place to hang anymore. So, I'm gonna send you a check for $150. I don't know if that's enough but at least it's something. So, just deposit it when you get it. Don't even mention that to Maury. OK? Love you, man. I'll see you soon."

What can I say? When you have class you always have class.

*****

Zoot Sims

Zoot played tenor, alto, soprano saxophone and clarinet. He worked with Benny Goodman, Stan Kenton, Joe Bushkin, Al Cohn, Gerry Mulligan …but he also was best known as one of the "Four Brothers" sax team with the Woody Herman band from 1947-49.

Zoot was in the store one day and for some reason he needed a horn to play. Maury told me to give him a mint condition Selmer Balanced Action tenor sax (with original lacquer). I don't know whether Maury just gave him the horn or loaned it to him. Anyway I don't think that was the horn Zoot always played. Zoot played a Selmer Super for a long time on a lot of his recordings.

I always like Zoot - his sound, his time and the way he swings. Zoot was from Inglewood, California. Maybe that's why he's got so much soul.

I have this picture of Maury and Zoot playing in Maury's living room at his Beverly Hills home. Zoot was playing soprano sax and Maury was sitting on the floor playing a clarinet. It seems that they were having a good time. I really like Zoot's soprano sound - big, fat and warm. You don't usually get that kind of sound from a soprano sax.

We all heard somebody asked Zoot what he thought about Stan Getz, and Zoot said, "Nice bunch of guys."

Lou Levy told me another interesting story about Zoot when they were in Woody's band. Zoot was a big fan of Pres (Lester Young). One time Woody's band and the Basie band stayed in the same hotel. As soon as Zoot found out Pres was in the hotel he went to find Pres and asked Pres to come to his room. He sat Pres down, and pulled up a chair. He sat right in front of him and played every solo that Pres had ever recorded. Lou said Pres was so impressed he didn't know what to say.

Well, Pres influenced almost every saxophone player. You can hear Pres in a lot of players. Pres also created his own language. He had a unique way of describing things. Donald Maggin talked about Pres in his book "A Life in Jazz". He wrote when Pres said, "Can Madame burn?" He meant, "Can your wife cook?" He called the police "Bing and Bob". And Al McKibbon (legendary bass player) told me when Pres gambled he said, "I bet two of my people." He meant he bet two dollars.

Al also told me that he asked Pres once, "Hey Pres, how come you hold your horn so high?" and Pres said,

"This fucking horn is so out of tune, Daddy! I have to play this way to play in tune."

Here's another one from Al:

When Pres was with Jazz at the Phil, one day Norman Granz was very upset with Billie Holiday and he literally yelled at her to tears.

Pres stepped in and told Norm, "You can't talk to Lady like that!"

Norm got so pissed off he actually punched Pres to the floor.

And Pres said, "Wow, you cup me a Sunday Daddy!" (Sunday punch- a knockout blow in boxing)

Anyway, Maury actually recorded several jam sessions in the back room with himself on tenor and a bunch of other guys. Lou Levy was on couple of them, and so were Jimmy Rowles and John Banister. The bass players were Leroy Vinegar, Jim Atlas and Harry Babasin. And there was one with guitar player Al Hendrickson. Anyway, Maury played mostly ballads. He had a very good sound and I liked the way he played.

He played that tape for Zoot, and Zoot told him,

"Well, I like it. See, some people like the way I play, and some people might like the way you play. Everybody's got their own thing."

Maury was so pleased with what Zoot said. He told me the same story at least a dozen times.

(John Banister told me the story about one of his classical musician friends who wanted to learn how to play Jazz so he called John in the middle of the night and asked, "John, how do you play jazz?"

Half awake, John said, "Fair, I hope!")

*****

Connie Stevens

Born in Brooklyn, New York, Connie is an actress and singer. She joined the vocal group called "The Fourmost" with three male vocalists when she was in her teens. Those three vocalists later on became the famous "The Lettermen".

The first time I heard about Connie was that song "Sixteen Reasons" that she recorded when I was a little boy in Taiwan.

Connie loved Maury. She told me her father was a bass player. She grew up watching her father play in all the studios and she loved to hang with the guys. That's why she is so hip.

One time Maury was playing at Donte's. Connie sat in and sang "There Will Never Be Another You" for Maury. I thought that was very appropriate plus she's got such a beautiful voice. She really touched everybody and Maury loved it.

Which reminds me that Sweets Edison (Sinatra's favorite trumpet player) did the same tune one night at the club Loa, he said,

"This next tune is dedicated to our president Ronald Reagan, titled 'I wish there will never ever be another you'".

Connie was rehearsing in my back room one day. She pulled in the parking lot in her brand new red Corvette. Styling! That same day Wayne Shorter (great composer and sax player) came to visit also. I took Wayne to meet Connie. They were both thrilled. Apparently they admired each other.

I remember in Taiwan watching that old TV sitcom "Wendy and Me" with Connie and George Burns. I don't think we had color TV yet. Last time I saw her at Alfonse's she looked the same. Some people just don't age.

*****

Sonny Stitt

Sonny was born in Boston, Mass, came from a musical family. Father was a college music professor, his mother was a piano teacher and his brother was a classically trained pianist. Sonny played alto sax with Getz and Dizz in 1945, later he played tenor sax more because he didn't want people to refer to him as a Charlie

Parker emulator. Personally, I don't see how that could be because they had different sound. Keith Fiddmont (sax player) and I both agree that Sonny's sound is a bit sweeter.

There were so many jazz clubs in those good old days. Carmelo's, Donte's, Hop Singh's, The Loa, Alfonse's, Money tree, Le Café, Chaney's, and Catalina's Bar and Grill... Whoever was playing in town, they would all stop by to see Maury.

I met Sonny just a few weeks before he died. Maury and Sonny came in from the back room to check out Maury's cockatiels. Maury introduced Sonny to me:

"Sonny, say hello to my son Gary the Doctor."

I was totally thrilled to meet Sonny because he is truly one of my all time favorite saxophone players. His melodic ideas and incredible time often made me say to myself,

"How the hell did he play like that?"

Not too many saxophone players can play tenor and alto equally well like Sonny.

It was really something to watch those two old guys singing, whistling and laughing with them two birds.

*****

Sir Charles Thompson

SIR CHARLES THOMPSON
COMPOSER OF ROBBINS NEST

Charles Phillip Thompson, a piano player, composer, and organist born in Springfield, Ohio, started his career in his early teens. Lester Young named him "Sir Charles Thompson." While with Illinois Jacquet (tenor sax player) in 1947, Sir Charles composed "Robins' Nest", which became a Jazz standard.

Sir Charles loved Maury. He always stopped by to visit. He got interested in playing Tenor sax, so every time he came in he would ask Maury to give him a few pointers.

Somebody gave me a videotape that was recorded in London 1964. It was a live Jazz show broadcast on TV. On that tape, Sir Charles was on piano, Harry Sweets Edison on trumpet, Coleman Hawkins on tenor, Joe Jones on drums and Jimmy Wood on bass. They were having a ball. Everybody was so relaxed and the band started to swing from the very first beat. Coleman Hawkins played some awesome solos with that powerful big sound. Sweet's got the most recognizable sweet sound on his trumpet. Joe Jones was swinging his ass off and posing for the camera the whole time. I love to watch drummers play with a relaxed wrist. You can hear the difference right away. I made a copy for Sir Charles.

A few days later, it was New Years Eve. Sir Charles called me at home and told me how grateful he was for that tape. He said,

"Gary, there's nothing like watching yourself play 20 some years ago and sounding good! You made me so proud of myself, and I thank you for that."

Then he told me, "Gary, did you know me and "Bird" used to room together?"

I said, "No, I had no idea."

"Yeah man, and most people didn't know this, at the beginning, all "Bird" was trying to do was to copy Tatum."

"Really? Yeah I can see that."

We ended up talking about music, life, people, for about two hours.

Not too many people that I can talk to on the phone for that long.

*****

Mel Tormé

Like Maury, Mel's from Chicago, a child prodigy who first performed on stage at age 4. By the time he was 9, he was already a veteran of Chicago radio series, while at the same time Mel was learning to play the drums. When he was 15, he actually got an offer from Harry James as a singer and drummer. He couldn't take the gig because of his young age. Torme' was best known as a singer, but he was also a fine pianist, drummer and arranger. His soft velvety voice with impeccable time and a great sense of jazz made him one of the greatest jazz vocalists. He is nicknamed "The Velvet Fog" and he IS one of my favorite male Jazz vocalists.

According to Maury, when he had his own sextet in the late 30's, he had Mel on drums and Barney Kessel on guitar. Mel and Barney used to room together. The story I heard was how Mel would talk to Barney about his singing all night long. And finally he took a break and said to Barney,

"Enough about me, Barney, let's talk about you, what do you think about me?"

One time Tormé was performing at the Hollywood Bowl, Maury and I went to see him. After the concert, we went to backstage to see Mel. When we got to the dressing room, there were so many people jammed pack in the room.

Maury took one look at all the people and said, "Fuck it! Let's get the hell out of here!"

As we were walking out of the room, we both heard this voice, "Maury Stein?!"

It was Mel. He saw Maury from the other side of the room and made his way through the crowd to give Maury a big hug. Evidently they hadn't seen each other for years.

John Leitham (now Jennifer - Mel's bass player) told me Mel loved movies and he always went to the theater and ate all the junk food. That's probably what killed him.

Leitham and I went to Mel's house once and Mel showed us his multi-million dollar old single action pistol collection. What an experience that was! I've never seen so many gorgeous old pistols in one place.

I had a chance to catch Mel perform with George Shearing. They had been working together since the late 70's. Like Shearing said,

"I humbly put forth that Mel and I had the best musical marriage in many a year, we literally breathed together during our countless performances. As Mel put it, we were two bodies in one musical mind."

What a great concert that was. Mel wrote some fascinating arrangements. He mixed his superb scatting chops with Charlie Parker's Be-bop lines, singing them perfectly in tune with complicated rhythmic patterns. You're talking about a true Be-bop vocalist. I honestly believe Mel was the last one who could do that at that level. That shit is lost.

*****

The French horn players

The French horn players - Vince De Rosa, Henry Sigismonti, and Art Maebe, they always came together to see Maury whenever they were between dates. I love them.

Vince is definitely considered a legend in the world of French horn players. He's been so active in the business for so many years, when he retired a lot of the young players thought he was dead.

I saw this videotape of one of Freddie Hubbard's recording sessions. He used only one horn player. Guess who that was?

Henry and I became very good friends. He was the principal horn player of Los Angeles Philharmonic under Zubin Mehta. Later on, like Vince, he quit LA Phil and became one of the first-call studio musicians.

What a great horn player Henry was. We started to hang a lot more after Maury died. I often took him to Monterey Park for good

Chinese food, and Henry was the one who hip me to that thin crust crispy pizza with no sauce, no cheese just fresh garlic, olive oil and anchovies. Henry always called me "Chen-Stein".

Not too many classical musicians were hanging out with Maury in those days. Those French horn players were special.

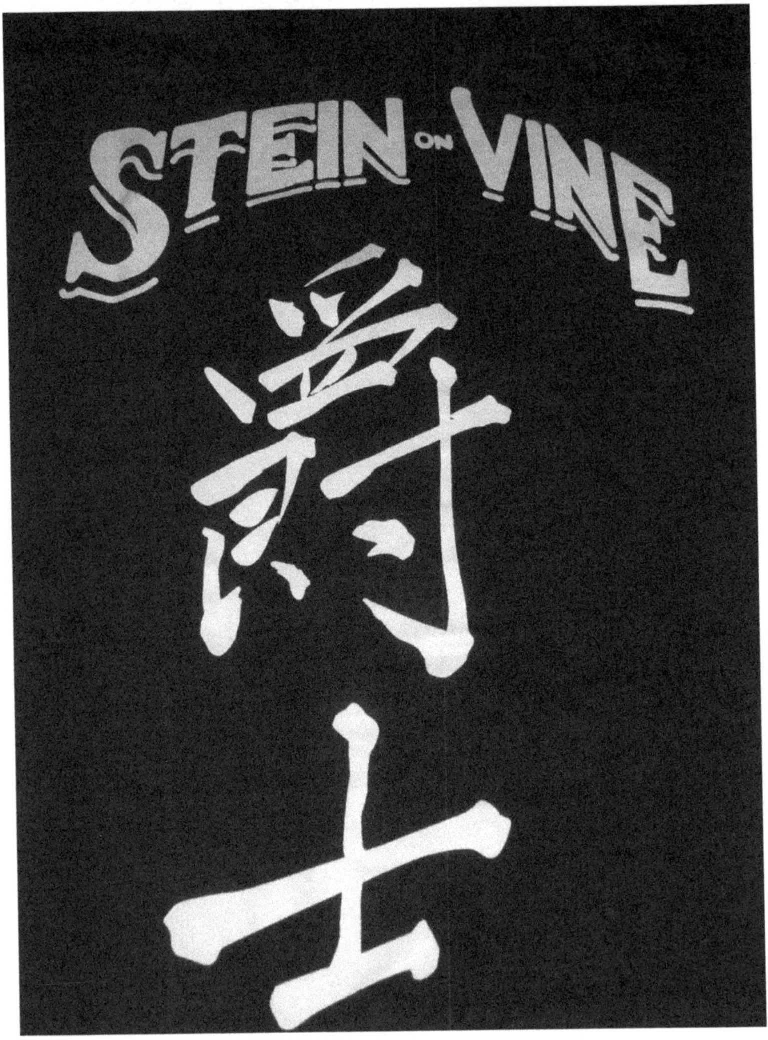
STEIN ON VINE
爵士

VII: MAURY'S DEATH

It was a Friday right after New Year in 1987.

I finished work, locked up the store and went to the parking lot to get my car. Maury was just about pulling out of the driveway when he saw me. He asked, "You want to have dinner with us tonight?" meaning him and Lynn.

I hesitated for a minute because we usually got together on Saturday nights since we don't have to work on Sunday so we could hang out late. But I said, "Yeah sure, why not."

So I followed him home like I always did. He was driving in the middle of the two lanes like he always did. We finally got to the house, and he lied to Viola like he always did. Something like, "We're working at the Paramount (or 20th Century Fox) tonight."

Maury told me more than once,

"I've been lying to my wife for 50 years. If I ever tell her the truth, she wouldn't believe me."

Viola was a very unusual woman. She was living in her own little world and she was content. She didn't want to have anything to do with Maury's active life. Maury provided her a comfortable simple lifestyle and she seemed to be ok with that. The only time Maury ever took her out was when her sister came to visit from Chicago. Maury took them to Carmelo's as he was playing that night. I ended up driving them home after the first set.

So anyway, that evening Maury and I walked the dogs (Peppi and Bengie) around Beverly Hills like we always did. Peppi was a black boy street dog Maury saved and kept, and Bengie was the sweetest white girl poodle. She's got a musician's union membership card that says "Bengie Stein."

Usually Maury would smoke some shit before we took the walk, and he would always say this to me, "Do you want to see this world the way it really isn't? Have a poke!"

We walked around the hills and he would ask me the same questions,

"That's what's his name's house?"

I said, "Smokey Robinson".

"That's right!" and then,

"That's what's her name's house?"

"Shirley Jones".

"That's right!"

So we took separate cars to Lynn's because I knew I was going home early since I had to open up the shop in the morning. Lynn cooked some kosher franks (from Gelson's) for dinner. Lynn drove all the way in from Orange County and she must have stopped by Gelson's.

Anyway, at the dinner table, after a couple of Jack Daniels, Lynn suddenly said to Maury, "You know Maury, I hate to nag you but, --- you really need to put something down on paper. God forbid, if anything happens to you, I hate to see Gary running around not knowing what to do."

Well, for the longest time I wasn't sure what I was going to do with my future because I was having such a good time with the old man. But I had finally decided I wanted to go back home and play, because that was what I came here for in the first place. But I never told anybody. So I was totally surprised when I heard Lynn say that. I said,

"Whoa, whoa, whoa, where did that come from?"

But right after I said that, I turned to Maury and told him,

"You know what? Maury, actually we should talk about this. As a matter of fact, I need to talk to you about this. You see, Maury, I never told you what I used to do. I never told you what kind of money I used to make. I certainly never told you what kind of offers I've been getting from back home in the past seven years. Some of the offers were so good and tempting. It's really hard for me. But I had to turn them down because I can't leave you. I love you, Maury. I don't want to leave you. But I didn't come to the United States to own a music store. This was not in my plan. Plus, the store is a trap. I don't want to be tied down. So, Maury, whatever you do with the store, don't count me in. I'm here as long as you're here. When you're gone, I'm gone!"

Maury didn't say a word, just sat there. A few minutes later, he said, "I'm not feeling very well, I need to go lay down." So he got up and went to the bedroom.

Lynn and I kept talking until it was almost 11 o'clock. I said,

"Oh, shit, I didn't know it's already this late. I gotta go, I gotta work tomorrow."

So I went to the bedroom and gave Maury a kiss, "I'll see you tomorrow Maury, love you, gotta go."

Well, I got home. For some odd reason, I felt like chanting for the first time since I started to practice Nichiren Buddhism about two weeks before. I had told both Maury and Lynn that I was introduced to this practice and went to a Buddhist meeting. I loved the sound of chanting. It really did something to me so I started to practice.

I didn't know how long that I'd been chanting until the phone rang. It was Viola. I knew right away something was wrong. She'd never called me at night especially midnight. So immediately I said, "Vi, what's wrong?"

She said, "Well, Maury came home and told the dogs he couldn't walk them because he wasn't feeling well, and then he just dropped on the floor."

"Oh My God! I'll be right over."

"Oh no, I've already called the paramedics."

"What hospital?"

"Cedars-Sinai"

"Ok, I'll see you over there!"

I hung up the phone ran out of the apartment, got back into my car and I started to curse, "God damn! Maury, I am so sick and tired of this shit."

Maury passed out a couple of times in the last year or so and one of them was in the bank. He went to do some banking and never came back. I had to call all the near-by hospitals to find out which hospital they took him to. I thought this was another one of those Maury Stein's episodes. So I started talking to myself, "All right Maury, I am really tired of this, from now on, nothing for you. No booze, no blow, no cigarettes, no nothing. I can't deal with this anymore."

I got to the hospital, walked right into the emergency room and saw Viola standing there. Before I even got a chance to talk to her I saw this doctor walking towards us followed by two nurses. I didn't like the look on their faces. Sure enough the doctor came over and said to Vi,

"Mrs. Stein? Mr. Stein just passed away."

I said, "No way! Not Maury!"

The minute I said that I knew it was true. It finally happened!

Lynn and I had been worrying about Maury for quite some time. He hadn't looked very well lately – watery eyes, pale and tired. Well, the way Maury lived, he could go anytime. I remember Lynn used to tell me, often when she came in from Orange County every weekend, as soon as she put the keys in her apartment door, she wondered when would be the last time she's ever gonna see Maury. He was still doing everything, partying hard at age 76.

I asked the doctor if I could go see Maury. Doc said, "Sure!"

He pointed at one of the rooms behind him. Vi didn't want to go so I went by myself. I walked in the room, pulled opened the curtain and there he was, lying there with his mouth open. The doctor did say that the attack was so massive he didn't even have time to feel the pain. Well, the look on his face says exactly that.

I started to cry. It was so weird. I was just with him two, three hours ago. Look at him now!

I don't know how long I cried. I finally pulled myself together, and suddenly, the first thing that came to my mind was,

"Oh my God! Who's gonna take care of the store...Man! ... Stein on Vine is gonna go down the drain. Oh my God!"

I never thought about the store!

All this time I was thinking about me, and what I wanted to do. This was the first time that I realized if I don't take over, Stein on Vine would be GONE! And I am not sure that's what I wanted and I don't know if I could live with that!

I took a good look at Maury and said to him, "Jesus, Maury, I think you got me. You got me good!"

I took Viola home then I drove to a nearby phone booth at the corner of Santa Monica and Doheny. (Cellular phone was nowhere in the picture) I got out of the car and walked around the phone booth and tried to decide whether I should call Lynn. It was 4 in the morning. Maybe I should wait, let her sleep for a couple of more hours…

I called!

"Lynn?"

She recognized my voice right away, "Yeah, sweetheart?"

"Lynn, eh… Maury just left us!"

(Dead silence)

Finally she said, "You want to come over?"

"Eh… yeah, I'll be right over."

So I drove back to her condo, she opened the door and burst into tears in my arms. She already started cooking - mashed potatoes. She didn't know what else to do. She was sobbing from time to time.

It was so weird! A few hours ago the three of us were sitting here eating, drinking and laughing, having a great time, and now just hours later, everything's changed.

I finally made it back to my apartment. I was exhausted and it was already 7 o'clock in the morning so I started to make phone calls. I called everybody.

Jews don't wait long for their funerals. So the very next Sunday, we had the funeral at Hillside Mortuary. I have no idea how many musicians and friends came to the funeral. Maury told me more than once that he wanted to be buried in Hollywood Forever Funeral Home on Santa Monica Blvd. right by the store so the guys can come over to visit him. But Vi chose Hillside.

Funny, I remember hearing Maury arguing with Vi about where he wanted to be buried, he said, "Why don't you get buried at Hillside and let me stay in Hollywood, we sleep in separate beds anyway."

Lou Levy sent me a postcard once and it was a picture of Hillside Cemetery. On the back, he wrote, "Remember separate beds?"

Stan Getz flew in from up north. Joey Bushkin drove down from Santa Barbara. It was funny when Vi saw Lynn. She thought Lynn was Joe's wife since Lynn was standing right next to Joe when everybody was standing in line paying respects to the family. Vi said to Lynn,

"Oh, I always wanted to meet Joe Bushkin's wife. It's so nice to finally meet you."

I was standing right next to Vi and I looked at Lynn, she looked at me, I just didn't know what to think.

Maury's cousin Bob Danziger mentioned Maury's funeral in his book. This is what he said:

> "The rabbi and Maury had never met, so when he got to the standard part of the service about 'And he was a good and faithful husband,' all in attendance.... and I'm not making this up.... put their faces in their armpits and chortled."

After the funeral, we all went to Alfonse's. Lynn arranged food and drinks for everybody. What a scene. Maury had touched so many people's hearts. I've never seen so many people crying and laughing at the same time. Everybody played and so did Stan Getz. I took quite a few pictures of that party.

*****

Now, Maury's gone, and of course there's no will and I'm nowhere in the picture.

Somehow I remember what Lou levy used to tell me,

"If you want to make God laugh, tell him about your plans."

Maury made his money with other businesses but as far as the store, we were losing money every year. I know, because I was the one doing all the books. That was probably one of the reasons why I wanted to leave, because it was frustrating at times that when I suggested something to Maury, he would agree right away, but next day after his first drink, forget it. Maury didn't care. He just wanted to have a place that he could get out of the house and have a good time with all his friends every day. I get that. But to sell a business that is losing money, you're gonna get 10 cents on a dollar and that's just the way it is. So, to make the best of it, we decided that I would run the business as usual, and Mike Stein, Maury's son, was my silent partner and I'd pay Viola weekly.

Mike is a funny guy! Every time he came to the store he always told me some jokes.

Here's one:

Walking along Fairfax Avenue (Jewish neighborhood), he witnessed - "Drive by nagging".

This one I like the most:

"Albert Einstein was an amateur violin player. One time he was practicing with Jascha Heifetz and Arthur Rubinstein. After just a few bars, Heifetz suddenly stopped playing and said to Einstein, 'Albert, can't you count?'"

Here's another one:

A casual bandleader was trying to find a piano player for a gig since his piano player called in sick last minute. As he was calling everybody, he heard piano playing right next door. So he went next door and rang the doorbell. A woman came out. The guy asked the lady,

"Ah, excuse me, Ma'am, could you tell me who's playing the piano?"

"It's my son Johnny."

"Can I talk to him?"

"Sure! Johnny, Johnny, somebody wants to talk to you."

A kid came downstairs and the guy asked him,

"Hey, kid, do you know any tunes?"

"Yes, I know 3 songs, 'God bless America', 'Happy Birthday', and 'Giant Steps'."

(This one is for all the guys. "Giant Steps" is a Coltrane composition. The tune is a total challenge to solo on because of its unusual chord progressions - most young kids nowadays, they don't know any standards but they want to play "Giant Steps".

You gotta know tunes if you want to be a jazz musician - a lot of tunes. In fact, most jazz musicians, when they listen to a solo, they should be able to recognize a standard in 4, 5 bars according to the changes and the indication of the melody.

Miles played tunes, Trane played tunes, Duke definitely played tunes.)

*****

I went to see Viola every Sunday for years. It was really sad to see Maury's two dogs. Without Maury, Peppi and Bengie were just two lonely old dogs. They tried so hard to get up to greet me. They both died after a while. Finally, Viola was getting to be too old to live by herself. Mike decided to send her to a very nice home. I still went to see her every Sunday. Funny! Viola was acting like a child. She wouldn't share the cookies I brought her with her roommate. I could tell she was looking forward to seeing me every Sunday. Mike called one day and told me Viola finally passed away.

After 20 years, with the help of my accountant Hal Kramer, I finally bought Mike out.

Now people call me Mr. Stein.

Never in my wildest dreams did I ever think that I would come all the way from Taiwan to become a Jew.

*****

Chinese fortuneteller

There was a very interesting story happened years ago when I first started working for Maury. I had some serious bad luck with car accidents, all 7 of them in one year. I know I'm a Chinaman but I ain't that bad a driver. My car was parked right in front of my apartment on the street and somebody hit it during the night. And I also got myself a ticket for jaywalking in Chinatown where everybody was jaywalking. Talk about bad luck! Something was wrong and I had no idea what it was.

Ernest (my Chinese buddy) suggested that I go see a Chinese fortuneteller. I thought it couldn't hurt. So I called the number that Ernest gave me. A Chinese woman answered and she sounded very nice. So I arranged to see her on the following Sunday. She lived in Tustin. I remember driving into this very nice big house and she greeted me at the doorway looking very serene. I told her why I was there, and she started to ask me a few questions and my date of birth on the Chinese calendar. Then she started to count her fingers, and she opened up a very old beat-up looking heavy book (later on I found out it was Yi Jing—one of the oldest of the Chinese classic texts which contains a divination system). And then she started to put things down on a piece of paper. It actually took her quite a while to finish writing. As soon as she stopped, she glanced over the whole page and sighed,

"Well, I've never seen anything like this. You've had quite a life so far, and you haven't even started yet."

"Oh yeah?" I said.

"Yes! And I can see that right now you are going through a dark period, but there isn't much to worry about because you are already at the end of it. But, Wow, What a life!"

I just sat there and waited for her to tell me more.

"Well, you were born HEAVY (in Chinese it doesn't mean weight), and you were one of the Emperors in a previous life (yeah sure). You had a pretty hard childhood but you did well in your early 20's. At age 25, you had a major change. (I came to the States at 25 that should be major enough) From 25 to 35, you have money signs all over the place but for some reasons you can't get them. But from 35 on, your life starts to change, by 37 your door is wide open and nothing could stop you. And also, you have such strong connection with Buddhism."

Well, all I cared about was all the accidents, as long as that was over with, I really didn't care about anything else.

That was 30 some years ago. I didn't pay too much attention to most of the things she said because I was never superstitious, and plus it was so long ago, I lost that piece of paper that she wrote me. But a couple of things she mentioned kind of made me wonder that maybe she really knew what she was talking about. For example, Maury died on January 10th 1987. A week later, it was Chinese New Year. In Chinese, everybody gains one year in age at New Year. I turned 35 that year. And I have been practicing Nichiren's Buddhism for over 26 years. So, go figure!

*****

VIII: MEMORABLE STORIES FROM THE STORE

*****

Stein on Vine logo

I wrote the Chinese character on my "Stein on Vine" logo. John Heard did the Stein on Vine part and I finished it with the Chinese character, which says "JAZZ", so it fits the store perfectly.

An old Chinese customer and friend of mine Mr. Sheng (an amateur violin player, very knowledgeable about old violins and bows) once visited me in the store and saw my tee shirt hanging on the wall. He asked, "Who wrote that Slim Gold style 'JAZZ'?"

I said, "I did."

He was surprised, "Gee, my little old brother, I had no idea you can write so well."

Actually I was kind of surprised myself because when I wrote that I hadn't touched the brush for god knows how many years, and that was my first try. Well, some things are just meant to be.

*****

One day this guy walked in the store and said to me, "You don't remember me, do you?"

I looked at him and said, "No, I don't seem to recall."

"Well, I was here about 9 years ago and you gave me the best advice!"

"Oh yeah? Now you got me curious. So tell me what did I do?"

"I came here one day and asked you if you could find me a trumpet mouthpiece that could help me play high notes. You went into one of the drawers and picked one out. I put it on my trumpet and played about 3 notes. You grabbed the horn from me, pulled out the mouthpiece and said,

'You don't need no mouthpiece, you need to practice!'"

"Yeah…? Well, I could have done that."

"I just want to tell you "thank you" because I AM a trumpet player now."

*****

Jim Atlas (bass player from Chicago) used to stay in the back room for quite a while and he told this true story:

When Jimmy Giuffre (composer, arranger, jazz clarinet and saxophone player) had his trio playing at a club in Orange County in the late 50's, he had Jim Hall on guitar and Jim Atlas on bass (Jim was hired to replace Ralph Pena). So there were three Jims in that trio. When Giuffre decided to let Jim Atlas go, he didn't know how to tell him.

It just so happened it was during the time when the US Air Force was developing and test firing the Atlas missile. So, the next day when Jim Atlas got into the club, Giuffre threw him the newspaper and told him to read the headline. Jim said he opened the paper and the headline reads,

"Thousands cheered when Atlas fired!"

*****

A guy came in the store wanted to buy a tambourine.

After I showed him several different types, he asked, "Do you have one without any jingles?"

I said, "What's the point to get a tambourine with no jingles?"

He said, "Well, to be honest with you Gary, I'm buying this for my bandleader's wife. She insists on being on stage but she has no time whatsoever."

How funny!!!

*****

I got a phone call from this guy one day and he asked me if we had any Leblanc trumpets for Maynard Ferguson (Canadian trumpet player and band leader known for his high note playing) to try. I told him "yes", we did have a couple of them.

Next thing I knew a guy ran into the store and told everybody,

"Maynard is here, Maynard Ferguson is here."

And then another guy walked in and he looked not a bit like Maynard except the grey hair.

Just so happened, Chuck Findley was in the store and Chuck looked at the guy and said,

"You're not Maynard."

Both guys totally ignored Chuck and still wanted to see those two trumpets. Maury asked Chuck to play something. Chuck grabbed one of the horns and just wailed on it. He played some of the most beautiful lines with incredibly gorgeous high notes. The room was still ringing after he stopped playing.

Those two guys didn't even look at us. Without saying a word they just left.

How 'bout that, a Maynard Ferguson impersonator.

This is Hollywood!

*****

Keith Johnson

Keith told me he has been coming to the store since the late 60's. He came to rent a clarinet from Maury while his clarinet was being repaired by another shop. Maury wouldn't rent him one. He just gave him a clarinet to use till he got his own clarinet back. And later on Keith bought his first Conn M6 alto sax from Maury for

$154 (it was a $500 horn then) and it took Keith 6 payments to pay it off. Not only was Maury the first guy gave Keith credit, he also offered Keith 6 free lessons. So Keith had been coming for clarinet lessons every week. Sometimes Maury was too busy. He would have whoever was in the store give Keith a lesson. I can just picture Maury asking Abe Most (one of the best clarinet players in town),

"Hey Abe, give this kid a lesson. Show him something!"

That was almost 50 years ago when the store was across the street.

Anyway, what amazes me the most is that Keith has always been visually impaired and he lives in Pasadena. He has to take two buses to get to the store. I just can't imagine how the hell he finds me every time.

One day I was sitting in the store doing some paper work and I just happened to look up and saw Keith walking past the store with his white cane. So I jumped up, ran outside and called him,
"Hey, Keith, I'm over here."

Keith turned around and said, "I know. I'm going to the drum shop next door."

"Oh… well, EXCUSE ME!"

I ran into Keith one day at Larchmont Village. I said hello to him,
"Hi, Keith!"

Without hesitation, he said, "Oh hi, Gary!"

In the old days, after 5 o'clock, I would have a beer with whoever was in the store. Keith loves beer and he loves to hang. So whenever he was in I always had a cold beer for him. Through the years, we got to know each other pretty well. He would tell me what was going on with his life, where he played or if he found a good restaurant.

Keith told me one time he was playing on the street in Pasadena and somebody stole his money from his saxophone case. Can you believe this shit? Stealing from a blind man? That's as low as it gets.

One day Keith told me that he was rehearsing with this band and he was talking to the guy sitting right next to him about how long he has been coming to the store. The guy asked him,

"So, is that Chinese guy taking care of you?"

Keith said, "What Chinese guy?"

Ain't that something? All these years, Keith never knew that I'm Chinese!

Keith Johnson

*****

Old man's Shoe

A guy came in one day and wanted to try out some alto saxophone mouthpieces. Well, there's something about the alto saxophone, it's such a listener-unfriendly instrument. I can name 20 great tenor sax players that I like, but there are only a handful of alto players that I enjoy listening to. The range of that particular instrument is very hard to please human ears if you don't have a sound.

This guy had a horrible sound to begin with and he was trying out a metal mouthpiece (usually they sound a lot more edgy and brighter than hard rubber ones) and he was SOOOO out of tune (you usually tune the horn by pushing in or pulling out the mouthpiece from the neck depending on whether you are flat or sharp). Apparently, this guy not only couldn't play he also couldn't hear. I waited as long as I could, finally I just couldn't stand it. I blew a loud whistle to stop him from playing and I grabbed the tuning hammer and hit the A tuning bar as hard as I could and yelled at the guy,

"Jesus! Man, you're so out of tune. Listen to the pitch and tune the fucking horn. ... Man, you're driving me nuts!!!"

The guy just stood there for a second and slowly he said, "Well... at least you didn't throw a shoe at me like the old man did."

I can easily picture Maury throwing a shoe at him.

*****

Mike Milan

Mike was an old violinmaker from Yugoslavia. He had been working for Maury in one of the back rooms for as long as I can remember. He was already there when I first came in. What an interesting character - old and grumpy. But he was one of the best violinmakers that I've ever met. His violins have the most gorgeous sound and look. I don't know how Maury found him. I know he was working in Chicago for years. Probably because he couldn't stand the cold weather, he contacted Maury and moved to California. Maury gave him a room in the back and he'd been there doing repairs for Maury and making instruments for himself ever since. Both Ray Brown and Andy Simpkins had their basses repaired by Mike when the airlines broke them. And so did Gene Cherico (bass player from Buffalo, New York) when he was traveling with Sinatra. I remember Jim De Julio (bass player from Pittsburgh) told me that old Mike was complaining to him about how Gene made him tired by talking to him nonstop. I knew Gene well, a bitching bass player but a nervous wreck. So I know exactly how Mike felt.

Don't remember how we started talking to each other. Somehow he took a liking to me. He didn't say much but he always let me watch him work whenever I needed some help with all the repairs. So I pretty much stole everything from the old man by watching him work. We got along well, especially after Maury died and I kept him in the back. He started to open up to me. We began to have conversations about not just instruments. He even taught me how to make cheese strudels. But he never talked about his family. I asked him once and he didn't seem to want to talk about it so I never asked again.

He told me when he first started to learn how to become a luthier at very young age, apprenticing under a few violinmakers in Italy, the very first thing he was told to do was sharpening knives, all kinds of knives in addition to sweeping the floor and all the cleaning in the shop. He did that for over 2 years before they even let him put is hands on wood. I don't know how long he had been working there, but he said,

"When it was time for them to give me the test for my certificate, three judges were sitting in front of me and one of them picked up a violin and smashed it against the table, then threw it at me and said, 'Go fix it!'"

I know he was playing in an orchestra somewhere when he was younger because he said his violins were always overpowering everybody else's. Every time he finished making a violin or viola or whatever, he always asked me for my opinion about the sound and the look. I have to say those violins and violas he made are just gorgeous, and each one of them has its own sound and look. His varnish was deep and lustrous, unique and brilliant. He's got a big shelf full of different color varnish. He never showed me how to mix them. We all know the story about Stradivarius - up to this day nobody can figure out Strad's formula for his varnish. Mike told me that good varnish could improve the sound 3 times better than violin in the white (without varnish). He usually puts on at least seven coats of varnish on each of his instruments. Mike was probably the most well kept secret in Hollywood. Only a few top-notch professional string players knew about him and he was cool with that.

One day in the early years I was in his shop and wanted to ask him to help me with some repairs. This fat old concertmaster was trying out one of Mike's own violins. He played so well and the sound of that violin just filled up the whole room. After he finally stopped playing, he said,

"Mike, what can I say? You are a genius." And he turned to me, "Nobody knows about Mike, nobody knows how great he is. Isn't that a shame?"

Mike's one big dream was to have a chamber orchestra playing all of his own instruments = 12 violins, 8 violas, 4 cellos and 2 basses. I was very fortunate to have the honor to see and play all those instruments. Well, I must say I wasn't too impressed with those two basses he made. They looked great, but the sound was just not quite there. Maybe they needed to be played. But the rest of them were just fantastic! Can you picture that? Standing in a room, full of the most gorgeous sounding brand new instruments made of at least 200 year-old wood, hanging there one after another and each one of them has its own unique color, sound and character. It was breathtaking, and with the maker (grumpy old man) standing right next to me. I felt so honored and privileged.

I asked Mike to give me one of his instruments so at least I have something to show people his work (I didn't tell him I wanted to have something to remember him by after he dies - that's what I really meant) and he did. He gave me one of the worst violas he made. I kept it in the shop for not even a year. He asked me to give it back. I was so pissed. What a fucking Indian giver.

But he did make me two bass bows, one German and one French. I noticed that there was a big old knot on the German stick. I wondered why he didn't see that. Eventually that bow broke right from the knot. What a shame! I still have that French bow.

I helped him a lot when he was getting to be too old and too fat and eventually he couldn't even move around easily. He finally had to stop coming to the shop because he couldn't even drive. So I helped him move everything to his rented house just off of Sunset Boulevard, not too far from the store. Mike had moved three times since I first met him. He set up a workshop in his living room and started working at home. I don't know how but he managed to go to Paris with this Frenchman violin dealer for a few weeks trying to sell some of his instruments. I wouldn't have known this except he told me he was riding a 3 wheel motor wheelchair on the streets of Paris. He never told me if he sold anything and I never bothered to ask.

I was buying him groceries once every few weeks for years. And he was a big pain in the ass to shop for. He wanted certain brands of almost everything. Celery, for instance, he wanted the ones with blue tie not red and the ones with more leaves; certain brands of organic milk, flours and a whole lot of other things. Who says beggars can't be choosers? Sometimes I had to make two, three stops to finish shopping for him. After I got married I took my wife with me to shop for him, and even my wife was impressed by how I treated him.

Mike had a huge collection of old wood in storage. I saw all the wood piled up in storage in the San Fernando Valley when I drove all the way down there to make a storage payment for him when he was 3 months behind. He told me some of his wood is older than 400 years. The wood came from an old church somewhere in Europe (Yugoslavia?), and the church was about 400 years old. When they tore down the church, Mike recognized some of the fine wood they used to build that church. So he bought it all (he probably stole it).

I asked him once, "Mike, what are you going to do with all that wood?"

He said, "I'm gonna make instruments with them."

"How much wood do you have?"

"Well, let's see, if I start from today on nonstop, 8 hours a day, it'll probably take me about 50 years to finish them."

I said, "Well, I hate to tell you this, Mike, I don't think either one of us will still be around in 50 years."

"Then I will burn them before I die!"

"You're not serious!"

"I am! Nobody deserves these wood."

"Mike, you are a sick man. I can't believe you just said that."

He didn't say anything. And I certainly didn't feel like talking to him after that.

One of my customers was looking for a fine violin. So I took him to see Mike. Mike had a couple of fine Old Italian violins. After several visits and trials, my friend finally bought one of the violins for $40,000. And I was very happy for both of them. I was supposed to get 10% commission out of that deal. But instead, Mike gave me $1000. And I was ok with that because even though I had no idea about his real financial situation, I do know he hadn't sold anything or done any repairs for a long time. So I was cool.

Months passed by. I got a call from another customer friend of mine whom I took to see Mike also. And he wanted Mike's phone number because he lost it. And we started to talk. He told me he ended up buying that viola from Mike months ago. That pissed me off. The old man was not being straight with me. He didn't even tell me that he sold the viola. It's not about money, I felt betrayed. I called him up, confronted him and told him how disappointed I was and I hung up on him. That was the last time I ever talked to him.

Later on I heard from this mutual friend of ours who told me Mike had moved to Florida to be with his relatives. I didn't even know he had any relatives in Florida. That was the last I've ever heard about him. He was 80 some years old when I last saw him. He's probably gone.

*****

William Claxton and Herman Leonard

I'd known Bill Claxton for a long time. He was born in Pasadena, California, an American photographer and author. He was best known for his photography of jazz musicians.

Herman was from Allentown, Pennsylvania. He was also known as a photographer for his unique images of jazz icons.

Bill had been renting quite a few instruments from me for his Jazz photo shoots. I only met Herman Leonard once when he dropped in the store to introduce himself to me.

What a pair of great jazz photographers those two were.

One day Bill called me up and asked me if he and Herman can use my store for them to do a little photo session. In other words, he'd take some pictures of Herman and Herman would take some of him. Of course I said yes.

So, when the day finally came, I had both William Claxton and Herman Leonard carrying all the equipment to the store and they spent a good 3 hours talking and taking pictures of each other. Too bad I never thought about taking some pictures with both of them. Wouldn't that be great? What a dumb ass I am.

*****

Frank Rosolino and Carl Fontana

Frank Rosolino was born in Detroit, Michigan. Carl Fontana's from Monroe, Louisiana. They were a couple of the most amazing trombone players.

Ernie Watts (saxophone player from Norfolk, Virginia) and his wife Patricia told me this story:

Not only was Carl Fontana a great trombone player he was also a fishing nut. One time Rosolino went to visit him in Vegas and they went fishing together. Afterwards, they stopped by a resort to have a drink and they were both in their fishing outfits. Just so happened, there was a band playing at the lounge and they had a trombone player who wasn't very good. So when the band was taking a break, Carl got up and went to the bathroom. Rosolino walked up to the bandstand, asked the trombone player,

"Say yeah, my man, I always love trombone but I've never had the chance to play one. I was wondering if it's possible for me to check out your horn."

The guy said, "Well, ah… I guess it's ok." So he handed Rosolino the horn.

Frank grabbed the horn, looking at it and then he said, "Whoa, look at this… ah… you think I can play a note on this? Do you mind?"

"Well, ah…yeah, … sure!"

So Frank faked cracking a couple of notes first and gradually he started to play a few real notes and then a couple of simple melodies, and then, he just wailed with some fast well-known Rosolino Bebop lines.

Fontana got out of the bathroom, Frank said to him,

"Hey Carl, come check this out, this horn plays by itself."

So Carl took over the horn and he whipped out some beautiful fast lines, up and down all over the horn.

That poor guy just stood there with his mouth open watching those two geeky looking guys in fishing outfits playing the shit out of his horn.

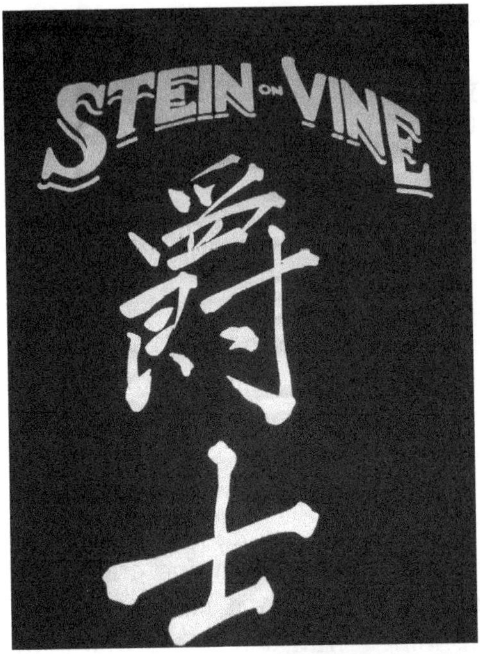
STEIN ON VINE
爵士

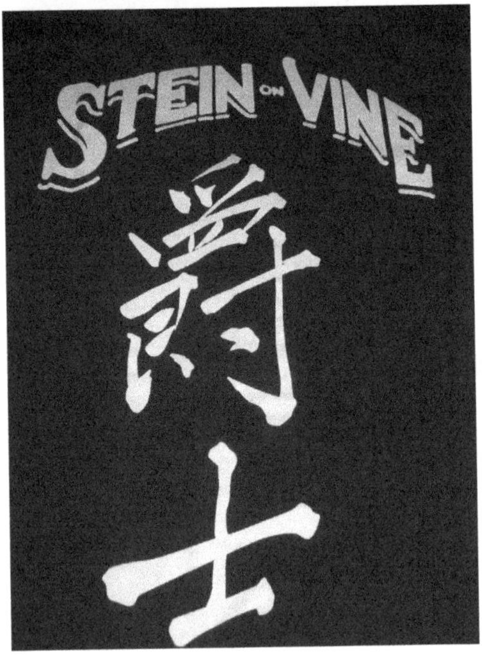
STEIN ON VINE
爵士

IX: SOME OF MY DEAR FRIENDS AFTER THE MAURY ERA

Chuck Berghofer

Chuck was the bass player who played that famous bass line on that song "These Boots Are Made for Walking" by Nancy Sinatra.

Chuck was in one day. I offered him some cranberry juice and he said to me,

"Boy, this place's really changed."

This reminds me of the joke about the store:

The going joke among musicians during the first couple of years after Maury died was,

"Do you know what happened to Stein on Vine?"

"What happened?"

"It's a music store now!"

*****

Ray Brown

Raymond Matthews Brown was born in Pittsburgh, Pennsylvania. He started to play the piano at the age of eight then moved to upright bass while in high school. Heavily influenced by Jimmy Blanton (Duke Ellington's bass player), young Ray Brown became known in the Pittsburgh jazz scene. He came to New York after graduating from high school and immediately started to play with Hank Jones, Dizzy Gillespie, Art Tatum and Charlie Parker.

Ray was also one of the guys that I first met in the store. Other than him being the most well known and highest paid bass player, what impressed me the most was how much he loved to play. Every time he came to the store, he would pick up the first bass in sight and started to play. I mean he would go up and down all over the fingerboard playing all the runs, arpeggios, diminished and whole tone scales non-stop for god knows how long. Al McKibbon told me whenever he was playing in a session with Ray, Ray would always be playing while everybody else was taking a break.

I asked him one time while he was playing in the store, "Mathews, after all these years, you still love it. Huh!"

He simply said, "Why play if you don't?"

Ray started me out with playing the bass. You can't find a better teacher. I was a guitar player, but I've always been fascinated by the sound of the double bass. There are so many basses in the store so I'd pick one up and fool around with it every chance I got.

One day I was playing the bass, and somehow I just felt that somebody was watching me. I turned around and it was "The Ray Brown". I was so embarrassed so I said to him,

"Oh man, you embarrassed the shit out of me!"

And Ray said, "No, go on, keep playing."

I said, "Hell no, I don't want to play in front of you."

He said, "No, no, no, go on, you got the feel, and I want to show you how to play this thing."

So, that was it. Ray Brown started to teach me how to play the bass.

Every time Ray came back from the road, he would come in to visit and he always showed me something. This is what he said, "Check this out. This is what Francois Rabbath (born in Aleppo, Syria, a French double-bass player, soloist and composer) showed me when I was hanging out with him in Paris..."

Ray was not only a great bass player. He was also a golf fanatic. He played golf between gigs all the time no matter where he was. Some people said Ray made more money playing golf than playing the bass. I wouldn't be a bit surprised if that was true.

We had a very special relationship. In some ways he was like a father to me. I remember one time he was trying to make a videotape about bass playing for the young beginners. The taping was at The Loa - the jazz club he and Marico (Ray's partner from Japan) opened in Santa Monica. He wanted me to help him demonstrate playing as he was teaching. Unfortunately, the night before the taping, I got a phone call from back home that my father died. So, I couldn't make it. Later on Ray called and left a message for me,

"Tell Gary he's a chicken shit!"

One day he came in from a long tour, and he asked me to join him for lunch. On our way to this sushi joint on Ventura Blvd, he asked me, "How's everything?"

I said, "It's ok."

"So, are you seeing anybody?"

"No, man, I'm just too busy to get involved with anybody."

He didn't say nothing first, a few seconds later, he said,
"Well, young man, for your information, the President of the world is married, you know. So don't give me that you're too busy shit!"

Another time he came in to have his bow rehaired and he needed a loaner because he was playing at Catalina's for the whole week. So I loaned him my bow. The next day he called, "Hey Gary, Ray Brown!"

"Matthews! What's up?"

"Well, when is my bow gonna be ready?"

"Tomorrow."

"Oh yeah?"

"Yeah!"

"Hey listen, that bow you loaned me yesterday, it's not bad."

"Of course it's not bad! It's my bow."

"Oh really? Can I have it?"

"Can you have it? Hell No! That's my own bow"

"But I gave you some strings and bags and some other shit!"

"Yeah, but you got them free."

He wasn't too happy about me turning him down.

Well, I went to see him play that night. When I walked in, Ray was already on stage playing. He saw me walking in. He smiled at me and nodded but kept playing. As soon as he finished the set, he put his bass down and walked straight to me. Gave me a hug and he asked,

"How did my bass sound?"

Now, that's Ray Brown!

I told him, "You know, to be honest with you, I don't really like the sound but the way you play, it don't really matter."

Boy, I can tell he was bugged. But I also said, "Man, you sounded so good with my bow. Keep that damn bow."

"Really?"

"Yeah, yeah, yeah, keep it."

I wished I had a camera with me (no camera phone then), for the first time in god knows how many years that I've known him, he picked up my check.

But you know what? Ray could be very generous too. John Clayton told me that when he was traveling with Harry James Band, he found this bass in Canada, but he couldn't afford it so he called Ray and Ray actually helped him get that bass. Some story!

Ray gave me this very deep road case with wheels after he cleaned up his garage. He said,

"I called this 'kiss my ass case'. Whenever your wife gives you shit, you put everything you need in this case and tell her 'kiss my ass!'"

I still got that damn case except I never had the chance to use it.

I hurt my back from jumping rope every morning in the late 80's. I really overdid it. When I first felt some pain in my lower back, I thought I could work through it but it only got worse. Until one night, I woke up screaming with this severe pain in my lower back. I started to walk around like a big old shrimp. I went to see at least half a dozen chiropractors and did all kinds of therapy but nothing really worked.

Ray walked in one day and saw I couldn't even get up to greet him. He said,

"What happened to you?"

I told him what's been going on and he said, "Go see my guy Adachi, see if he can help you."

Well, that's probably one of the best things that anybody could have ever done for me. Dr. Adachi is totally amazing. Not only did he cure me, he has become a dear friend. I told everybody about how amazing he is. He's not only gifted, he also has such compassion.

Like everybody else, Ray sent me postcards from all over the world. One day I got a phone call from him, "Gary? Ray Brown!"

"Man, I didn't know you're in town."

Ray said, "Oh no, I'm in Japan"

"Really? Are you ok?"

"Yeah, yeah, yeah, the hotel gave us free phone calls so I thought I give you a call."

Ain't he sweet?

Sometimes Ray would call me up and ask me to meet him for lunch. If I couldn't join him, he would bring me some lunch back from wherever he was. It was so nice to see him with a bag of food and that big smile walking in.

Bobby Haggart (bass player who wrote "What's New") came to the store to visit one day with his wife Wendy, and Ray happened to walk in. The minute they saw each other, they cheered and hugged. Apparently they hadn't seen each other for a long time.

Ray said to Bobby, "You know Bobby, I actually studied your book."

Evidently Bobby had written a bass study book and Ray had read it.

Bobby said, "Really? May be I should take another look at it myself."

Every Christmas Ray always brought me some gifts, usually a bottle of champagne, vodka, and some wine. This one Christmas Eve, I stayed open till around 3 o'clock in the afternoon and it was pouring rain outside. I locked the door and tried to finish up work so I could take my Mom to Vegas and spend Christmas with my sisters. It was dark and wet outside. Suddenly I heard knocking on the door. Somebody was outside with a raincoat and a hat on standing in the heavy rain. I couldn't tell who that was until I opened the door. It was Ray! He was soaking wet with a soaking wet brown bag full of stuff. And he said,

"Well, if I'm in town, I just have to come over to see you. It's the tradition."

I was so touched I said to him, "Man, are you trying to make me cry or what?"

We always had lunch together whenever Ray was in town. There were a couple of places that he loved. One of them is a Japanese noodle joint on Vine Street, not too far from the store. They have real good miso Raman. One time we were sitting at a table by the door, a woman walked in, I hate to say this, but she was one of the most unpleasant looking women that I've ever seen. Without even thinking, I said to Ray,

"Whoa! That's a real Willophant!"

Ray said, (with that high pitch voice)

"Willophant? You've been hanging out with Big Mac too long."

He's right. I did learn that from Al McKibbon.

Ray made a trip to Alaska to see his son Jr. After he came back, he came over to see me and during lunch he said,

"I just went to Alaska to see my son. When I was on the plane as we were ready to land in Anchorage, the Captain announced, 'ladies and gentlemen, we are about to land, and the outside temperature is 50 below.' So when I saw my son, the first thing I said to him was, 'you take a good look at me. Next time if you want to see my black ass, you come to me. I ain't coming here no more.'"

Ray loved baked eel at this sushi joint that Al McKibbon and I always went. First time I took Ray there, he showed me this novel that he was reading on the airplane on his way back from Japan (he went to Japan at least 2-3 times a year) and opened the page that he folded and had me read the part that he highlighted, it reads,

"An FBI agent named Maury Stein..."

He told me he was laughing his ass off on the plane when he read that and he got a real kick out of watching me stunned by the coincidence.

Later on in the restaurant as we were eating at the bar, this kid came over to us, (I recognized him, nice kid who had been coming to the store for saxophone reeds and stuff) and he bowed to me,

"Hello, Mr. Stein!"

Ray almost fell out of the chair. He laughed so loud with that high pitch laugh. I was actually a little embarrassed and I said, "Oh hi, how are you?"

And I saw the kid's mom standing by the entrance and waved at me.

That was the first time I've ever heard anybody call me Stein outside of the store. Usually that's what all the old black men would call me,

"Hey, Stein!"

Again, how the hell did I get here?

When Maury died, Ray was in Hawaii. As I mentioned, Jews don't wait long for their funerals. So, by Monday, everything was taken care of. I pretty much learned everything about a Jewish funeral. Ray called me from Hawaii asking me if it was true that he heard Maury was gone. So I told him. A few months later, I went to see him at the Loa, we talked a lot about Maury, Ray was still sad. He really loved Maury.

One day this 20 some year old kid came in the store and he wanted to check out some basses. After about two notes, I knew he couldn't play. Just so happened Ray walked in. He gave me a hug and just stood there, watching the kid fooling around with the bass. Finally Ray said to the kid,

"Well, young man, this is how you play this thing."

So Ray grabbed the bass and started to show him how to hold the bass first. And the kid asked Ray, "Well, who are you?"

Ray said, "My name is Ray Brown!"

"Oh, My God..."

Jeff Hamilton (drummer from Richmond, Indiana) joined the Ray Brown Trio when Ray had Benny Green (from NY) on piano. That was some trio. They worked together for quite a few years. One day Jeff came in to say hello. He told me he was so tired of being on the road all the time and he was ready to leave Ray.

Ray came in right after Jeff left. As we were driving out of the parking lot to get some lunch, I said to Ray, "So, Jeff is leaving. Huh!" and I heard this voice with a disturbing tone,

"Come again?"

"Oh, Shit! Man, I didn't know that Jeff hadn't told you yet. Oh, Fuck me."

Well, I guess he had to find out sooner or later, one way or another. Maybe I was doing Jeff a favor.

Ray told me one day, "Every time I come home, I hear some bad news. Last time it was Sweets. Now I just heard they cut my ex-wife's (Ella Fitzgerald) leg."

I didn't know what to say. All these giants are dropping like flies.

Ray had a knee operation. And he recovered very well. Dr. Adachi spent a lot of time treating him to make him heal much faster. He played at Catalina's right after he could move around. I went to see him and that was the first time I saw Ray play sitting down and he still sounded great. He told me he was feeling fine and he was leaving town again right after Catalina's.

One night around midnight, I got a call from Cedar Walton. He told me, "I'm sorry to call you this late but I just want to tell you that Brown's gone!"

"Brown? Which Brown? ...You don't mean Ray?"

"Yeah!"

"Oh my God! How could that be? I just saw him!"

Well, from what I've heard, after the surgery, Ray's knee was retaining water (I remember seeing him with a swollen knee). So the doctor gave him some pills to pass water. When Ray got to Indianapolis, he played golf all morning without drinking a drop of water because he didn't want to look for a bathroom all the time. After he finished playing, he went back to the hotel room, lay down for a nap and he never woke up.

There were so many people at Ray's funeral. People came from all over the world to pay respect. I saw quite a few old friends that I hadn't seen for years. This young Japanese bass player came all the way from Japan. I remember him from a few years back when Ray was producing his album recorded at David Abel's studio and I took the whole band out for dinner after they finished the recording.

Wilfred Middlebrooks (bass player with Ella) and I rode together to the funeral (now Wilfred's gone). John Clayton had to organize people to go inside the service hall because there were just way too many people. John was like Ray's son, which reminds me of this story:

I was delivering a bass to the Hollywood Bowl one day for the Jazz Festival. As I was carrying the bass to backstage, I saw John running out. I asked him, "John, are you OK?"

John said, "Yeah, man. Ray told me to go home and change. He wants me to wear a tux tonight."

I just laughed!

Only Ray Brown can make John Clayton go home to change.

Oh, that concert featured three generations of bass players, Ray, John and Christian McBride. They put on a great show.

*****

Monty Budwig

Monty was born in Pender, Nebraska. He started playing bass in high school, continuing in the military band while in the Air Force. Moved to Los Angeles in 1954, and went on to record and perform with great jazz musicians: Barney Kessel, Carmen McRae, Woody Herman, Scott Hamilton and Shelly Manne...

Monty was probably one of the most underrated bass players. He told me he had recorded over 200 some albums (nearly as many as Ray Brown). Monty played pretty good piano too (so did Ray). I really like Monty's solos. He was such a melodic player. You can tell he listened to horn players. The few times I saw him play as a sideman with different top names, he stole the show. Monty's wife Arlette was a piano player and singer. She was the one came up with the famous line,

"So many drummers so little time".

Pretty cool!

I liked Monty. We were hanging out at the bass convention at UCLA in 1988. That was the first time people in LA got hip to Edgar Meyer (bass player from Tennessee). I remember Monty and I went to have Mongolian BBQ first in Westwood, and then we went back to check out Edgar. He played Bach cello suites and that was the best I've ever heard from a bass player. Monty was sitting right next to me and said,

"Man, this guy is really talented!"

I said, "No shit!"

Monty had two basses in the shop for me to sell. One of them was a 100 some year old English bass, and the other one was a French about the same vintage. He bought that French bass from me years ago and that bass really has a beautiful big sound. He called me up one day and said,

"Gary, those two basses of mine, I want $18,000 for the English bass, and $12,000 for the French. If somebody wants to buy both of them, I'll give him a deal. I'll take $30,000 for both."

I said, "Monty, 18 and 12 is 30. So what kind of deal is that?"

He goes, "Oh yeah, you're right!"

Monty could be pretty funny too. When he heard that Michel Petrucciani (French jazz pianist who suffered from birth with osteogenesis imperfecta which caused him short stature) got divorced, (his wife usually carried him on stage) Monty said,

"You mean she finally dropped him?"

*****

Cachao

Grandfather of Mambo.

Israel "Cachao" Lopez was born in Havana 1918 into a family of musicians and many of them were bass players. His parents wanted him classically trained, first at home then at a conservatory. In his early teens he was already playing bass with the Orquesta

Filarmonica de La Habana. He actually played for big name guest conductors including Herbert Von Karajan, Igor Stravinsky and Heitor Villa-Lobos. He also played with the orchestra from 1930 to 1960.

Cachao performed with Machito's orchestra (Machito - raised in Havana, formed the band "The Afro-Cubans" in 1940, brought together Cuban rhythm and big band arrangements in one group - my favorite Latin band) and was one of the most in-demand bass players in New York City in the 60's. He won several Grammy Awards. He has a star on the Hollywood Walk of Fame, and he's considered a master of "descarga" (Latin—Jam session).

The first time I met Cachao was in the late 80's when Andy Garcia (actor) brought him over to rent him a bass for the concert. We became friends right away. Since then every time he came to the store, he'd always call me,

"Maestro Galee" and I would call him,

"Maestro Cachao".

Andy invited me to all of Cachao's concerts - House of Blues, Universal Amphitheater, Hollywood Bowl --- Cachao always had an all-star band. All the best Latino musicians would play with him. I tell you, those guys they can really swing. You can't stop tapping your feet when you listen to them play. Latin music is a total different trip. All them jazz licks just don't work unless you know what you're doing. I love Cachao! What a natural bass player. He had a very unique style of playing. I love his feel and his unorthodox style of bowing.

Andy kept me posted by sending me all the new CD's every time Cachao recorded one. So I have a collection of old masters' recordings. Too bad, I never got the chance to hang with him. But I have quite a few pictures of us taken in the store. Cachao always looked serious. I look like a little kid right next to him.

*****

Pete Candoli

Pete's birthday and mine were only a few days apart. We're both Cancers. Not only was Pete a great trumpet player, he was also a dashing and good-looking man.

Jack Sheldon once said, "Had Pete been in the right place at the right time, he could have been a movie star."

Jack also said that somebody told Pete's Mom that Maynard Ferguson could play higher notes than Pete. And Pete's Mom said, "Bullu Shiiit!"

Sheryl (Pete's wife) put together a surprise tribute dinner party for Pete in 1990 at The Sportsman's Lodge. Sheryl asked me if she could get Stan Getz to play so I called Stan and asked if he would be interested in playing for Pete's tribute. Stan said,

"Sure! I always like Pete."

So, for the first time I got to see Stan playing in a section as 2nd tenor.

It was funny because Pete had no idea about the party, a total surprise for him.

During the day, I got a call from Pete. He said,

"Gary, Conte got me this gig at Sportsman's Lodge tonight, and he asked me to bring a Harmon mute. Man, I don't have one with me and it's an early gig it starts at 6 and I don't have time to go home. Do you have one?"

I said, "Yeah sure, as a matter of fact, Pete, I'm not doing anything tonight so why don't I bring one over to Sportsman's Lodge for you."

He said, "Really? You don't mind doing that for me? Oh man, I can't tell you how much I appreciate that. You don't know how much shit I have to take care of today."

Anyway, I got to Sportsman's Lodge right after work. There were a whole lot of people there already. I remember there must have been 12 trumpet players (Jack Sheldon, Bill Berry, Steve Huffsteter, Chuck Findley, Carl Saunders, Frank Zabo, Bob Summers, Sal Marquez…can't remember them all) on stage. Bill Berry was leading the band trying to do a fast rehearsal of 12 trumpets playing in unison of Monk's "Straight no Chaser" when Pete walks in. After a couple of false alarms, Pete finally walked in with Conte. I greeted him at the entrance. The band started to play. Pete suddenly recognized all the familiar faces, totally confused, he shouted,

"What's goin' on? What the hell's goin' on? What the fuck's goin' on?"

And Jack Sheldon grabbed the microphone and said,

"Yes! Pete Candoli! This is a tribute to you!"

Everybody applauded and I saw tears running down Pete's cheeks.

Stan showed! He was wearing my Stein on Vine T-shirt. He kept saying, "I want 10% commission."

Hank Mancini was right next to us and overheard Stan, he said, "10% of what? I'll take 10% too."

Incidentally, Lou Levy told me how Hank wrote the theme song for Pink Panther. He said after Hank saw the clip, he already had some idea. By the time he got home, it only took him 15 minutes to write it down. Pretty damn good, wasn't he? And, let's face it, he couldn't have found a better tenor sax player than Plas Johnson to play that theme.

What a great party that was. Sheryl did a great job putting everything together. So many great musicians played. Pete was so well loved by everybody. Hank conducted a couple of his own hits with the band, themes from "The Pink Panther", and "Peter Gunn". Bill Berry did the rest. It was so great to see Stan playing second chair in a big band. When he started to play Billy Strayhorn's "Blood Count", it was Sooo beautiful. That haunting sound he gets out of that horn. Forget it!!

Stan told me he went to visit Strayhorn when he was dying in the hospital and "Blood Count" was the last tune Strayhorn wrote. The title says it all.

Pete was so happy that night. Everything went beautifully. He and Conte were having a ball. As a matter of fact, you can go to YouTube and check out the night.

Pete had been one of the regulars for my routine dinner parties at my house, but he was always late. One time I was complaining about him being late again, Lou Levy said,

"Well, Pete's been late for 50 years. What do you expect?"

Boy, did Pete love his dogs. He always had dogs. I remember he was totally crushed when he lost his dog. I told him to get another one. He said he'd never do that again, it was too painful to see them go. But, a few months later, he got another one.

Pete always called me. This is what he said every time he called: "Hey, young man, I thought I give you a call before you decide to disown me."

He was so sweet. He loved to sit right in front of me asking me how everything was and telling me what was going on with his life and he always asked me about my mom.

Pete had a Porsche 911 and a VW mini bus. He spent a lot of time fixing those two cars. I don't know how many times I drove him to different repair shops to pick them up. When he finally bought his Toyota Camry, he kept telling me, "Man, this is the best car I've ever had."

Pete's health was going down as he was getting older. He was the kind of person who never told anybody about his problems. I'd been noticing him getting more and more pale and moving slower and slower. I'd walk him out to his car every time he came to see me. I wondered each time how many more times that I'd get to see him. Finally, one night in 2008, not too long after New Year, Sheryl called and told me Pete was gone.

I miss him! I miss his beautiful smile and the cologne he was always wearing. I miss that every time I told him I found a good restaurant, he would try it out the first chance he got and call me the next day to tell me how much he enjoyed it.

I've got this picture of him in a Superman outfit hanging on my wall, taken when he was with Woody Herman.

Jack was right. Pete could have been a movie star.

*****

Benny Carter

Benny was born in Harlem, August 8th 1907 in New York. In Chinese, the number 8 is pronounced "ba". Since August is the 8th month of the year, August 8th is "ba ba". That's why father's day in Taiwan is August 8th, the "ba ba" (pa pa) day. I always remember Benny's birthday. I used to call him every year to wish him happy birthday.

Benny took his first music lessons on piano from his mother. Mainly self-taught, Benny played alto saxophone, clarinet and trumpet. He was also a composer, arranger and bandleader. In the late 1920's and early 30's, Benny had already played with clarinet-soprano sax player Sidney Bechet and piano players like Earl "fatha" Hines, Willie "The Lion" Smith, Fats Waller and Duke Ellington. In 1958, he performed with Billie Holiday at the legendary Monterey Jazz Festival. He won many awards including Grammys and received a star on the Hollywood Walk of Fame in 1987. He was also awarded the National Medal of Arts, presented by President Bill Clinton in 2000.

I had lunch with Benny not too long before he passed away. He looked great. He took me to this private club not too far from his house. I remember when we were entering the restaurant, all the guys working there they all bowed to him,

"Good afternoon Mr. Carter."

During lunch, Benny started to tell me about how lucky he'd been all his life. When he found out he could play the saxophone and make a living at age 14, he'd been doing it ever since. Benny had a very distinguished sound and style on his alto and he played good trumpet and clarinet too. Old black men like Benny who grew up in the Depression, they had to deal with a lot of racial bullshit and Benny had always been a tough guy. I think Miles mentioned how much he respected Benny for his toughness in his autobiography (not too many people get that kind of respect from Miles).

I went to see Benny play at The Loa one night. They already started the first set when I got in. Quietly, I walked past the stage to get to the table on the other side. Benny saw me, but he couldn't be sure because the spotlight was so bright and it was right on him.

I think John B was taking a solo when Benny called my name, "Gary? Is that you Gary?"

The whole place was so quiet. I was kind of embarrassed, but Benny actually got off the stage to give me a big hug. I'd never forget that.

I think it was Steve Edelman (bass player) who told me that when the Russian Ballet was performing at the Music Center in the 80's, he took some of the guys from the Orchestra to see Benny play at The Loa. Just so happened when they got to the club entrance, Benny was pulling into the parking lot. They saw Benny's Rolls, and the Russians thought all famous Jazz musicians are doing that well. Everybody's driving expensive cars.

How funny!

We'd been talking about making a trip to the East Side for some good Chinese food for many years but we never made it.

*****

John Clayton

John was born in Venice, California, a jazz and classical bassist, arranger, composer, bandleader and educator. John studied bass with Ray Brown, as a matter of fact, John is like Ray's son.

John toured with the Monty Alexander Trio and the Count Basie Orchestra after he got his degree from Indiana University's School of Music in bass performance in 1975. Later he took the position of principal bass in the Amsterdam Philharmonic Orchestra in Amsterdam, Netherlands.

Ray Brown came in one day and told me, "This guy Clayton just came back in town from Amsterdam, you should check him out."

One day, this tall good-looking, well-mannered man walked in the store and asked me if he could check out some basses. I was helping somebody with a trumpet. So I told him,

"Go ahead, be my guest."

A few minutes later, suddenly, I heard this gorgeous arco sound coming out of the back room where all the basses are at. So I told the guy I was helping, "excuse me for a minute!"

And I went to the back and asked, "Are you John Clayton?"

"Yes!"

"Man, Ray had told me about you, and I'd love to get together with you sometime."

So, I started taking lessons from John.

What a fine musician and gentleman John Clayton is. He is such a whole package. He plays well, writes well, and he has so much love for everything he does. I don't think I know anybody who is that together at that young age.

John is the co-leader of Clayton-Hamilton Jazz Orchestra with his brother - alto sax player Jeff and drummer Jeff Hamilton. He also served as Artistic Director of the Jazz for the Los Angeles Philharmonic program at the Hollywood Bowl from 1999 to 2001.

John won a Grammy for Instrumental Accompanying Vocalist(s): "I'm Gonna Live Till I Die" (Queen Latifah) John Clayton, Arranger in 2007. And the album "Brother to Brother" by The Clayton Brothers received a Grammy nomination in the Best Jazz Instrumental Album, Individual or Group category in 2009.

I had one of John's basses in the store on consignment. Just so happened, I sold the bass right before John's 40th birthday. I put all the cash in this leather bow case that I picked out for his birthday gift. When I told John to open the case at the party in his house, you should have seen the look on John's face and everybody else's as he found all the cash stuffed inside. Jeff Hamilton immediately told me when his birthday was.

Jeff Hamilton

I remember that day John's 8-year-old son Gerald played a Boogie Woogie tune on piano for us. He already had the feel and time. Excellent! I knew then he's gonna be a good piano player. I was right, look at him now. Gerald has become a well-accomplished jazz pianist and composer. He joined several world tours with the Roy Hargrove Quintet. In December 2009, he was also nominated for a Grammy for Best Improvised Jazz Solo, for his solo on Cole Porter's "All of You". In 2010, Gerald was again nominated for Best Instrumental Composition for "Battle Circle".

What a great kid. Can you imagine how proud of him John must have been?

*****

John Collins

John Collins was a great guitar player born in Montgomery, Alabama 1913. He had worked with Art Tatum, Roy Eldridge, Billie Holiday, Lester Young and Nat King Cole.

John and I became very good friends since he started to give some private lessons in one of my back rooms. I told him how much I enjoyed his playing with Nat. He told me that he actually had to woodshed at home to get his chops back after Nat died because Nat wanted him to play exact same solos every night. Evidently all the hard work paid off, he sounded so good especially the way he played all those beautiful voicings.

Every time he came to the store he always gave me a big hug, "How are you doing my old buddy?"

I love listening to John telling stories about all the people he worked with - "Lady", "Pres", and Nat. John had this old and faded yellow picture of himself in his wallet. That picture must have been at least 60 years old. He looked so young with that silly grin on his face.

John Heard told me the only time he could get a raise from Nat was when they were at the airport.

"Eh-- Nat, I can't go!"

"What do you mean you can't go?"

"Well, I need more bread."

"You ^&#? @#!"

And he got it.

*****

Eric Von Essen

Eric was a bassist, pianist and composer. He played in the Young Musicians Foundation Debut Orchestra in 1978. He was very active on the West Coast jazz scene from the late 70's to 90's. He replaced Monty Budwig as the bassist for the Light House All-star band in 1992. He also worked with Frank Morgan, Jimmy Rowles, Bob Brookmeyer, Mike Campbell and the Jazz Tap Ensemble.

Eric and I have the exact same birthday so we always felt like brothers. Eric was very shy, but what a talented musician. He was not only a good bass player, he also played excellent piano and was a good writer. Some of his compositions are incredibly beautiful. Kind of got that Bill Evans flavor.

Later on, Eric started to play chromatic harmonica, and he'd gotten real good at that too. When he got interested in cello, I sold him an old Italian cello for 500 bucks and I let him pay it off because he sounded so good and he didn't have a lot of money.

Such a talented guy but such a fuck-up. Quite a few times that he came to visit me he didn't even have shoes on. I took him out for dinner many times and we always had a good time. When he was playing with Bob Brookmeyer (valve trombone player from Kansas City, Missouri), he was finally making some money. He fell in love with the French bass that I had. So I told him to keep it and pay me when he could. He called me up a few weeks later and told me he finally came up with all the dough, but he couldn't make it in the store. So he asked me if I could meet him at the Money Tree since he was playing there that night. We met at the Money Tree. After he finished the first set he came down to the back of the club and counted all the cash to me. That was pretty funny, we both felt like drug dealers.

When he was in Paris recording Lou Levy's CD "Ya Know", he played both bass and cello. That was a great album. Lou used two bass players - Eric and Pierre Michelot, Alvin Queen was on drums. I remember after they came back, Lou told me he was really upset with Eric. Evidently Eric got really fucked up during the recording session. Lou said he was lying on the couch in the studio trying to recover from whatever he was on. But anyway, regardless, the album came out great.

Eric got a teaching gig at a conservatory in Sweden. He seemed to like it a lot. He stayed there for quite a few years, and he visited me a couple of times when he was on break from the school. Then the next thing I knew somebody called and told me Eric OD'd and died in Sweden.

*****

Stan Getz and Herb Alpert at Stein on Vine

Stan Getz

Stan Getz; Photo by James Johnson

Stan was born in Philadelphia, Pennsylvania on February 2, 1927, and was considered one of the all-time greatest saxophone players.

The first time I met Stan was in the store. Maury and Stan came in from the back door. Maury introduced me to Stan and he was very nice to me. What a thrill to meet The Stan Getz. Right away Stan asked me what instrument I played and wanted me to play him something. So I grabbed a guitar and played a chorus of "My One and Only Love". Stan said to Maury,

"He's a musician!"

Coming from Stan Getz that was the best compliment I ever had.

Then, he asked me, "You like Jimmy Raney?"

"Of course, he's one of my favorite guitar players."

"Isn't he something?"

One night Stan was playing at Hop Singh's in Marina Del Rey. He had George Mraz on bass, Jim Mcneely on piano and I think Ralph Penland on drums. As soon as Maury and I walked in, Stan saw us and he walked to the edge of the stage, put his right hand on his left chest, and bowed to Maury but kept playing the horn with only his left hand.

After he finished the tune, Stan grabbed the microphone, "Ladies and gentlemen, I just want to introduce my mentor and very best friend, Maury Stein, the first man who ever taught me to never wear a tuxedo with white socks."

Stan's pictures are all over the store. Some of them are very old pictures taken when he was just a boy. One of them was with Maury and Jule, and they were all dressed in tux. Another one was with Maury in Jack Teagarden's band. Stan was sitting right next to Maury holding an alto sax. In that picture you can see Stan had a pair of white socks on.

Teddy Edwards (tenor sax player from Jackson, Mississippi) once told me that he ran into Stan in Germany at a big jazz festival. They were hanging out backstage, and Maury's name came up, Teddy said,

"Stan kept saying, 'Maury Stein, my only friend.'"

Well, Maury actually taught Stan saxophone when Stan first came to LA as a kid. Maury got Stan the gig playing with Teagarden and Maury told me when Stan had to go on the road with the band, Stan's Mom kept telling Maury,

"Please take care of my son Stanley. Please take care of my son."

One morning, Maury was doing some paperwork and I was sitting right next to him. The phone rang and it was Stan, He said, "Gary, this is Stan, is Maury there?"

"Sure Stan, he's right here."

I said, "Maury, Stan Getz!"

Maury picked up the phone, "Yeah, Stanley... God Damn Stanley, how can I afford to buy your fucking Mercedes?"

Well, Stan wanted to sell his car. He wanted to give Maury the first shot. I guess he called him at the wrong time.

Stan told me when Maury was in the hospital one time, he happened to be in town. By the time he finished the gig, it was way past visiting hours. Somehow he found out where Maury was, so he climbed the fire escape all the way up to Maury's floor with his horn, got in through the window and played "Desafinado" while walking into Maury's room. Stan said,

"I was so scared, I thought for sure they would throw me out, but everybody loved it and applauded."

One day in the early 80's, Stan walked into the store, gave me a big hug and went straight to the back room to see Maury. Couple of hours later, this guy came in and asked me,

"Where is Mr. Getz?"

"Why?"

"I'm the cab driver. I'm still waiting for him."

I ran to the back to get Stan, "Stan, the cab driver's still waiting for you."

Stan said, "Let him wait!"

There was another time when Stan was in the store and this guy was so thrilled to see Stan in person, he walked up to him and said, "Mr. Getz, I just want to tell you I love your sound. It's so soft and so warm!"

Without thinking, Stan said, "Yeah, so soft and so warm, like shit!!!"

Stan and Lou Levy had a long history of friendship. They played together since Woody Herman's 2nd Herd with The Four Brothers (Stan Getz, Zoot Sims, Al Cohn, and Serge Chaloff). Later on they traveled together with Norman Granz's Jazz at the Philharmonic. That was a total all-star band. Anyway, like Lou said about Stan,

"We lived together, we ate together, we traveled together, we played together, we practiced together, and we even got high together. I don't think anybody can know Stan any better than I."

Lou told me the story that when they traveled to London with Jazz at the Phil, Stan couldn't wait for the bus to stop. He jumped out of the window. After Lou settled in the hotel room he rang for the house doctor. In those days the house doctor can prescribe any drugs for them. But the operator said,

"Sorry Mr. Levy, the house doctor is in Mr. Getz's room."

After Maury died, Stan and I became real close. He called me from time to time just to make sure I was ok.

We were hanging out one day and Stan told me,

"You know, when I first came to LA, it was beautiful here. We never heard of "smog". The air was clean, everything was green and they only had one freeway - Pasadena Freeway."

Then he said, "There was a motel on Western and Santa Monica and there was this one room that when you entered, there was a shelf right above the doorway, if you reached up you would find a joint and it's yours. You could do whatever you want with it but you just had to make sure to replace it when you checked out. It was like an unwritten rule and everybody followed."

Stan called me one day and told me he was moving to LA, Malibu to be exact. He asked me if I could find him a guy that he can trust to help him move all the furniture from Palo Alto to LA (Stan already moved some stuff into the Malibu home and he had to go do a recording session so he couldn't meet the movers). I thought about it for a second and told him I would take my horn repairman Karlo to help him move. Stan was so thrilled, he said,

"Really? Will you do that for me? Oh man, that would be so great and I'd love to see you."

So, I flew up with Karlo early in the morning on a Sunday to Palo Alto. Stan was already waiting for us at the airport. As soon as Stan finished hugging me he asked Karlo what instrument he plays. When Karlo told him he played sax too, Stan said,

"You must play like Trane. I can tell!"

Which was kind of true, Karlo is a deep kid and he did listen to a lot of Trane.

We drove to the U-Haul place first to rent a big old truck and then Karlo drove the truck followed us to Stan's house. We started to load everything onto the truck. We're moving pretty fast. By 3 o'clock in the afternoon, we were all done. Stan had to leave to do the recording session so I took Karlo to San Francisco to get some BBQ first. We left SF about 6 pm. We didn't get back to LA until 3 in the morning. We parked the truck in front of the store and came back around 10:00 am and drove all the way to Malibu. Halfway through unloading, Stan called. He kept thanking me and kept telling me,

"Man, I can't tell you how much I appreciate you. I owe you one!"

I was visiting Stan one day, and I saw a silver soprano saxophone lying on his bed. I asked, "I didn't know you play soprano. Are you any good?"

Stan said, "I'm bad!"

"Really? Good bad or bad bad?"

"Bad bad!"

We laughed!

Later Stan told me, "You know, I gotta tell you something about Lou (Levy). I am very pissed off at him..... I asked him once, 'You like Al (Cohn) better huh!' and he said, 'Yeah, don't you?'"

Stan was so pissed. He said, "Why did he have to say that? I'd listen to Al any time but why did he have to say that?"

Boy, was he pissed. And for that, Stan stopped using Lou for a long time.

There was a Long Beach Jazz Festival that I didn't get a chance to go, but the next morning I got a phone call from Lou, (He called me two, three times a day) He said, "God, I'm exhausted."

I said, "What happened?"

"Well, you know I played that Long Beach festival yesterday. Man, I must have played with 20 saxophone players. It was exhausting! But you know what, when Stan came up, the minute he started to play, it was all over with. He sounded Sooo Good."

Of course! I've never heard Stan not sounding good. After I hung up the phone with Lou, I made a call to Stan, I said, "I heard you sounding good yesterday."

He said, "Oh yeah? Where did you hear that from?"

I told him what Lou said.

Half an hour later, I got another call from Lou, he said, "Guess what?"

"What?"

"Stan Just called and he gave me a gig."

Lou also told me this story:

One time Stan was playing in town, the promoter called the last minute because the drummer got sick couldn't make the gig,

> *"Stan, Joe couldn't make the gig but we found this guy, he is not the best drummer in the world but he sure is a nice guy!"*
>
> *Stan said, "Find me a prick can play!"*

Another time I was at Stan's Malibu home. The phone rang and it was Stan's physical therapist Donna (the Chinese girl flew in from San Francisco once a week to work on Stan). I heard Stan said,

"Yeah Donna, how was the flight? ...Good! All right, come up then. Oh... did you bring my laundry? ...Neh... never mind!"
He hung up the phone and with that grin on his face said,
"These 2nd generation Chinese, they don't know shit!"

I said, "Yeah, you dirty."

Couple of my friends came to the store to visit one day and told me they saw Stan Getz on PBS playing with the Boston Pops backing up a pop singer who was trying to sing standards (I eventually saw the same show). When Stan was taking a solo, she was scatting all over Stan. It was annoying! After the song finally came to an end, as the orchestra was fading out, Stan played this simple melody of "they're singing songs of love, BUT NOT FOR ME."

It was perfect!

The later days of Stan's life, he was trying to be a better human being so he started practicing Buddhism with me. I helped him enshrine his Gohonzon (the scroll we chant to).

One day I got this phone call from him. He said,

"Jew boy!" (That's what Stan called me sometimes)

"Yeah, Stan!"

"You know, I'm moving my furniture around. Can I move the Gohonzon?"

I said, "Of course!"

So I told him how to do it over the phone.

And he said,

"Yeah? Is that kosher?"

After hanging out with Maury, Stan and Lou for so many years, I can actually speak a little Yiddish. Stan knew that. That's why he signed that picture he gave me hanging on my wall,

"To Gary and Maury, I love you both. Gornisht Helfin. (Nothing helps)"

I remember I was talking to my accountant Hal Kramer once and we were discussing something. I said to him,

"Yeah, I needed that like a loch in kop (a hole in my head)."

Hal laughed so hard. I told Stan that and he was laughing hard.

It is kind of funny to hear this Chinaman talk like an old Jew.

Actually Jews and Judaism in China have had a long history. Jewish settlers are documented in China as early as the 7th or 8th century CE. In the first half of the 20th century, thousands of Jewish refugees escaping from the 1917 Russian Revolution and the Holocaust in Europe arrived in China (mostly to Shanghai, Hong Kong and Harbin).

Maury told me this story:

A Chinese Rabbi from Hong Kong went to San Francisco to attend his Granddaughter's wedding. On his way back on the airplane, he was having a conversation with a gentleman sitting right next to him. The guy asked the Chinese Rabbi what does he do for a living. The Chinese said,

"I'm a Rabbi"

The guy said, "Really? I'm a Rabbi too."

The Chinese Rabbi took a good look at him and said, "You don't look Jewish to me!"

That reminds me of this cute joke Stan told me:

Two old Jewish jazz musicians sitting on the park bench, one of them let out a long sigh,

"---Oy Veh!"

And the other one followed, "---Yeah, I'm hip!"

One thing I love about Stan was that he was so confident with his own playing. He was never threatened by his sidemen sounding good. Lou Levy told me that every time he played with Stan, he always encouraged guys to play their best. Lou said,

"That album 'Dolphin' we recorded in Keystone Korner, San Francisco, after we finished recording, Stan listened to the playback and said to me, 'you sounded so good, it's your album.'"

Same thing with that album "People Time" Stan recorded with Kenny Barron (great pianist from Philly). What a great album. Stan sounded good, but Kenny was SUPERB! He sounded like a small orchestra. He played so beautiful harmonically, rhythmically and melodically, wonderful ideas after ideas. Just when you're totally knocked out by some great lines or some hip changes, he came up with another one and yet another one. I was totally blown away. Those two match so well you don't miss anything. Incredible! When I mentioned how much I enjoyed that album to Stan, he said, "Isn't Kenny great?"

Can't remember who told me this story:

Stan was playing in a club. Someone in the audience kept requesting "Girl from Ipanema" (or may be Desafinado?).

Stan finally got tired so he asked Kenny, "Where's Canada?"

"Up U.S."

Stan told me once that he was invited by one of the major reed manufacturing companies to visit their reed making facilities. He said,

"They showed me how they selected the cane, how they cut them, how they number the reeds…. so when they asked me what did I think. I told them 'Well, that's all good but what I'd really like is to meet the asshole who makes sure to put only one good reed in each box.'"

When Ahmad Jamal (great piano player from Pittsburgh) was in town playing at Catalina's in the late 80's, Stan called me up and asked if I'd like to join him and Lou to go see Ahmad. I love Ahmad. "Of course!" I said.

We walked into the club as Ahmad was already playing. It was very dark inside and they had a spotlight on Ahmad. We sat in the booth a few tables from the stage. Ahmad couldn't have seen us. But when he finished the tune he grabbed the microphone and said,

"Ladies and gentleman, my greatest honor, Mr. Stan Getz."

He waited till everybody finished applauding then said, "And Mr. Lou Levy."

I had no idea how the hell he found out about us. We didn't tell anybody that we were coming. We certainly didn't see anybody walking up to the stage to tell Ahmad that we were there. So, go figure!

That night we had so much fun. We talked, and talked, and talked. I told a couple of jokes. Everybody was laughing. Stan suddenly said, "Maury is here."

I said, "Oh yeah? Do you feel his presence?"

Stan said, "No! You are Maury."

Stan asked me one day, "Gary, did you ever write anything?"

I said, "No, other than when I was at Berklee, I haven't written anything."

"Why don't you write me something? I'll play!"

I was really flattered. But, I never did write anything for him.

We're trying to decide where to have dinner one night and I remember asking Stan, "You like sushi?"

Stan said, "You like sushi like I like sushi?"

I laughed because I knew he was referring to that old song "If You Knew Susie like I Know Susie" sung by Sinatra and Gene Kelly in that old movie "Anchors Aweigh".

Lou told me when they were with Woody Herman, they arranged a baseball game with Harry James's band at the local high school in the suburb of New York City. Everybody knows Harry James was a baseball nut. I heard when he auditioned a player he always asked him what position he played first. Anyway, James got a real team, uniforms and all and they practiced routinely. They showed up early and practiced. Woody's guys finally showed, and everybody was still in tux. I asked Stan if that really happened. He said,

"Oh sure, we beat the shit out of them."

Lou also told me that Oscar Pettiford (bass player from Oklahoma) threw his arm out. He said he was right next to Oscar and heard this weird bone cracking sound when Oscar tried to throw the ball.

That must have hurt!

I do remember well that it was 1989 New Years Eve. I went to Lou's house (actually it was Pinky's house) to have dinner with them. Johnny Mandel was there too. Afterwards when I got home, there was a message on my machine, and it was Stan. The message goes,

"Jew boy, this is the old Jew saxophone player Stan. I just want to wish you a happy, happy New Year. 1990's gonna be a mother fucker."

I asked Stan once (way before youtube) if he'd ever played with Trane. He said, "Oh sure, he liked me and he mentioned me in his book, 'if we could all sound like him.'"

I can tell Stan was so proud that Trane liked his playing. Who wouldn't be?

Stan had liver cancer. I don't know who recommended him to this herb doctor from San Francisco. Stan flew the doctor down every week to treat him. In addition to that, Stan also changed his diet to macrobiotic, which means no grease, no dairy, everything natural. Stan told me he was fine with the diet except he missed cheese a lot.

His house in Malibu was right next to the Pacific Ocean. You opened the front door you can see the ocean right away across the room. Stan took advantage of it – he went swimming in the ocean every day. He told me, "Something about that salt water, Gary, it does something to me. I don't know how to explain it. It just makes me feel so good after being in it for a while."

I don't know how long that herb doctor had been treating Stan. I just noticed Stan was looking better and better, healthier and healthier, and that tan from swimming under the sun in the ocean every day. So I asked him one day, "Stan, how are you? I mean as far as your health?"

He said, "Well, just between you and me, Jew boy, I just had a checkup. The tumor had shrunk so much they had a hell of a time finding it. But you know what pisses me off? They didn't even ask me what I've been doing. I was leaving the room and I had to turn back and ask them, 'How come you people never even ask me what I have been doing. According to you guys I should have been dead a year and half ago.' Well, nobody said anything. Can you believe that?"

Stan called me one day and asked me if I was doing anything on that coming Sunday. I said, "No! Not that I know of. Why?"

He said, "Would you mind coming up to see me?"

I said, "Course not!"

So I went to see him. He started to talk to me,

"My ex-girlfriend wants to come back to me."

"So?"

"Well, I'm not sure what to do with her."

I didn't know what to say. First of all, I didn't know his ex-girlfriend that well and also I didn't even know they were not together anymore. So I told him,

"Well, I don't know Stan, it seems like you still want to be with her. Why not? If you guys don't get along then forget it."

After that, I didn't see Stan for a long time.

When he came back from Europe, I called and asked him how the trip was.

"A total disaster!" He said.

Next thing I knew Stan got really sick again. The herb Dr. told me Stan asked her if she would mind that he went to see another doctor in New York.

"Of course not", she said.

I did talk to Stan on the phone once after he came back from NY. He sounded real weak. I told him a joke and he didn't get it. I knew he was seriously ill.

Well, that stupid joke was, "What do you call a Chinese baby with red hair?"

"Some-sing Wong"

The herb doctor told me later that Stan begged her to come back to see him. She did. She took one look at him and told him to call his family. She said she knew Stan didn't have much time left. Stan died not too long after that. I remember I was in the store that day and Sal Marquez (trumpet player) was hanging out with me. I told him,

"Something tells me that I gotta call Stan."

I did. Beverly answered the phone and told me her Dad just passed away.

Lou Levy went to see Stan with Shorty Rogers right before he died and he told me afterwards, "You're better off not seeing him. He weighed about 90lbs., you couldn't even recognize him. He looked terrible."

Lou attended Stan's funeral. He said they went out to the sea on Shorty's boat and Chris (grandson) tossed Stan's ashes in the Pacific Ocean and that was that.

*****

Eddie Harris

Eddie was born and raised in Chicago. He studied music from high school all the way through College and played piano, vibraphone and tenor sax. He played with Gene Ammons (Chicago tenor sax player) while he was still in college. His best-known compositions are "Freedom Jazz Dance" and "Listen Here". I personally also like that tune "Eddie Who?"

Eddie had been a dear friend for a long time. He always came to visit me whenever he was in town. We used to talk about all kinds of shit. He told me when Trane left Miles, Miles was actually considering him as the replacement. But he was on the road. By the time he finally heard that Miles was looking for him, he called and Miles told him,

"Where the fuck were you? Now I got Wayne."

Can you imagine? Had Miles got Eddie Harris instead of Wayne Shorter? History would have had to be rewritten. But, let's face it, that 2nd generation of Miles Davis Quintet with Wayne, Herbie Hancock, Tony Williams and Ron Carter that was just meant to be.

Oscar Brashear (trumpet player from Chicago) once said, "When you talk to Eddie Harris, all you talk about is Eddie Harris." Which is funny but true.

Eddie was a talented innovator. He always came up with some wild ideas and tried something new. He introduced amplified saxophone, and experimented with new instruments of his own invention = trumpet with saxophone mouthpiece and saxophone with a trombone mouthpiece. Sometimes it worked, sometimes it didn't. But he was always trying.

I love the picture he gave me. He wrote,

"To my friend brother Chen, who knows when being outside is in."

Eddie got a rare blood disease = I can't remember the name of it.

But I do remember what Oscar Brashear said, "Eddie was so different from everybody, even when he was sick he had to be different."

Anyway, Eddie got real sick real quickly. One day he called, "Gary, Eddie Harris! How you doin' my brother?"

"I'm all right, Eddie, how you doing?"

"Well, I ain't doing too hot. But you know what man, somebody gave me a remedy for this sickness I got, and they said it really worked. But it was written in Chinese. I was wondering if you can read it for me."

"Sure!" I said.

A few days later Eddie came to the store and I read the remedy for him, which was a list of different Chinese herbs. I took him to Chinatown to get him all the stuff. He was so weak he couldn't even walk for a block, so I told him to sit on the bus bench and I'd go get all the herbs for him.

A couple of days later I was sitting by my desk in the store. I heard somebody honking the horn outside. I looked up and saw somebody was waving at me in the car. I went outside, it was Eddie. He rolled down the window.

I said, "Eddie, what the hell are you doing here?"

He handed me a bag and said, "I know brother Gary loves fried king fish from the hood so I brought you some."

"Jesus, Eddie!"

"I'll come by see you some other time, my brother." Then he drove away.

That was the last time I saw him.

*****

John Heard

JOHN HEARD

John was born in Pittsburgh, Pennsylvania. He taught himself to play the bass as a teenager. Played with Sonny Rollins in the late 60's, moved to the west coast where he became one of the most in-demand bass players for bands like the Ahmad Jamal Trio, the Count Basie Orchestra, Toshiko Akiyoshi and many small recording groups. Later on he traveled with Louie Bellson, Oscar Peterson, Cal Tjader, George Duke, Joe Williams, Nancy Wilson and many other famous singers and jazz musicians.

What a unique individual. I don't think John knows how talented he really is. I loved what Don Thompson (one of my favorite bass players and piano players) said about John, "He is one of the greatest bass players and the only person who doesn't know that, is John."

But if you want to talk about a guy who always tells the truth and speaks his mind - John is it.

John is an artist! I don't know much about art, but I like everything he did - painting, sketches, and sculpture. I have quite a few paintings of his hanging on my wall in the store.

John's all natural! He has the most natural feel. I love the way he plays - no bullshit just play the bass. When he plays, he swings. I always say this, you can learn all the licks, scales, arpeggios, all the notes on the fingerboard, inside out, up and down, but you cannot learn the feel. That's something either you have or you don't. John's got it. And what tone he gets out of that bass, dark, warm, distinctive and powerful.

John was another one of the guys I met the first day I walked in the store 30 some years ago. God, I just realized that he is the only one still around. He looks so good considering the health issue he had to go through last year. I say to him every time I see him,

"Man you look so good, you look better than me." And he does.

We both love that thin crust pizza Henry Sigismonti had turned me on to. No sauce, fresh chopped garlic, olive oil and anchovies. That restaurant down the street was the place that would make those pizzas for us. Too bad they moved to Hollywood Blvd, and somehow they just don't taste the same. Last time we tried some it didn't knock me out.

John found this Mexican food joint on Los Feliz. They have the best tacos and burritos. John knows how to put a big smile on my face by showing up with one of those big burritos. They are YUMMY!!!

Charlie-O's was the club that John played every weekend and he also booked all the bands. What a great job. Guys loved to play there. Too bad it didn't last longer.

John's working on a bust of Clifford Brown. I can't wait to see how that turns out.

*****

Freddie Hubbard

Freddie started to play mellophone and trumpet in his high school band in Indianapolis, Indiana. He played with the Montgomery Brothers when he was just a teenager.

Freddie was also one of the guys that I met on that very first day at Stein's.

I always prepare all the tax info for my accountant Hal Kramer (the smartest Jew) every quarter. I usually sharpen all my pencils before I start the work. I've been doing it for over 30 years. I still hate it.

This one day as I was sharpening the pencils I said to myself, "You know, come to think of it, the only other person that I know of ever used this sharpener is Freddie Hubbard."

And Freddie walked right in!

I said, "Freddie? I.... never mind!"

Now, Freddie Hubbard, what a trumpet player!

We're hanging out in the store's back room one night. I told Freddie, "Hey Freddie, I was listening to you last night. Do you remember that tune 'Bock To Bock' that you recorded with the Montgomery brothers? Man, you sounded good."

He said, "Man, that was my very first recording session."

I remember one time he invited me to his gig at "Concerts by The Sea" in Redondo Beach. Freddie was late. But as soon as he got on stage, he wailed! That powerful, big fat tone he got! He started to burn on the very first note. The band immediately got into the "Groove".

I went to the dressing room after the first set. The minute he saw me he reached in his pocket and took out $15 and gave it to me.

I said, "What's this?"

Freddie said, "Man, I'm so sorry I was late. I didn't get a chance to put your name on the guest list."

"Oh, come on, Freddie?"

John B Williams was right next to us, he said, "Take it Gary. I've never seen him do that for anybody!"

Freddie busted his lips and he could never play like he used to. I can't imagine how hard it must have been for him. I was trying to convince him to play valve trombone instead, since the mouthpiece is much bigger than a trumpet's, maybe he would have a better chance with it. He was actually tempted. So I gave him a valve trombone and a big trombone mouthpiece to try. He played for about 5 seconds and he started to crack on a few notes. He handed the horn back to me and said, "Neh… fuck it!"

I told him, "Freddie, I don't care if you can play or not, to me you are still the BADDEST MOTHER FUCKER!"

He liked that, and I was telling the truth. In my book, when it comes to Bebop, nobody can touch Freddie!

*****

Harold Land

Harold was born in Houston, Texas in 1928 but grew up in San Diego. He got his first tenor saxophone at age 17. His early influences were Coleman Hawkins and Lucky Thompson.

Clifford Brown and Max Roach (drummer) hired Harold after they listened to him play in a session at Eric Dolphy's house (Eric

Dolphy = reed man from Los Angeles, best known for his bass clarinet playing).

"Eric was beautiful. We had known each other since the San Diego days." Harold said, "He loved to play anywhere, any hour of the day or night. So did I. In fact, I still do."

Harold moved to Los Angeles in 1955 and worked with Blue Mitchell (trumpeter), Red Mitchell (bass) and Bobby Hutcherson (vibraphonist). He played regularly with Cedar Walton on piano, Billy Higgins on drums, Buster Williams on bass and Curtis Fuller on trombone since the early 1980s through the early 1990s.

Harold had been coming to the store for saxophone reeds and stuff for as long as I could remember. Always with that big warm smile every time he walked in. Harold loved to play tennis. He often asked me to join him but I never did.

I liked Harold. Very soft-spoken man but played with such a big sound. I like the way he played. He had a different sound from the early days. You can hear some Trane in his playing. What a fine gentleman Harold was. He never bitched about how bad the reeds are nowadays.

Harold was a Buddhist too. One Saturday morning when I first started practicing Buddhism, I went to a men's division morning Gongyo (sutra reciting) at 7AM in Santa Monica. It was painful. I had never been a morning person. Mornings and musicians just don't get along, especially 7 o'clock on a Saturday morning = that was brutal. But anyway, I made it, sitting all the way in the back, chanting and yawning away. Suddenly I noticed this guy sitting right in front me. I couldn't see his face but somehow I felt that I knew this person. So I leaned forward and looked at him. It was Harold! I tapped him on his shoulder and said,

"Harold!"

He turned around and his eyes grew bigger. I just loved that surprised happy look on his face. He said, "Gary, oh whoa, I didn't know you chant."

I said, "I didn't know you chant either."

That reminds me of one of Cedar Walton's lines, "I Don't Stand a Ghost of a Chant"

*****

James Leary

James is from Little Rock, Arkansas, a talented bass player, arranger and composer living in Los Angeles. He has worked with Frank Sinatra, Sammy Davis, Jr., Nancy Wilson, Monk, Dizzy, Stan Getz, Eddie Harris, Sonny Rollins, Buddy Rich, Boston Pops and Count Basie Orchestra.

Like Ray Brown, James called me from Japan one day and told me that the hotel he stayed in gave everybody free phone calls so he just wanted to say hello.

That was very nice.

James has been a dear friend ever since I first met him. He too always comes to the shop whenever the Basie band was taking a break. God, time really flies. I have no idea how many years he has been playing with the Basie band (off and on). I remember I was so happy for him when he first got the gig.

Ray Charles came in one day to rent an alto saxophone. Not too many people know that brother Ray could really play the alto. He had a great sound. James happened to drop in when Ray was trying out my Selmer Cigar Cutter. James picked a bass and they played a chorus of blues.

James has written some very interesting arrangements for all basses and vocal choir. He toured with the musical "Five Guys Named Moe" in 1995. He always gave me a copy of everything he did.

I like the way he writes and I like James.

*****

Jennifer Leitham

Jennifer Leithem, photo by Thomas Westerlin

Born in Philly, PA, Jennifer is a talented left-handed bass player. Worked with Woody Herman, George Shearing, Gerry Mulligan, Peggy Lee, Louie Bellson, Bill Watrous… she's best known for long associations with Mel Tormé and Doc Severinsen.

Like everybody else, I've known Jennifer since she was "John" when he first came in town in the early 80's.

Leitham told me he was born right-handed but when he first got hip to Paul McCartney, he switched to play left handed. That must have taken some commitment.

We get along well. We used to hang out having sushi together whenever he was in town from the road (mostly with Tormé). We even went to a Dodgers game together with Rudy Regalado (timbale player from Venezuela) once. Never did I ever suspect that he had a tendency of being a woman until he confronted me one day that he'd always had a "gender problem".

"Gender problem?" I asked. "What do you mean? What kind of gender problem could you possibly have?"

"Well, ever since I was a little kid, I always felt that I should have been a girl."

" Wow..."

Now that's some gender problem!

Man! I can't imagine what he had to go through all those years trying to hide that from people. So when he told me he was thinking about having a sex change, both my wife and I totally encouraged him. I'm not making this up. The doctor who performed the surgery? His name is Dr. Alter.

The film "I Stand Corrected" (The journey of Jennifer Leitham) won the Audience Choice Award as best film of the 2012 American Documentary Festival in Palm Springs, California. I saw the film. I really liked it. It was very well made and honest. Plus, I'm in it.

I remember one day both Ray Brown and Jennifer were in the store. They played a few chorus of blues together. Since I didn't have any left-handed basses at the time, Jennifer had to play a right- handed bass left-handed. She actually got through it ok. I was impressed! She wasn't. She said,

"The only time I got to play with Ray Brown and I had to play a right-handed bass!"

*****

Lou Levy (Label)

"Label" was Lou's nickname. It seems that Jews call everybody named Lou - Label.

Lou was born March 5, 1928 in Chicago, started playing piano at age 12. His main influences were Art Tatum and Bud Powell. At age 19, he worked with Georgie Auld (tenor sax player from Toronto who played the solos for Robert De Niro in the movie "New York, New York"), Sarah Vaughan, and Chubby Jackson (bass player from New York), later on Woody Herman's Second Herd, Tommy Dorsey and Flip Phillips (tenor sax player from Brooklyn, New York) and Ella Fitzgerald.

(I ran into Georgie Auld in a restaurant not too long before he died and he took care of my tab without telling me.)

Lou was also one of the guys I first met in the store and became very good friends with immediately. I learned about him in Taiwan from listening to all of Ella's records. One of my favorite albums was "Ella in Rome". Lou was on piano, Max Bennett on bass and Gus Johnson on drums. Lou actually gave me a new CD as a gift after I told him that was how I first heard about him.

I knew he was an excellent comper (accompanist) for singers but I had no idea he was such a good soloist too. He told me he started to play with Sarah Vaughan when he was still in high school. He said,

"Somehow Sassy heard about me so she asked me to play for her at this little club in Chicago. I was underage at the time, so Sassy had to come to my house to pick me up every night and drove me home after the gig."

He also said, "The first time I played with Bird (Charlie Parker), I was only 16 and he told me to go listen to Bud Powell."

We hit it off right away. I remember he used to tell me, "I always like Chinese people. I remember when I was a kid, my parents used to take us for Chinese food all the time (of course, Jews and Chinese food), and I always watched the people working in the kitchen. They were so interesting!"

Jews and Chinese are very much alike in a lot of ways.

Lou cooked the best skirt steak. Every once in a while he would buy some beautiful skirt steaks from this Danish meat market in the valley and ask me to come over to have dinner with him. Between the Martinis and skirt steaks, we were two happy Jews. Oh, Lou made the best Martinis. I got shit-faced every time I hung with him.

Lou was telling me about this skirt steak joint in Chicago called "Joe Stein's" (it's probably long gone). He said his Mom and Dad used to take all the kids to Joe's every weekend. The minute you sat down they would bring to the table this big aluminum bucket full of all kinds of pickles, and then you order the steaks. I can just picture that old Jewish restaurant, and those pickles made my mouth water. Lou hated Canters (famous deli). I can hear him right now,

"The worst!"

Lou's mom must have been a hell of a cook because I remember Maury used to tell Lou, "Every time I think about your mother's matzo ball soup, I get a lump in my throat."

Lou told me Benny Goodman and he actually went to see Sinatra at the Sands. He said Sinatra saw them in the front row, so as soon as he finished the song he said to the audience,

"Ladies and gentleman, the King of Swing, Mr. Benny Goodman."

And then he said to Lou,

"Hey, Louigie, how you doin?"

Lou said, "He thought I was a Wop."

Lou also told me that when he was with Norman Granz's Jazz at the Phil, he was playing for Ella. They were in Germany playing a big concert. Everybody played: Pres, Stan (Getz), Diz (Dizzy Gillespie), Hank Jones, Buddy Rich, Ray Brown, Oscar Peterson, Flip Phillips, Roy Eldridge, ====. Anyway, Ella was on last. The whole joint broke down. They just loved her! They wouldn't let her go. She did a couple of encores and they still wouldn't let her go. Ella refused to come out but the audience just wouldn't stop applauding. Norman finally asked Dizzy to play something and Diz said,

"Uh uh! Not after sister!"

Lou was probably one of the most honest musicians that I've ever met. His honesty actually cost him the gig with Sinatra. He told me the story about how Sinatra screwed up on stage forgetting something they rehearsed and Lou had to improvise to cover his ass. When Sinatra called Lou about something else, Lou confronted him with his fuck up;

"Hey Frank, weren't you supposed to do this on that song...?"

Sinatra said, "Oh.... yeah, I forgot about it."

Little did Lou know the next thing he knew he got a phone call from the management office and they decided to let him go.

Lou was so good at sending me postcards from all over the world. He wrote such good one liners. A few words tell the whole story.

One of my favorite cards was an Indian parade in the 1940's in Flagstaff, Arizona. In the background, there were quite a few stores. And Lou wrote;

"Hip Indians! One hotel, two drug stores." Signed Later, L.L.

Only Label would notice two drug stores in the background.

He would address me differently on those cards every time. "Chen Gang" was the one he used most. And the rest of them were:

"Chen Stein",
"Shrine on vine",
"Chen Shrine on Vine",
"Chop Shop",
"Bruce Stein",
"Gary & Gang",
"Stein & Staff & Stuff",

"Chop Chop Shop",
"Mother Chen",
"Dudeville",
"Charlie Chen",
"Music Chop on Vine",
"Chen & Co.",
"Stein - Way",

Evidently he got lot of time on his hands.

One of my favorite things to do is reading all the postcards that Label sent me. A lot of them were sent from outside the States, so he often wrote, "I'll probably see you before this card gets to you!"

He was right. Sometimes I'd get a call from him first and then receive the card later on that same day.

Here are some of the postcards he sent me:

1) Sat. 11/13/91, 7:30 AM

"Hi, back in Tokyo last nite. Concert & 5 hr. ride on bus. Vodka & poker, today hangover. 3 more concerts & TV show & then home. People have been nice but I can hardly wait to get home & see some unfriendly faces. Now to unpack & see if there is any clean laundry left. Your name comes up alot & of course Maury's. "Sweets" (Edison) has been terrific fun. Sayonara. Label."

2) Nov. 3, 8:40am Tues-Kochi Japan

"Well its "erection" day (I wish) in Japan but since we're a day ahead still have to wait 24 hours. Going out in a little while to eat more noodles. But I'm enjoying it. Still no booze. Weather has been sunny, rainy & snowing. Snowed in Sapporo. Today I'm going to stick around & hear rest of concert (we open) - this is the best the band has sounded since I've been with them. Sherman (Ferguson) is doing a real good job & it's great to have Conte (Candoli) on it. Eric (Von Essen) is fine & always finds good noodle shops. I think I'll make him Jewish and call him Eric

Noodleman. - Or maybe Eric Von Noodleman- I sorta like it- or somethin' like that- Sayonara. Label"

3) Friday Nov 22, high noon from London town

"Got here easily & went right to eight hour rehearsal, now to another rehearsal & then sound check & then concert. And then fuck everybody. I'm going to Paris. Gotta get downstairs for ride to rehearsal. All the guys Conte (Candoli), Shorty (Rogers), Coop (Bob Cooper), all send regards. The weather is typical London but comfortable. See you probably before you get this card. Label"

4)   This postcard is about some dudes playing pool in a parlor. And he addressed me as Bruce Stein.

"Oscar day. High noon. Talkin' bout some bad dudes! You hear what I'm saying? Time now to start getting my shit together for governor's ball tonite - Someday gotta' get a real gig, but if I ever do, have someone arrest me. Never did get together with Konitz. Easier eating home in p.j.'s. Bye for now. Agent Double L."

5) Sunday high noon 7/29/1990 Fort Lauderdale

"Hello to Hollywood from Hollywood. Got here last nite in time to catch Mel Lewis band. Good band but it could use Mel. If you don't believe me, ask him when you see him, which eventually we all will. (Chinese proverb) See ya L.L."

6) Post card from Rihga Royal Hotel New York.

"Tues. Day of gig. Man, is this town a rip off. I've had 3 or 4 meals that cost a lot & stunk. But I did find a good bkfst place. $4.50, room service Hamburg came to $20 w/tip. You dig? Anyway, it'll all be over today & I'm looking forward to getting back. You hear what I'm saying bro? Label"

7) This one is a winner.

He cut down two lines of ads from MCI phone co., one in Chinese and the other one in Korean. And he pasted them together on the card and wrote, "No starch please!" and addressed to Chen & co

8) This one is a winner too.

He sent me a thank you card for the dinner party at my house with all the guys, Al, Cedar, Pete, and… The card was a picture of Ella dressed in a red outfit and wearing a red hat standing in the garden. (So cute) He writes, "Great dinner! Thanx. P& L (Pinky and Lou), Label."

But on the envelope he put down Quemoy & Matsu on the upper left corner. It took me a long time to finally figure it out what he was trying to tell me. See, after Chiang Kai-shek lost the civil War to Mao and retreated to Taiwan, Quemoy and Matsu are two small islands located closest to Mainland China and basically acted as two guards to protect Taiwan from being attacked by Mao. I can't believe that Label was hip to those two islands. That goes to show you how well read he was. That's incredible. I was so impressed.

9) Monday 10/8 7am (Osaka, Japan)

"Last nite walked into lobby of hotel & there was Cedar, David Williams, Billy Higgins & Ralph Moore. SURPRISE! They had a gig earlier. - Catch train in couple of hours for next gig. The band now sounds about as good as it will ever sound, which is not too good. Well, it's a gig. Hang out mostly with Joe Ramano, Nimitz too. Not much else to tell. I'll be seeing you about the time you get this. Later, Label."

10) This card is a picture of Thelonius Monk sitting in front of a piano.

"Actual incident at bar in New York City. --- Scenario---Jimmy Rowles sitting at bar, in walks Monk. Monk says to bartender, "Say M.F. give that M.F. another one of those M.F.'s." Thought you should have this classic motherfucker for your rogues' gallery. Nice Yarmulke huh? Later, mother Label."

11) This one is right after the election. From Japan. And it goes:

"Friday, Well, We got Flucked again. So at least "Bird lives"! Maybe someone will take a shot and that maybe me. Sounds like a good idea but a shot of what? Do you think I'd do well in Taipe? Excuse the spelling. So I've been around Reagan, Nixon, Ford, Ike, F.D.R & J.F.K. luckily never Bush League. Somehow we'll survive. But Maury would help. God bless him and the Democlats. Lou, LL."

12) This card is a picture of Ella singing with Dizzy, and Ray Brown is in the background Photographed by William P. Gottlieb in New York, 1947. Label and Pinky went to Dick Nash's for the weekend. And it goes like this:

"Sunday, 10:30am Super Bowl. Well, tonight's the night. Football at 5p.m. Right now getting the stuff ready for breakfast. I brought * (Jew) food for the Goyim. Lox, cream cheese, bagels etc. Oh, oh!! They're setting the table right now. Gotta sign off. Chop Chop * LL."

13) This one from a gig at Le Meridien hotel in Chicago:

"Mon.11am. Well, it's over. Actually went o.k. – Nothing that took too much thinking, now for the fun. Teddy Edwards is going to leave my bread for this gig with you (I think). If he doesn't, get your guns ready - you dig! Gotta pack now. Lou L. LL."

14) This one is a sign that says, "If assholes could fly this place would be an airport" and he wrote, "Kung She Fa Tsai" (New Year's greeting in Chinese). Wright Bros. LL. "

And he addressed to Chen Gang.

15) This one is a picture of bunch of naked Japanese women taking bath Quarreling and scuffling in Women's Bathhouse. And he writes:

"3/8/90 6:20 Am
Well, up with the rising sun. All is well. Nice gig & club. One show for 1 ½ hrs a nite. Weather nice. Crisp & clear. Hotel nice. I'll probably be home before you get this but thought you like the picture. Like I said this is better than working for a living, see how happy I am. (He had a mean-looking Samurai face stamp pasted right after that). L.L."

16) This one is a picture of a man and woman standing in front of the big spider web in Sax Rohmer's "Tales of Chinatown". His book included ten stories of England's Chinatown, "Where life moves in devious paths and subtle intrigues of the Orient challenge all resources of New Scotland Yard" Ten stories of macabre mystery by the creator of the famous Dr. Fu Manchu. And Lou writes:

"Wed. 10 am
See, them English Chinamen know where it's at. You dig!?! Have to find opium den, then I will have led a full life. Right now the defendant, Dr. Fung is still being questioned by * (Jew) – BORING!!!!!!!!! But, better than working. Now time to pay some bills & put some bread in bank. Later from the Valley. Label, LL."
And he addressed to Charlie Chen.

17) This one is the night view of new Chinatown, Los Angeles. And he writes:

"Where's the den?
So it's Friday & got stuff to take care of. Always something! Did Mandel call? If not, give him a call. Love & happy trail from the San Fernando Valley. Label LL."

18) This one's from Washington D.C. when he was with Sinatra 1987

"Sunday 5 pm. Hi from your capital. Finishing 1st week today. Nice gig. Good piano & sound system. Nice apt. in lovely old Alexandria Va. Tomorrow on to N.Y.C. for 2 days. Plans include Village Vanguard (M. Lewis Orch.) & old blue eyes at Carnegie Hall. Lots of side activities. Too numerous to mention also on agenda. Back here wed for 2nd week. We'll be home Monday. Can't wait to get back to corn & tomatoes. But we're enjoying this & also enjoying news about all the help now coming to the old woodchopper. See Ya Soon. L.L."

19) This one is sent from Holiday Inn Downtown Bayfront, Florida. 1997 and he wrote:

"Friday 28th, 9:45 am

Good morning. At this moment I'm waiting for Mr. & Mrs. Lovely to pick me up for lunch. They have a good condo here. --- Last nite did Terry's set ...HELP!!! The worst... It was like trying to put a fan belt on with the motor going. Well, at least I got a terrific room & the weather isn't too hot. Tonite play with big band & tomorrow Super sax. A Glick A Tear Gitrofen (another shit I don't need). Later, Label, L.L."

20) This one was from Lee Katzman's (trumpet player) house in New York in 1998. And he writes:

"Monday, 6:30 am

So here I am, up early as usual. Did gig yesterday aft. Very nice. Good music & good food & good bar. Weather's cool but o.k. Then we watched Jets murder the Buffalo Bills in football. Glad Marv (coach of Buffalo Bills) wasn't there (Marv Levy is Lou's cousin). No plans today. Have 2 days to goof off before blue eyes bash. Having good time with the Katzmans in the suburbs. Later—Label L.L."

And Lee wrote the following: "let's hear it for Levy. Playing be-ootiful. And behaving grand. Tomorrow we're playing tennis. Lee."

And he addressed to Chen Gang.

These are just a few of all the cards Label sent me through the years. You can see why I enjoy so much reading them.

I remember one time I had to fly to San Jose to see my mom and my sisters. And Lou had to fly to Chicago to play a gig with Conte Candoli. We were coming back to LAX around the same time. So, I agreed to pick him up since I drove myself to the airport and left my car at lot C.

It was real cute to see him standing on the sidewalk waiting for me, holding a card that said "Gong Hi Fa Choi" in Chinese, which means "Great fortune to you" (usually we use that phrase on Chinese New Years).

We took La Brea all the way. We were listening to my tape of Paul Desmond and Jim Hall. Lou told me that the problem with Paul Desmond was he fell in love too easily. No wonder he played the way he played. He was romantic. And Lou also said that Paul got the idea of writing "Take 5" from playing the slot machine in Vegas. I can see that too, you know, "Ching ching ching, ching

ching." "Ching ching ching, ching ching." 1, 2, 3, 4, 5, and 1, 2, 3, 4, 5.

How interesting!

When we passed Washington Blvd, Lou said, "Look over there! There was a club that I used to go see Trane play. And over there, that motel Conte and I used to stay there. What a strange place. It was dark and weird."

Lou used to go to the Tabia market (produce place in the valley) from time to time and he would always pick up some bagels, fresh tomato, few ears of corn, and a bag of unsalted peanuts and brought them to the store for me. That was very sweet of him.

Lou loved the original Tommy's Hamburger. Every once in a while we would make a trip to Beverly and Rampart, standing there eating greasy chiliburgers and washing it down with 7 Ups. It's kind of funny to see an old Jew and a Chinaman standing outside gulping down greasy burgers with all the Mexicans.

Musso and Frank on Hollywood Blvd. is one of my favorite restaurants. They've been in business since 1919. They've got the best steaks, great bar and they make the best Martinis. Maury took me there years ago, and I've been going there ever since.

One time Lou and I were eating there, the waiter came over and said, "Good evening gentlemen, my name is Oscar, the second best waiter in the world."

Lou said, "Who's the best?"

Oscar said, "Everyone else."

Later on, we were talking about all the songs I'd like to record with him (we were thinking about doing an album together). Lou knew a lot of songs and lyrics as well. It must have something to do with him working with all the great singers all his life. He asked me if I knew who wrote "Everything Happens to Me?"

I said, "Matt Dennis".

He said, "Not bad!"

Lou called me one morning and told me he was invited to a BBQ party the night before and all they served was hot dogs, burgers, ham, pork chops, macaroni and cheese.

He said, "I woke up this morning felt like somebody put a plug up my ass!"

I think it was Lou himself who told me when he was asked which was his favorite rock group, he said, "Mount Rushmore".

Maury, Stan Getz, and Lou Levy, they were like The 3 Musketeers. They were always hanging out together. Lou lived in town, so he came to visit Maury almost every day. You always saw Lou Levy at Stein on Vine. He was like an in-house piano player. I can just see him standing by the doorway in Maury's famous back room smoking that skinny cigar that he always smoked. Every gig that Maury played, he always used Lou. Why not, like Miles said about Bill Evans when he was asked why did he use a white piano player in his band, Miles said,

"Find me a better one."

According to Lou, in the old days, Stein on Vine was like a casual, convenient stop for all the guys. People would come in just to use the room to change and get their horns tuned up for the gigs, or just killing time between gigs or simply having a drink hanging out with the old man. You'll never know, you might pick up a gig or two by hanging out at Stein on Vine. Actually it was still like that before the economy took a nosedive.

(I came back from the bank one day and found this note on my desk and it reads " took 5 dollars, will pay back - James Moody." I still have that note)

A lot of people who may not have seen each other for years often ran into each other at Stein on Vine. It happens all the time. I have seen enough guys in the store cheering, screaming and hugging each other trying to remember when was the last time that they saw or played with each other. It's real neat!

Well, Maury and Lou had a fall-out one time. It was kind of a long story:

An old friend of Maury's from Chicago was celebrating his birthday so he called Lou to play for the party and he also wanted him to put together a band. So, Lou immediately mentioned Maury,

"How about Maury Stein?"

And the guy said, "Absolutely not, no Maury Stein."

So, Lou used Plas Johnson.

Somehow Maury got invited to the party, and when he saw Lou playing with Plas, Maury got very upset and hurt. He felt betrayed and he didn't want to talk to Lou nor let him come around anymore.

I wasn't that close to Maury and Lou yet, so I never asked Lou why he didn't try to explain the whole story to Maury. Until years later I asked Lou and he told me he did try but Maury just didn't want to listen.

But anyway, for months, Maury didn't want to have anything to do with Lou. I guess Maury was so hurt because he probably thought Lou didn't want to play with him because he wasn't good enough.

One night, Lou was playing at the Money Tree, Maury showed up, and he was standing right next to the stage watching Label play. And he said to him,

"You sounded good."

And that was it.
Just like that, like nothing ever happened.

For the longest time I was pretty pissed off at Lou too before he told me the story. As a matter of fact, Lynn was really upset with him. But after I told her exactly what happened, she felt so bad that she had held a grudge against Lou for so long, she said she needed to apologize to him. I don't know if she ever did.

Well, Lou was always bugging me about finding him an opium den. He used to joke about what kind of Chinaman I am that I couldn't even find an opium den. He was convinced that there must be one somewhere in Chinatown.

One time my Mom was visiting me and when I told Lou about Mom's visit, he said, "Hey, by any chance you think your Mom might know where the opium den is?"

We made a visit to Stan Getz's with Pinky once. It was fun to watch Lou prepare all the Jew food for Stan: smoked whitefish, cream cheese, water bagels, red onions, and fresh tomato. Stan loved it. It was precious watching him gulping down all the Jewish food that he wasn't supposed to eat (he was on a macrobiotic diet to save energy to fight liver cancer).

Lou was probably one of the fastest-minded guys that I've ever met:

During the LA riots in 1992, I had to stay in the store 2 nights to protect it from the looters. One time I was catching myself looking ridiculous, holding a shotgun in the back room, sitting in the dark so I could have a clear view of both the back parking lot and the front door. Anyway, the image was, here I am in Los Angeles, in 1992, sitting in the dark in my own store holding a shotgun trying to protect myself. -----THIS IS RIDICULOUS!!!

Next morning Lou called, and I told him how I felt. I said, "You know Label, for a minute, I looked at myself, I felt like I was Judge Roy Bean!"

Lou said, "You mean Soy Bean."

Lou told me a story about Bill Evans. It was real cute. They were very close:

One time when Bill was in town playing at Shelly's Manne-Hole, he was staying at the Beverly Hilton. Lou went to see Bill for lunch at the hotel garden restaurant, and Bill said to Lou, "You know, I just wrote a little piece, and I'd like to play it for you."

Lou said, "Oh, I can't wait to hear it."

So Bill got the restaurant manager over and asked him if he could use the piano in the Lobby for a minute. The manager reluctantly said,

"Well... I guess it's ok."

Bill went upstairs to get his music. The manager had to come back to Lou and asked him,

"Say yeah ....., is he any good?"

Lou just laughed and said, "I don't think you got anything to worry about."

Lou also told me that not only was Bill Evans a great jazz piano player, he was also a world-class snooker player, and an excellent marksman. That was interesting. But I would never go shooting with him because he was high all the time.

Lou was supposed to play a gig in Santa Barbara. Right before he left the house, he got a phone call from the doctor. The doctor told him that he needed to come into the hospital right away because they found a tumor in his head. Label said,

"But..."

Doc said, "There's no but, you need to come in right now."

So, Lou cancelled the gig and had an operation instead. Thank god the operation was successful and he was ok after that.

Later on Lou started to hurt real bad from his diabetes and arthritis. Just like Maury at the end. But he still didn't lose his sense of humor. He told me he went to the grocery store. The woman at the checkout asked him if he needed help carrying the groceries, he said,

"Do I really look that bad?"

Lou couldn't stand the pain, so he went back to using hard drugs again with the help of a "friend". Herb Alpert helped get him to rehab. But Lou was acting like a child. I went to the rehab place in Pasadena to see him. It was a real nice place. He was ok for about a week then he started to call everybody trying to get us to help him get the hell out of there. He basically sat by the payphone all day calling everybody and waited for everybody to call him back. This is what he said to me on the phone:

"Listen! You got to help me out. You got to get me out of here. I just can't stand it anymore."

I don't know how he managed to stay and finish the whole thing. He sure was bugging the shit out of me and everybody else.

All the dinner parties we had in my house, Lou was always the first to show with Pinky. As the party went on I'd notice he was drinking very heavily. Even my wife was telling me that Lou was drinking way too much. I guess it was getting worse and worse because he was hurting so bad.

Finally he couldn't and didn't even want to play the piano anymore. That really made things worse. He often called and complained about how much pain he had to suffer. He was telling me that he slept so hard every night. His body was so tight from all the pain and he could never relax. He said he woke up every morning exhausted.

One morning Lou called and sounded cheerful. He told me he was going to Max Bennett's in Newport Beach for the weekend. I was really happy for him because I thought the sun and the beach might do him some good.

Pinky called me that night and told me Lou had a heart attack and died at Max's.

Maybe it was because when Maury died, I had too much business to take care of so I didn't really have that much time to think about him. Maybe it might have been too painful to think about Maury all the time. But Label was a totally different story. I really miss him!!!

*****

Stan Levey

Stan was born in Philadelphia in 1926. He was considered one of the most important drummers in the Bebop years along with Kenny Clarke and Max Roach. He worked with Dizzy in Philly in 1942 when he was 16, then moved to New York and played with Dizzy, Charlie Parker and Oscar Pettiford. That album "For Musicians Only" - Stan's crisp, melodic style of drumming and Ray Brown's steady walking bass lines really drove the whole band.

Stan came in to see me one day. When he saw that famous picture behind me by William P. Gottlieb in 1948 with "Bird" and Miles at 3 Deuces in New York. He screamed,

"They missed me, they missed me. I was sitting right next to Bird."

I had no idea that Stan was on that gig.

Stan loved boxing and he actually became a heavyweight boxer. Lou told me Stan won 14 bouts straight and had his jaw broken on the 15th bout. So he quit. Later on he became a photographer. It seemed that he was doing all right.

Stan was the one that Lou told me once they were in a restaurant, and Stan asked the waitress,

"Miss, ...oh Miss... could you bring me something can kill the taste of this food?"

Stan asked Lou if he was "getting any" lately.

Lou said, "If I can only get it up!"

Stan said, "IF, now that's a big word!"

Stan was one of the guys that used to join us at Langer's deli in downtown LA for corned beef and pastrami sandwiches. We had so much fun talking, bullshitting, gulping down sandwiches drinking Dr. Brown's soda pop.

*****

Warne Marsh

Warne was a tenor sax player born in Los Angeles. He and Lee Konitz (sax player from Chicago) studied with Lennie Tristano (Chicago born jazz pianist). He was one of the most faithful adherents of the Tristano philosophy of improvisation. Not like most jazz musicians, you hardly ever heard him play any clichés or licks.

One of the few true improvisers in my opinion.

I always liked Warne's playing. He had so much facility and ideas. One time I went to see him at Donte's. Jack Nimitz (Bari sax player, nicknamed "Admiral") and I were sitting together and he kept buying me drinks. Warne was playing his ass off that night. I could really hear what he was trying to do. His ideas were just pouring out of his horn and his lines were flowing beautifully in and out of the changes and everything made sense. Stunning! It was such a joy to listen to Warne play.

Warne came to visit me one day. We had some coffee and cookies together. Those cookies were made by Kay Simpkins (wife of Sarah Vaughan's bass player Andy) who always made a big jar of the most delicious chocolate chip cookies for me.

Warne was looking fine and he said to me, "Gary, I'm playing at Donte's tonight. If you're not doing anything, come by to see me."

I said, "Of course!"

I never made it. The next day I got a phone call from somebody, and he told me Warne died on stage last night at Donte's.

*****

Al McKibbon

Al was born in Chicago 1919. Known as a bop, hard bop and Latin jazz bass player. He had worked with big names like Coleman Hawkins, Dizzy, Miles, Monk, Basie, Sinatra, Sammy Davis, Jr., George Shearing and Cal Tjader. He recorded his first album in his own name "Tumbao Para Los Congueros De Mi Vida" which was nominated for a Grammy at age 80.

I don't remember when I first met Al. I just remember the first time Al took Allison (his daughter) to the store. She was only 9 years old - a beautiful, tall, skinny girl.

Al McKibbon and me at Stein on Vine

Al always came to the store whenever he was in town, and we started to hang out more after he left Sammy Davis, Jr.. Later on he did the show "Black and Blue" for a couple of years in New York, and after that he worked in Laughlin (Nevada) for a while. After Jeannine (Al's wife) died, Al was in the store almost every day. There's a tall stool right next to the telephone and credit card processing terminal. That was Al's chair. He was like a fixture in the store. He loved to sit there and watch people come in and out. Sometimes when I was busy, he would even help me make a sale especially when people were looking for upright basses. Al was very generous when it came to sharing his knowledge about bass playing. He would invite anybody to his house and let him play his Stainer bass (Jacob Stainer- born in Absam, Austria in the 17th century. He was the best-known Austrian luthier) if you showed him any interest in learning. He never hesitated giving people free lessons.

Al's got big hands and fat fingers. I often told him, "That's how you get your sound with those well padded fingers".

He said, "You think so, huh."

This was his outgoing message on his answering machine with that deep baritone voice, "If you want to talk to a big, tall, dark, handsome bass player, please leave a message."

Jeannine was a trip! She was the hippest Southern gal. She used to call me "Ornamental Prince". She was a beautiful red head. Jeannine was a great cook and she loved to cook. She used to make all kinds of desserts for Al to bring to the store for me. They were to die for - Key Lime pie, Apple pie, Cheesecake, Chocolate Mousse cake, Peach cobbler ... you name it. The funny thing was she never asked Al if I liked them. She only cared if Al had brought back her dishes.

One time I took Al and Jeannine to this hole-in-the-wall Chinese restaurant in Monterey Park. Their pot stickers are the best in town. I've been going there for over 30 years and they're still owned by the same people. Now, you can imagine how the folks in the restaurant are looking at us - a big tall black man, a beautiful red head, and a Chinaman, laughing, pigging out as dishes are piling up on the table. They had no idea what to make of us. I'd been taking so many people to that restaurant – Al, Lou Levy, Cedar Walton, Ira Coleman, Mulgrew Miller, John Heard…can't remember them all but everybody loved it.

Al loved Chinese food. He always told me that when it comes to food, he loved variety and taste and Chinese food is totally that - variety and taste. Especially those live shrimp. What you do is you order live shrimp by the pound from the fish tank, and they will bring to the table a bucket to show you what you've ordered, and then they will steam them. You break the heads off and peal the shell then dip them in this light soy sauce with cilantro, ginger, sesame oil and scallion. Yum!!!

I can just hear him calling me, "Hey Black, (that's what he called me) let's go get some swimps (that's how Al's father JC pronounced shrimp)!"

One Sunday morning, I got up early and called Al, "Home (That's what I called him), let me take you to Gladstones (a restaurant on the beach in Malibu) for brunch."

He was thrilled, "Really? ALL RIGHT! ... Oh, you know what I have to do first."

I said, "Yeah, yeah, yeah! Go wash your big ass."

He had this old black man thing that he had to wash his ass before he went out.

Anyway, I got to his house on the hills. He was already sitting at the bottom of the steps waiting. He looked so cute! I got out the car and said,

"Home!"

"What IT IS? Black!"

"Bad English, Motherfucker!"

We laughed.

One time Al and I went to this sushi joint on Beverly and Hobart. As we were standing at the entrance waiting for seats at the bar, we both saw this lady sitting at the far end of the bar, reaching into her purse. She took out a pair of glasses and put them on looking straight at us just to make sure that what she saw was right, a big tall black man and a Chinaman wearing a hat. I guess we did look kind of unusual. We always felt people were eavesdropping on us, especially when we were talking about Jazz, naming all the cats …Horace this, Horace that, Ray Brown this Ray Brown that...

Like Lou Levy, Al knew all the standards. Not only the melody & chord changes but lyrics as well. It's amazing how many songs he knew. Some of them I'd never heard of and I know a lot of songs. We used to go out almost every night. He would be sitting in the store on his private stool, waiting for me to finish up and then we would go to wherever we felt like eating. Mind you, rush hour traffic in LA could be as bad as New York. Sometimes it would take us a good hour, hour and half to get to where we wanted to go. But it didn't matter, I'd put on a tape of Sinatra or Ella, or anybody else, and we would be singing along with the tape having a great time driving.

This is how Al described how touched he was by the way Sinatra sang 'I'm a Fool to Want You'. He said, "Man, he's ready to lick her ass."

One of Al's neighbors tried to hook him up with a lady. So Al went on a blind date for the first time since Jeannine died. The next day he called,

"Man, the woman looked like Fred Mertz" (in "I love Lucy").

I told that to Ray Brown when he came to visit. He was laughing so hard he couldn't stand straight. Immediately, he called Al and left a message for him,

"Big Mac, Ray Brown. How's Fred Mertz?"

Sometimes when there were no customers in the store, Al and I would play a tune or two. I played guitar and he played bass. Every once in a while, Al would sing a song or two and so would I. He knew this one song called "My Mom", the lyrics are so touching. Al and I both had tears in our eyes when he sang. He told me more than once how much his parents loved him and how proud of him they were. Al loved to play in the store with me. He always asked me, "When are we going to do this again?"

One Sunday, we had lunch in Malibu. After that, we went to Brown's Deli on Wilshire (no longer there) right next to The El Rey theatre. Years of hanging out with Maury and Lou, I know all the good deli's.

When we got out of the car, we noticed there were a lot of people going into the theater. Some of them dressed very funny. After living in Hollywood for so many years, you just don't think too much about much. After I grabbed everything I needed and put it on the counter, the woman behind the cash register (kind of looking at us funny) asked me,

"So...ah, you guys going to the party?"

"What party?"

"The party next door."

"Oh...oh, no, no, no, we are not going to any party."

No wonder some of those people went into the theater dressed like village people. I finally got it. They were having a big old gay party next door at The El Rey. And the woman thought Al and I were going to the party. I know we looked kind of funny together. So I laughed and said to Al,

"Hey Home, she thought we are going to the party next door..."

With that sort of annoyed deep voice, Al said,
"Shiiiiiit!"

I was laughing and I could tell Al didn't think it was funny!

When Al was playing with George Shearing, he told me one time he and another guy (can't remember who) put Shearing in the driver's seat and let him drive. Cops finally stopped them. And when the cop asked George for his driver license,

George told him, "I don't have one."

The cop said, "What do you mean you don't have one?"

George said, "I'm legally blind."

Al could be naughty. He told me he was driving with Shearing one time and Shearing was eating a strawberry ice cream. Whenever Shearing was about to take a bite, Al would step on the gas and Shearing would smear ice cream all over his face. Shearing kept saying, "You're terrible! You're terrible!"

Al had played with Shearing for over 6 years. One time they were playing at a club in Chicago. Ahmad Jamal trio (with Israel Crosby on bass and Vernell Fournier on drums – one of my favorite trios) was the opening act. Anyway, Ahmad was rehearsing at the club in the afternoon, and Al went to check them out. That night, when Al got to the dressing room, the first thing he said to Shearing was,

"Hey, George, did you check out the house band?"

Al told me one time Billy Eckstine had to meet Lena Horne early in the morning at her house. Later, Eckstine told Al, "7 o'clock in the morning, bitch is beautiful!"

Al said he played with Monk at Minton's Playhouse in Manhattan in late 40's for a couple of years; they took the subway home together every night. Sometimes they'd share a cab and Al'd drop

Monk off first. Monk usually got off the subway two stops before Al.

Al told me, "Sometimes Monk would not say a word to me for weeks on the subway. One day when the subway got to his stop, Monk got up, walked to the door, as soon as the door opened, Monk suddenly turned around and said to me, 'you ugly, nasty, stinking mother fucker!' and then he jumped off the subway!"

Al also said, "Sometimes Monk would come to my apartment and sit in the living room with a matchbox full of weed for 2, 3 days without saying a word."

Al had a natural feel for Latin music. His bass lines came naturally. Some of his bass lines became standards. I remember Rudy Regalado told me that some foreign Latin musicians thought that Al had died a long time ago. I guess most people just assume that once you are considered a legend, you must be dead.

Al once said, "Afro-Cuban music is probably the closest thing to Afro-American root."

Al had a chance to go visit Cuba with Allison. He asked me for some used strings or anything I could spare. He said people there are still in need of almost everything especially musical instrument accessories. So I put together a bag for him. After Al came back, Allison told me Al cried a lot in Cuba. I thought that was deep, he must have felt some deep connection with the Cuban culture.

Al had a surgery at St. Vincent hospital. By the time I got there, they'd already put him in the recovery room. I don't know how but they let me go straight in. In no time I was standing right in front of him, watching him hooked up with all the tubes. He suddenly opened his eyes and pointed his finger to the side and said,

"Get rid of that mother fucker." (Miles said that when he was in the hospital).

Al tried to be funny, but it hurt him so when we're both laughing. It was hard to watch him laughing and moaning at the same time.

Al was on the top floor in Northridge Hospital when that big Northridge earthquake happened. He actually got thrown out of bed. Electricity went out, so all the nurses kept calling him in the dark, "Alfred, Alfred, are you OK?"

Alfred? Apparently they had no idea who Al McKibbon was.

Al was a hell of a cook himself. He could BBQ his ass off. I had so many great dinners at Al's - leg of lamb with mint sauce, roast beef, collard greens, fried pizza... He cooked the best fried-chicken and catfish. We used to watch boxing at my house. The usual guys would join us: Cedar Walton, Lou Levy, Pete Candoli, Rudy Regalado, and whoever else was in town. Al's fried chicken was famous. He could never make enough. He even showed me how. I tried catfish once under his supervision at my house and it turned out great. The secret is buttermilk, paprika and a brown bag.

Al called me one morning and told me he didn't sleep well because somebody called him up at 2 in the morning and bugged the shit out of him. I told him,

"I'd never call you at 2 in the morning."

He said, "You could, if you got something to say!"

Al was very upset when he found out I was alone in the store for 2 nights during the Riots. I told him,

"Man, I can't let you stay with me. I didn't know what was gonna happen. It's my store, if anything happens to me, so be it. But I can't let anything happen to you. Jeannine's gonna kill me."

He said, "Well, you still could have called."

I have this old picture of Billie Holiday hanging on the wall in the store. "Lady" was lying on the floor with her bulldog. When Al first saw that picture, he was laughing his ass off,

"Ha ha ha...that dog's name is Mister and he bit the shit out of Coleman Hawkins."

Al told me that one time Art Tatum (born 1909 – one of the greatest jazz pianists despite being nearly blind from birth) was comping a singer, halfway thru the song Tatum told the singer, "Don't fuck with the blues, bitch!"

I've been a sharpshooter ever since I was in the service back home. There was a time I would go to target practice at least 3 or 4 times a week. I don't need to use the sights with certain guns. Within 20 feet, I hardly miss! Like everything else, all it takes is practice. I have taken a lot people shooting. Al would come along with me from time to time.

Allison decided she wanted to join us one day since she never handled a handgun before. We got to the range in downtown LA. Everything went smoothly until I heard a strange sound coming from the booth right next to me on my left while I was shooting. I turned my head and saw a pair of earmuffs flying in the air then drop to the floor. The next thing I saw was this guy falling backwards to the ground with a big hole in his forehead and there was blood everywhere. Al and Allison were stunned and turned their heads away. I jumped over the guy's body, went outside and screamed,

"Call the ambulance, somebody shot himself."

The woman at the counter picked up the phone, immediately called 911 and said, "I knew it, I knew it, I shouldn't have let him shoot. He looked way too weird and nervous."

So the guy committed suicide right next to us.

Cops came within minutes. They were all hiding behind the walls with their guns drawn like there was gonna be a big gun battle. We're all just standing there watching them inching in. Kind of funny!

Can you believe this shit? First time and last time for Allison. I can't even remember if she even touched the gun.

When I told my dear friend doctor Nick about this incident, he said, "I don't mean to sound cruel, but do you know what caliber he was shooting?"

One day I came back from the bank and Al had called earlier so I called him back. He said, "So you were doing the lone ranger shit, huh!"

"What? ... What are you talking about?"

"You know, 'to the bank, to the bank, to the bank, bank, bank.'"

Al told me the story about one time Duke Ellington was coming out of a dressing room with some white shit on his mustache. So Al said to him, "Edward Kennedy (Duke's name), wipe your nose."

Duke smiled at him and said, "Love you madly!"

When Bags (Milt Jackson - vibe player from Detroit) was playing at Catalina's, Al and I went to see him. It was so funny to see Bags acting like a little kid around Al. Of course, Al told me they went to the same high school and Al was a few years older. I've never seen Bags talk so much.

We went to see Percy (Heath) too when he was playing in town. Al and I took him to Chan Dara (Thai restaurant) for lunch. We couldn't shut him up. Percy's bass was a 200 year-old blonde Ruggeri (well known Italian family of violinmakers from Cremona since the mid 17th century). I played that bass at Catalina's kitchen. It had a wonderful tone. Percy also played cello tuned like a bass. He was actually pretty good! Percy's got a lot of soul.

Al played quite a few local restaurant gigs after he stopped touring. I hardly ever went to see him because I can't stand watching him play at places that nobody gives a shit. It breaks my heart. Guys like Al they are American treasures in my opinion. They deserve so much more. A few times I did go, he was so happy to see me.

Al always had bad kidneys and we'd tried to watch his salt intake. When he was around 84, he started to have all kinds of problems. Within one year, he was having dialysis every week, later on twice a week. Finally Allison had to put him in the hospital.

I was going to the hospital to see him almost every day. It was so hard to watch him lying in bed not knowing if he's going to get better. Often, I had to stop at the door for a minute to try and put myself together before I walked in. And I would ask,

"How do you feel, Home?"

"Like shit! How do you feel?"

Did I ever mention that Al was one of the most honest people that I've ever met?

That reminds me of another story that Al told me:

When Miles had his first quintet with Trane, Cannonball, Bill Evans, Paul Chambers, and Jimmy Cobb, they were rehearsing one afternoon, Al walked in. As soon as Miles saw Al, Miles leaned over and asked Al,

"Hey man, do you want to play?"

"No man, I don't know your shit!"

"Yah you do!"

Al never played.

He told me, "I probably could, but I just didn't feel like playing something I don't know very well with those guys."

I don't blame him. Can you imagine? Trane, Cannonball, Bill Evans, Paul Chambers and Miles (all the guys from that classic album 'Kind of Blue')? I wouldn't play either. The thing is Miles asked Al to play. That should tell you how much Miles liked Al and his playing. Not too many people that Miles would ask to play with him.

Al also told me one time he was checking out somebody's rehearsal and Mingus (bass player from Nogales, Arizona) was supposed to play but he didn't show. So Al played. When Mingus finally came he got pissed that somebody took his place. He said,

"Who played the bass? Who…. oh, oh, oh it's you, Bigon."

One day when I was in Al's room in the hospital, I saw him breathing hard even with the tubes stuck in his nose. I tried to lighten up his spirit so I asked,

"Home, do you know 'With Every Breath I Take?'"

"Sure!"

And he started to sing, "I think of you with every breath I take…"

Since I knew the song, I sang along with him (we always did that). After the verses, I thought he was going to stop but he kept going to the bridge, and I followed him. By the end of the song when the lyrics go to "every breath that I take, is a prayer that I'll make you mine", we both had tears in our eyes because we kind of knew that was probably the last song we're ever gonna sing together.

It's so hard to watch your loved ones deteriorate. Al had always been big, tall and strong. Now watching him being a sick old man, it was breaking my heart.

John Clayton called. He wanted to go see Al with me. We made a trip to this rehab place in Silver Lake, except they had just moved Al to a different hospital. It took us a minute to find him. When Al saw us, he started to cry. I knew then he didn't really have that much time left.

Poor Allison, she was really having a hard time trying to take care of Al day in and day out and watching him getting worse. Al finally went into a coma.

One night at around 8 o'clock, I told my wife, "I need to go see Al." And I did.

I sat with Al in his room watching him gasping for air with his eyes closed and mouth open, tubes stuck in his nose and body everywhere. I don't know how long I'd been sitting. Finally, I said to him,

"Home, you gotta go! Man, this is too much for you and everybody else. I know you are worrying about Allison, but you know what? She's gonna be ok. We all gonna look out for her."

I don't know whether he heard me or not. I walked outside and called Allison. I said, "Allison, I'm here with your dad. I think he's waiting for you to let him go. You've gotta let him go. He is suffering way too much."

Allison didn't say a word. I waited for a minute, she finally said, "Alright, I'll tell him tomorrow."

I went back to the hospital next morning. Al died.

*****

Rudy Regalado

Rudy and Me at Sushi joint

Rudy was born in Venezuela, a Timbalero, bandleader and composer. He was one of the top Timbale players in LA. In addition to being a regular member of "El Chicano", and the leader of his own band "Chevere", Rudy had recorded with Joe Zawinul, Quincy Jones, Alphonse Mouzon, Caravana Cubana and many others. I have a video copy of him playing a Timbale duel with the king of Timbale -Tito Puente.

Before Maury died, I often saw Rudy going in & out of the drum shop next door and he always stopped at the front door waving at me or hanging out in the parking lot listening to the music coming out of Maury's back room.

You know, come to think of it, when Bob Yeager (owner of Professional Drum Shop next door) was very sick in the hospital with cancer, Maury and I went to visit him, but Maury died first and Yeager soon followed. That was the end of that era and the beginning of a new one. Two owners of two landmark Hollywood music stores both died within a month. Ain't that something?

Now it's the new generation that carries the same tradition. Stan, Jerry and Tom are doing a great job with the drum shop and I'm here trying to be a good Jew.

Anyway, I can't remember exactly what happened, I guess somehow I invited Rudy to come in the store, and we started to hang. Eventually we became very best friends. We were going out to hang all the time. He took me to all the good Latin restaurants and clubs and I took him to the best Chinese food. I even took him for sushi for the first time and remember him looking at the raw fish in his plate. He said, "Goneo, Gary, I'm not sure I can eat this."

He tried it, and loved it. He even got his Mom hooked on it.

Rudy's got one of the hottest salsa bands in town - "Chevere". He was an excellent timbale player himself and he had the best Latino musicians in the band. You know, the kind of musicians always got "clove" in their heads. Oscar Mesa was the bass player and the pillar of the band as he wrote all the arrangements. Oscar has written some great charts. I love Oscar. What a great bass player, composer and arranger. His son Jr. is playing for the LA Phil.

I remember one time Oscar was playing with Rudy at a club and he was in the bathroom. One of the guys was snorting some shit not knowing Oscar was right next to him. So, when the guy came out of the toilet, Oscar said, "So, you're gonna play better now huh!" He embarrassed the shit out of him.

Rudy had a unique taste in colors when it comes to his wardrobe. His color combination sometimes surprised the hell out of everybody. I remember Al McKibbon told me that when his album was nominated for a Grammy, he ran into Rudy at the Grammy party. Al said, "Everybody was dressed in tux, and Rudy had a green suit on."

I can totally picture that. I forget who told me that Rudy's nickname was "Poco Royal", in Spanish that's "peacock". When I told that to Al, he was laughing so hard. So whenever he mentioned Rudy, he always used "Poco" instead. Like, "How's Poco?"

Rudy was a total boxing fan. No, he was a boxing nut. He told me, "Gary, if I liked music as much as I like boxing, I would have been an even better musician."

Well, for him to make such a statement (as he really was an excellent musician), he must have a true passion for boxing. As a matter of fact, often times when I watched boxing on TV, nine times out of ten, I'd see Rudy sitting ringside if the fight was taking place at the Great Western Forum.

Rudy knew all the Latino boxers and baseball players as well.

One time he asked me if I wanted to go to a ballgame with him.

"Sure!" I said.

So we drove to Dodgers Stadium. I went straight to ticketing to get some tickets, but Rudy stopped me and told me to wait. As a matter of fact, he took me to one of the exits and just stood there.

I said, "Well? What are we waiting for? Aren't we gonna get some tickets?"

Rudy said, "No, no, just wait!"

So, we stood there for a couple of minutes, I felt stupid standing there. Suddenly one of the exit doors opened from inside and Rudy motioned me to follow him. As soon as we got in, Rudy started saying hello to everybody. Everybody knew Rudy.

Rudy and I celebrate my 40th birthday at L.A. Forum

"Hey, Rudy", "Hola, Rudy", "C'omo esta', Rudy"…

He asked me where I want to sit.

I said, "I don't know, wherever. There really isn't any bad seat in this stadium."

We ended up sitting right next to the dugout. We could see all the guys sitting there waiting for their turn to hit. The guy holding the speed gun with a hat on told me that I look like Bruce Lee.

What an experience!!!

Rudy even took Pedro Guerrero to the store to meet me once. What an honor that was.

Same thing with boxing, Rudy took me to see so many fights. On my 40th birthday, he took me for dinner at the Forum and then we watched 3 fights. He even managed to get somebody to take a couple of pictures of us. I don't know how he managed to get them pictures. I still have them framed in the store.

Years later I took my wife to see a fight for the first time. She ended up crying when she saw the guy's face got busted open with blood all over his face. Well, so much for going to the fights with my wife.

When Golden boy Oscar De La Hoya fought Julio Cesar Chavez in Vegas that was the fight everybody was waiting for. Tickets were sold out in no time. For some reason there was no Pay-per-view on TV and everybody wanted to see the fight. Rudy went to Vegas (of course). I don't know how but he managed to get a hold of a few tickets and he saved one for me but he called me around one o'clock in the morning and I was sound asleep.

"Gary, are you awake?"

"No, who is this?"
"It's Rudy. Do you want to see the fight?"

"I don't want to see no fucking fight, I want to sleep!"

And I hung up on him.

Then, suddenly, I realized which fight he was talking about and I said to myself,

"OH, SHIT!"

I didn't even know where the hell he was calling me from. We didn't have cell phones in those days. I couldn't call him back to tell him that I changed my mind. God Damn! What a fuck-up.

Well, the next day was the fight day and since I couldn't go to Vegas I called Al McKibbon to see if he wanted to join me to go watch the fight at the LA Coliseum. They had a giant screen over there. By the time we got there, there were a lot of people already and 90% of the audience was Latino. Everybody was rooting for Chavez. Al and I we just wanted to see a good fight and didn't really care who won. But when Chavez lost the fight, it was a big shock for almost everybody. The whole stadium became so quiet it turned into a ghost town. Nobody was talking. People walked away in disbelief and disappeared in no time. That was so weird. Even Al said,

"Man, this is weird!"

I gave Rudy a red silk nightgown since I never wore it. One Halloween day I was driving home from work and I saw Rudy coming out of that Peruvian restaurant by the store, walking on the street with that nightgown on and a pair of boots. I didn't know what he was supposed to look like but he sure looked funny as hell. I laughed in my car, didn't even bother to stop. Just drove away. He's really something else.

Rudy's a great bandleader. He not only played well, he also knew how to work the crowd. His gigs usually were fun times. Well, let's face it. Those Latinos do know how to party.

Rudy told me this funny story:

He called this trumpet player for a gig and he told the guy it pays 50 cents (fifty dollars). The guy later on called Rudy back and told Rudy that he had to cancel Rudy's gig because another guy offered him a gig that paid 30 dollars. Rudy said, "Are you crazy? When I said 50 cents I meant 50 dollars. Now you cancelled a fifty-dollar gig to take a 30-dollar gig. This has to be the joke of the year."

Rudy at his wedding

I was the best man at Rudy's wedding. Now, that was some experience!!!

254

Me at Rudy's wedding

First of all, I arranged for my friend Robert to be the driver for Rudy, his Mom and me since Robert has a classic Rolls. The night before when we were having a rehearsal in the church, I called Robert just to make sure that he was still on for the job. But he told me he wasn't feeling the greatest. So I told him, "Well, that's ok, why don't you get some rest. If you're still not feeling well tomorrow, call me first thing in the morning."

Next morning I waited till 10 o'clock and called Robert again. He didn't sound too hot.

Now, the wedding was scheduled at noon all the way in Southgate. I tried to call for a Limo but nobody could make it on such short notice. So, I jumped into my Jeep and drove it to the nearest car wash. I had it washed, waxed, and shampooed. Here I am, showed up at Rudy's around 11:30 and both Rudy and his Mom weren't even dressed yet. I said,

"Jesus, Rudy, Robert couldn't make it so I have to use my car to take us to the church and its already 11:30. For Christ's sake, you need to hurry. It's gonna take us at least half an hour to get there."

Rudy said to me S-L-O-W-L-Y, "Don't worry! We have plenty of time."

We finally got to the church and I was speeding the whole way. Thank god it was a Sunday, the traffic was very light. But guess what? There was nobody there and it was already past noon. So, we sat in the parking lot in our white tux and waited. Justo Almario (sax player from Colombia) showed up first. He was playing for the wedding (great job). And then people started to come. After everybody showed, the church door was still locked. So we all stood outside waiting. Finally, the Pastor came in and opened the door for us.

Well, the truth is, the pastor had totally forgot about Rudy's wedding and he went to a picnic in the near-by park with other people and he happened to come back to get something from the church, when he saw all the people waiting outside. That's when he finally remembered Rudy's wedding. Can you believe that?

So, after the ceremony we all drove to the reception, which was in a park supposedly not too far from the church. But because the Limo driver that everybody was following didn't study the directions and whoever volunteered to lead the way had no idea what he was doing, we all got lost. It took us more than an hour to finally get to the place. There was supposed to be music and refreshments waiting for us. We found out we couldn't serve any alcohol because of the park center regulation. To make things worse, it was so damn hot! Everybody was standing around sweating away not sure what the hell was going on. So finally I had to take Michito Sanchez (conga player) and a couple of guys to the nearest 7-11 to get a bunch of cold beer, wine and soft drinks and served them right there in the parking lot so at least people could have a cold drink while waiting.

The AC was broken and we couldn't rent one without a day's notice, so we had to rent a couple of big coolers. The sound guy finally showed. They went to a different party (in the same park) and played music for the wrong wedding. It took them a while to finally realize the name of the bride and groom was not right. Later on, the food guys finally showed. The chef cooked all night and crashed in the morning and overslept. He didn't wake up until 2 o'clock in the afternoon. Quietly sneaking in, they set up the buffet table.

Joe Zawinul (jazz keyboardist and composer from Austria) and his wife were there the whole time. Couple of times Joe and I we were just looking at each other and shook our heads. But you know what? Everybody ended up having a great time. So again, you got to hand it to Latins. Man! They do know how to party!

Rudy loved my Mom. He'd been enjoying Mom's cooking ever since the first time they met. Every time he saw Mom's pictures in the store, he immediately cleaned them for me and he would always say, "What a classy lady!"

Rudy moved to Vegas. He had to drive back and forth to LA to play all the gigs and he started to have some health issues. He seemed to get sick a lot. He had to call a sub to play one of the gigs. Finally he had to stay in the hospital.

I'm not sure how old Rudy really was. He looked the same for the last 30 years. I have a picture of him with Machito taken in 1960 in the Big Apple. He looked so young. He said he was 17 then. So he must have been in his mid or late 60s'.

Gloria (Rudy's wife) called and told me Rudy's home and I should go see him. So my wife and I drove all the way to Vegas one Sunday. We took off at 6:00 in the morning. It was still dark outside. Rudy was lying in bed in the living room but he looked great! Good spirit! He didn't look sick at all. He was so surprised to see me. Happy! My wife brought him some Ginseng tea. He drank the whole cup and loved it. He had some other visitors. Rudy was telling them all the stories that he and I went through, about the store and all the people we know. He seemed very relaxed and comfortable. Gloria walked me out and she told me the doctor started to give Rudy morphine. I knew right away that was not a good sign. We left Vegas around 6:00pm and we didn't get home until 11:00. Boy! Was my ass sore!

November 5th 2010, early in the morning Gloria called. Rudy died last night around 8:00 pm.

I still can't believe Rudy's gone. For the last 30 years that I'd known him, he always looked so happy, so vibrant and so full of life. It's so weird that I will never see him or hear from him again. So weird!!

I guess death is finally approaching my generation.

*****

Wayne Shorter

Wayne was born in Newark, New Jersey, a True Genius in my opinion. He went to Newark Arts High School and graduated from New York University. What a talented saxophone player and composer. He worked with Horace Silver and Maynard Ferguson before he joined Art Blakey's Jazz Messengers along with Cedar Walton and Freddie Hubbard in 1959, joined the Miles Davis Quintet in 1964. Many of his compositions such as "Footprints", "E.S.P.", and "Nefertiti" have become jazz standards. Wayne formed the fusion jazz band "Weather Report" with Joe Zawinul in 1971. Among all the excellent musicians that made up the Weather Report Alumni through the years, the most notable member was the revolutionary bassist Jaco Pastorius.

I can't really remember when I first met Wayne. I just remember how low key and nice he was. I'm a "straight ahead" kind of guy but when it comes to fusion jazz, I always like "Weather Report". I remember I got so excited every time I listened to Joe Zawinul's "Birdland" when I was still in Taiwan. The tune was named after the famous New York jazz club "Birdland" on 52nd street. Wayne, Zawinul and Jaco were superb on that album "Heavy Weather". According to Jaco, the studio version of "Birdland" was recorded in just one take.

Not too many people know that Wayne and Stan Getz were very close friends. One time I was at Stan's house with Wayne. Stan was so happy to see us. He had this German girl sent by the government visiting him from Germany, and he said to Wayne,

"Wayne, this is so and so. She won the saxophone competition in Germany, and they sent her over to me and wanted me to give her a few lessons. But you know me, man. I don't know how to teach. Can you help me out and show her something?"

Wayne said, "Sure!"

So Wayne asked the girl to play something. I remember she played "Stella by Starlight". She actually sounded ok. After she finished playing, Wayne thought for a moment and said,

"You should listen to Stravinsky more."

And that was it, that's all he said.

Brother Wayne is deep.

I used to go to Wayne's house before he moved to Florida. We both practice Buddhism, so we chanted together from time to time.

One time I finished overhauling Wayne's Mark VI tenor sax, I brought it to his house. As he was trying out the horn, Miles called. Wayne was so happy, he said to Miles,

"Hey, Miles, listen to my new horn."

Then he put the phone down and started to play to the receiver. And then he said,

"Listen to me play Trane."

Then he started to play like Trane. Then he said, "Listen to me play Stan Getz."

Then he started to sound like Getz.

He was having a good time playing for Miles over the phone.

Sometimes we'd be talking at the dinner table. He would say something that I had no idea what the hell he was talking about. But, hours later while I was driving home, it would suddenly hit me, "Oh, that's what he meant."

The man is way ahead of me.

Wayne is so deep. He told me years ago that I would marry a Chinese girl. I never paid any attention because I never felt the need to get married. But, here I am! When I told Wayne about what he said, he said, "Gary, when I said that I didn't just say that out of nothing. I actually felt that's what was gonna happen to you."

Wayne loves movies. He loves movies so much he's got this giant movie screen in his house. I really enjoy talking to him about all the great old movies.

We went to see "Terminator 2" together at Universal Studio Cinema. Right before that, we had dinner at this sushi joint on Ventura Blvd.. The restaurant was very busy and very crowded, so we had to stand by the entrance waiting for table. There were a lot of young people there, valley dudes and gals, loud and annoying. I was really bothered. So I said to Wayne,

"Man I just can't stand these fruity Californians!"

I probably took the words right out of his mouth as he just smiled.

We just had dinner, but Wayne got himself a big bucket of popcorn. We had a great time. Schwarzenegger is a bad dude.

Another time Wayne and I visited Stan Getz. We got there early in the morning. Stan was really being a great host. He fed us all day and we watched a lot of classic jazz videotapes. I should have taken some pictures of them two. When we were watching "Bird" playing with Dizzy, both Stan and Wayne were glued to the TV screen sitting side by side. Stan finally said, "Look at him, perfect fingering!"

Later on we watched Miles with Herbie, Ron Carter, Tony Williams and Wayne. When Wayne started to play "Footprints", Stan gave Wayne a couple of elbows and said,

"Yeah, Wayne! Yeah, Man!"

It was precious to watch them.

We didn't leave Stan's house until almost midnight. I was driving along the Pacific Coast Highway. Suddenly, I had this incredible realization - I was just hanging out with two of the greatest Jazz musicians who ever lived, and they both love me not because I'm a bitching musician but because I am who I am and do what I do. I actually felt this incredible relief, because for the longest time I had this chip on my shoulder that I sacrificed my playing for the store, and there was a lot of anger that I was carrying. Now I finally realized that the store is my real gig in this lifetime, not playing. --- That's deep!

But on the other hand, had I not had the passion and spent so much time working hard on my music, I wouldn't be able to handle this gig, and I wouldn't have had all the respect that I'm getting from all these giants of jazz. It seems that everything I've done in my life was basically preparation for this gig.

Now, that's real deep!

*****

Horace Silver

Horace was born September 2, 1928 in Norwalk, Connecticut. He started out playing tenor sax and then switched to piano. His unique funky and almost gospel style of piano playing and his simple melodic sense of composition set him apart from all piano players. You can recognize his playing anytime!

Horace had been using my rehearsal room ever since he first found out about me. We used to go to lunch together every time he rehearsed at the store. Horace is another one of those few mainstream Jazz musicians who made it by playing his own compositions. Tunes like "Song for My Father", "Nica's Dream", "Sister Sadie" "Strollin'"…they're all jazz standards.

We both agreed that among all the jazz musicians, the ones that have the most character are Monk and Pres.

Horace told me one day when we were on our way for lunch that he was thinking about releasing this album that he recorded live in New York with Lou Donaldson (alto sax player from North Carolina) in the 50's. And I told him I would love to have a copy when he did.

Months later, I came back from the bank and saw this new CD on my desk of Horace and Lou Donaldson, and Horace was rehearsing in my rehearsal room. Later on, Horace came up and I asked him,

"Hey, Horace, is this CD for me?"

Horace said, "Ya ya ya ya, If you pay for it."

"How much?"

"Eh…15 bucks."

"How much you owe me for the rehearsal room?"

"Twenty!"

"Well, let's call it even."

"Oh, oh, oh, OK!"

Horace told me when he first started to play he was working in a Jazz club "Sundown" in Hartford Connecticut. He said,

"The club owner was pretty hip. Every once in a while he would hire a star to play with us for one week. This one time we had Stan Getz for the whole week. That was great! Stan was so good and he forced me to get my chops together. He would play every tune in all 12 keys. Every chorus he would raise half a step until we came back to the original key. Man, I can't tell you what a challenge that was for a piano player. But I got my shit together!"

And then he told me, "Later on, when Stan was leaving, he asked me for my phone number because he said he liked the rhythm section and he wanted to use us. He said he would call and I thought he was just bullshitting because a couple of months ago we had Lucky Thompson (tenor and soprano sax player from South Carolina) and he said the same thing but he never called. But Stan came through. Not only did he call, he used the whole rhythm section on tour for 2 years. But every once in a while he would tell us the club owner didn't pay so we had to work for nothing. We were so young then we actually believed him."

Horace did call me one day and asked me if he could treat me for dinner for all the favors I've done for him. But it was a last minute invite and I couldn't make it.

Last time I saw Horace was at the Walt Disney Concert Hall when they had a tribute to him. Christian McBride put the whole thing together and he did a great job. He had Cedar Walton on piano, Randy Brecker and Tom Harrell on trumpet, Bennie Maupin and Joe Lovano on Tenor sax and the old time drummer Roger Humphries. They played all the hits by Horace. Dee Dee Bridgewater sang a couple of Horace's songs too. Cedar played with that master touch. Both Bennie and Joe Lovano played some mean, totally different style solos. I always love Tom Harrell's taste and that beautiful trumpet sound. I like Randy Brecker since the first time I heard him on that Brecker Brothers album "Some Skunk Funk". Christian McBride has become a master himself with both his bass playing and as a bandleader. Everybody sounded great. The whole concert went so smoothly. Horace was in a wheelchair but he was in very good spirits. We had a moment of silence for Michael Brecker who just died 3 days before. First time I heard about Michael Brecker was the solo he played on James Taylor's "Don't Let Me Be Lonely Tonight" when I was still in college. That was one of the most gorgeous solos that I ever heard.

After that concert, nobody heard anything about Horace for quite some time until Red Holloway (sax player from Arkansas) came back from the Apple and told me the family had put Horace in a home and he went to see him and he said Horace looked ok (now Red's gone).

I just can't imagine Horace being in a home after decades of a colorful music career.

*****

Cedar Walton

CEDAR WALTON

My man Cedar's from Dallas, Texas. He started out learning piano from his mother who was an aspiring concert pianist herself. She also exposed Cedar to a wide range of jazz greats such as Nat Cole, Errol Garner, Earl Hines, Hank Jones, Oscar Peterson, Lester Young and Dizzy Gillespie.

Cedar went to the University of Denver as a composition major and left for New York in 1955. He joined Art Blakey's Jazz Messengers in the early 1960's along with Freddie Hubbard and Curtis Fuller. Many of his compositions have become jazz standards - "Mosaic", "Ugetsu", "Bolivia"...are some of his best-known compositions. Like Benn Clatworthy (tenor sax player from England) said, "Every tune Cedar wrote is a triumph".

I love Cedar's playing. His unique harmonic sense with that masterful sensitive touch and impeccable time made Cedar one of the most distinctive piano players of all time.

I love Cedar!

I met Cedar when he first came to live in LA (Santa Monica to be exact). He needed a place to practice because he hadn't found a piano for his apartment yet. He called me up and since I have a halfway decent Chickering baby grand in the back room, he'd been practicing there ever since. In addition to his beautiful style of playing, Cedar is also very funny – great sense of humor. We became very close friends. Often after work we would head out to the east side to have some awesome Chinese food.

Cedar is unique, just like his music, which has such strong character. I remember he told me once, "You know Gary, I'm very lucky that I can play my own stuff and making it. It's not easy to do nowadays."

He's right. Not that many mainstream jazz players can make it by playing their own stuff today.

Cedar can also swing his ass off. I remember Lou Levy told me once,

"I can out-swing a lot of people, but guys like Cedar, they just got it."

Cedar told me when he first came to Los Angeles to record an album with Ray Brown, Ray sent somebody to pick him up from the airport. As soon as Cedar got off of the plane, this guy walked up to him and said, "Mr. Walton?"

Cedar said, "Yes!"

The guy said, "Well, Ray sent me to pick you up."

After they got in the car, Cedar had to ask the guy, "Say, my man, how did you know it was me?"

"Well, Ray told me to look for a big Chinese looking mother fucker!"

David Williams (bass player from Trinidad) has been playing with Cedar for many years. Sometimes Cedar calls me Mr. Wong. One time they were playing at Catalina's. I went to the dressing room to say hello before the gig. I knocked on the door and I heard David say, "Who is it?"

I said, "Wong here!"

"Wong place!"

Then he opened the door, and all three of them (Cedar, David and Billy Higgins) were laughing their asses off. Funny Huh! But you got to admit these guys are fast.

One day I went to Cedar's to watch the second rematch between Evander Holyfield and Riddick Bowe for the heavyweight championship title. What a fight that was. That's probably one of the last real heavyweight fights in my opinion. They beat the shit out of each other.

After the fight, I wanted to go home because I was feeling weird for some odd reason. It was like I kind of knew something was going to happen. Cedar wanted to show me some vintage videotape of Duke Ellington. I could never refuse that. So, we watched the tape for quite a while. But that hairy feeling was getting stronger and stronger. So I left.

After I got into my car, I said to myself, "You better drive carefully".

So, as soon as I got on the freeway I stayed in the slow lane and drove with my eyes wide open. Everything was cool except suddenly, the car two cars in front of me made a complete stop right on the freeway. The car in front of me made a squeaky sounding stop and so did I. But when I looked up in the mirror, I saw this Datsun 280 ZX sports car coming at me from behind so fast and I said to myself, "Oh my God!"

The next thing I knew that car slammed right into my car, so hard, my jeep actually jumped up in the air and fell down hard. I was going east but my car was facing south after it finally came to a complete stop. Everybody got out and they all came to me trying to find out if I was ok. I was still in shock. I couldn't feel a thing. I got out of the car and moved around.

"I guess I'm ok."

Thank God nobody was seriously injured.

The tow truck came by in no time and so did the police. After we all exchanged the insurance info, I was driven by the tow truck to drop my car at some repair shop and then they took me home. I called Cedar as soon as I got in,

"Man, you wouldn't believe what just happened to me…"

After I finally took a bath and tried to relax, my whole body was hurting like I just got run over by a truck. Literally!

Cedar moved back to New York after he and Martha got married. I really miss them. Even though we still talk on the phone from time to time, it's just not the same when you can just hop in the car and go see each other.

Cedar was inducted as a member of NEA (National Endowment for the Arts) 2010 class of Jazz Masters in January 2010. He stated, "It's quite an honor because it represents the endurance of an artist and his output as an artist and his ability to keep a certain stream of good performances throughout his or her career."

It is quite an honor and I am so proud of him (I told him so on the phone).

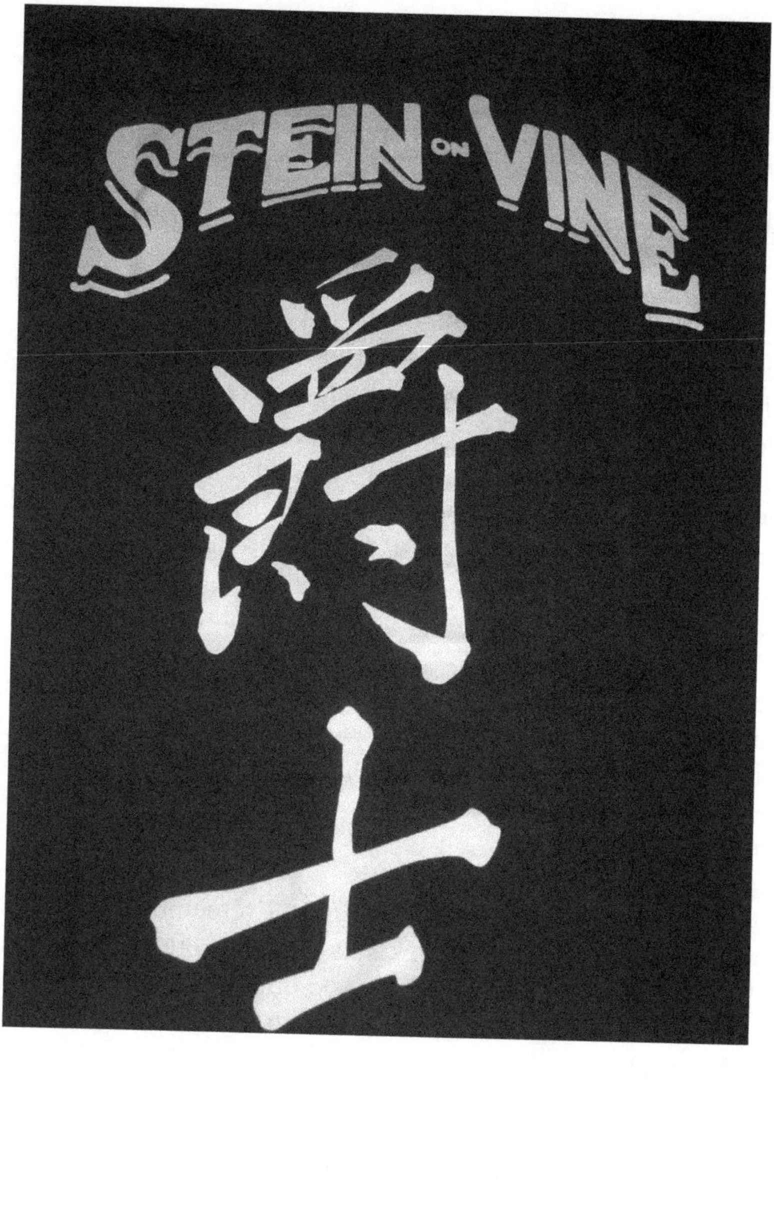
STEIN ON VINE
爵士

X: MY FATHER

I didn't have any contact with my Dad ever since I left Taiwan.

It was in early August 1988. My Dad decided to come to the United States to visit. He almost died of stomach cancer a year before. They operated on him and he seemed ok. I hardly ever talked to him after he and Mom divorced. He came to the club to see me play one night with his wife and her daughter when I was still in college. I could tell he was very proud of me after he saw me perform. I was a little uncomfortable seeing him and his family. In those days divorce was not common at all in Taiwan. Dad told me his wife's daughter was a big fan of mine and she'd really like to get to know me. I pretty much shined them on.

Anyway, so Dad was with me after he spent some time with sister Tina in San Jose and Grace in Vegas. It was so weird to be with him after all these years not seeing or talking to each other. Now he was right in front of my face and God knows how long he was gonna stay!

After spending only one day with him, I remember exactly why I couldn't stand his ass. He was just a natural big pain in the ass - selfish, demanding and sarcastic. And on top of everything else, he got real sick again. So I had to take him in and out of the doctors and hospital.

There was a big International Society of Bassists Convention in UCLA that August. I had a booth there. And August was the Buddhists campaign month. So, between the store, the Bass Convention and the campaign, I was going nuts, and I had a sick old man to take care of.

My apartment was on top of a hill. It was a big old mansion converted it into 8 units. It had open beams, high ceiling and nice hardwood floor, real nice for a single guy. But there are about 50 steps to get to the building. It was ok to carry Dad going down but when we came back from the Doctors, it was a bitch carrying Dad up those steps. Often times I thought about my military training.

One night, I woke up in the middle of the night by Dad's howling. I jumped out of the bed and went to him,

"Dad, are you ok?"

I was so afraid that he might die on me only to find out he was crying,

"What did I do to deserve this?"

That just pissed me off! So I screamed at him,

"What did you do to deserve this? What did I do to deserve you? I'll tell you what you did. I tell you what you did to Mom, and I tell you what a shitty father you have been..."

I was screaming at him at the top of my lungs.

Dad was like a balloon out of air. He just sat there looking down, stunned.

After I finally calmed down from screaming, I started to feel bad for him because he really looked like a sad old man.

So I said, "Dad, that's all bygones, let's not talk about it anymore. The main thing right now is to get you home. You have to go home. I can't take care of you Dad. We have to get you home."

And Dad said, "I know! But I'm too weak, I can't fly."

"Alright! Dad, why don't we set a goal? Today is Monday. Let's plan on this coming Sunday that you'll be able to fly home. I don't know what else to do other than let's both chant about it" (Dad had already started to practice Buddhism with me).

The next day, Dad was looking a little better and he could actually get out of the bed and walk around a little. The following day he was even better... Friday night, after I finished everything, I came home and found Dad was cheerful to see me because he cooked a couple of dishes for me.

'My Dad cooked for me?'

I was so touched and tried so hard to hold my tears I couldn't even swallow.

Sunday! I got up extra early and Dad was already up. I asked him, "Dad, what do you feel like for breakfast, I'll go get it for you."

He said, "Why don't we go out and have some dim sum. We never go out together."

"You're sure you are ok?"

"Yeah, I feel fine!"

"Alright then, let's go."

So I took him to Chinatown to this big old restaurant. Dad had a natural way of being his old self - a big pain in the ass. He was driving the waiter nuts. I just laughed.

Food was good and the atmosphere was even better. I had never been alone with my Dad in a restaurant. We talked and talked, having a great time.

So, it was time to go to the airport. I took Karlo (my horn repair man) along because it would be so much easier to have him park the car so Dad didn't have to walk too far.

We got to China Airlines and Dad just kept walking toward the counter. I called him,

"Dad, the line is over here. We have to stand in line."

But he just kept walking. I followed him and I saw Dad motion to one of the guys behind the counter to come to him. He said, "My name is so and so, the president of this airline is a dear friend of mine and I'd like to have a better seat," then he showed the guy his ticket.

The guy looked at us for a second and said, "Well, excuse me for a minute" and he went to the back office.

A few minutes later, another guy came out and said to Dad, "Yes sir, how can I help you?" Dad told him the same thing.

The guy said, "Ok, let me see what I can do." Then he walked back to the office again.

We waited for a while. The second guy came out and said, "Well Mr. Chen, just so happens, the pilot of this flight is the President's son and he said he knows you very well. So we're going to upgrade you to Dynasty Class and the wheelchair will be here in just a few minutes!"

Five minutes later I was wheeling Dad to the gate. As a matter of fact, they actually let me wheel Dad on board. There was nobody on that 747, not even the flight attendants. I sat Dad down in this big seat and made sure he was comfortable. Still, we were the only people on the plane.

Well, it was time to say goodbye. Dad held my hand tight and said, "Thank you! Thank you for everything. I never knew I have a wonderful son!"

Karlo was waiting for me outside. I drove. We didn't say a word to each other. Finally Karlo spoke with that Czech accent,

"He is kind of a pain in the ass, huh!"

I had this grin on my face.

Three days later, I got a phone call. This lady on the phone couldn't speak English at all. It took me a minute to find out that she was my Dad's wife calling me from Taiwan. She said Dad wanted her to call and let me know he got in ok and they took him straight to the hospital.

Two weeks later, Mom called and told me Dad died in the hospital.

Maury died in 1987. My dad died in 1988. I lost two fathers within one year.

Harry "Sweets" Edison

Lou Levy, Me and Horace Silver

XI: MY FIRST VISIT HOME

Grace called one day and asked me if I would like to go home to celebrate Mom's 70th birthday with everybody. I hadn't been home ever since I left which was 18 years ago. So I said, "Yes!"

Can't describe my feelings sitting in LAX waiting for the flight to go back home after all these years. It seemed so unreal! I always love flying, especially long flights. I have no problem sleeping on the plane and I love movies. Nothing like making myself comfortable, watching all the new movies and have people bring me food and drinks whenever I want.

When we were asked to fill out the declaration form, at the very bottom, I did see this one line of small print in red that says, "Any narcotics, death penalty".

You should have seen me with tears in my eyes watching the 747 landing at Tao Yuan Airport. 18 years! I finally had both my feet on home soil. I can't explain how I felt. Again, it seemed so unreal.

Brother Steve came to pick me up and it was drizzling. Of course, May is the rainy season in Taiwan. That hasn't changed in 18 years. It used to be my favorite season.

I'm really not used to seeing so many motorcycles riding so close to us. I was stepping on the brakes from time to time forgetting that I wasn't even driving.

Mom had no idea about my coming home. We rang the doorbell, and Mom opened the door. She knew Steve was coming over and she thought I was one of Steve's friends since Steve always brought friends over to enjoy Mom's cooking. So as soon as she opened the door she turned around and walked back into the living room. Everybody was there, Grace, Charlie, and Tina. Finally, Steve had to say to Mom,

"Mom, somebody is here to see you."

Mom turned around and looked at me. Suddenly she was confused! She didn't know who I was. I saw that confused look on her face. I had to tell her,

"Mom, it's me, little dragon. I'm home to celebrate your birthday."

Mom suddenly recognized me, and she burst into tears (so did I and everybody else). I hugged her until she finally started to smile. Immediately she asked me if I was hungry. I remember she cooked some homemade Wong Tong soup for me. I was so excited I couldn't even taste the food.

It's not like I hadn't seen her in 18 years. She'd been coming to the States almost every year to visit. But this was the first time I came home to visit her. She was Soooo happy.

I slept on the couch every night for the rest of the trip but I slept so well. Mom told me she couldn't sleep worth a shit (she didn't say it like that) over the excitement and I could totally understand. She got up early next morning and took me to have Chinese breakfast. I hadn't had traditional Chinese breakfast for so long and it was so good, even better than I remembered. The thin crust bread was so crispy and the lightly salted soymilk was so thick and tasty. My mouth is watering right now just thinking about it. I don't know how to fully describe Chinese breakfast, but let me try:

Basically there's a deep fried flour stick and you wrap it with a thin crust flaky flour jacket, then you dip them in soymilk (which can be either sweet, salty or a blend). You can drop an egg in it if you want to. There's another dish called egg-scallion pancake with soy paste. Yum! There's also a rice dish made of sticky rice wrap with crushed deep fried flour stick, shredded dried pork, and pickled radish, kind of like a bigger version of Japanese sushi. It is so delicious. There are some Chinese restaurants here in LA that serve Chinese breakfast, but it's just not the same. As a matter of fact, they are pretty sad!

After breakfast, we went to the traditional market to buy all kinds of my favorite tropical fruits. Guava has always been my very favorite. Something about the soil, water and weather in Taiwan, Lee Chee, Star Fruit, even Pineapple and Papaya are so sweet and flavorful. There are fruits like Long-En and Liam-Mu that you've never even heard of. Needless to say you can't find them in the States.

Every night, I was taken out to different restaurants. God! You want to talk about good Chinese food. Man, I can make a long list starting from breakfast. All the pictures I took, they are all foods!

Mom's birthday party was such a hit. Grace and Charlie picked this big restaurant right next to Mom's apartment. They booked a room big enough for 8 big round tables. They invited all of Mom's old friends and they even prepared one table for all my old buddies (did I mention that my brothers and sisters are the most considerate people that I'd ever known?). Mom was so happy! She was dressed in a long, red silk gown. She looked so elegant and beautiful.

HARRY KIM

One day I was hanging out with a couple of my old buddies. I made a call back to Mom's just to check in to see when I needed to come home (again, cellular phone was nowhere in the picture). Grace told me that Harry Kim called.

"Harry Kim?"

How the hell did Harry know where to find me? (I knew Harry from Rudy Regalado. Harry's been playing trumpet with Rudy's salsa band "Chevere" for years).

Later on I found out that Harry was touring with Phil Collins as a trumpeter and music director and they were doing a concert in Taipei. Knowing that I'm from Taiwan, he called the store to see if any of my family would like to go to the concert (how sweet). Rudy was in the store when Harry called. He told Harry that I was in Taiwan and gave him Mom's phone number, and, just so happened that Grace answered the phone (Mom couldn't speak English). So Harry was able to leave a message for me that he was staying at the Jin-Hua hotel.

When I called, the minute Harry picked up the phone, he said,

"Stein on Vine!"

That was just precious!

What were the odds that we ran into each other in Taiwan on my first home visit in 18 years? Anyway, I couldn't make the concert because I had to go to Stan Lai's to have dinner with his family. I had no idea Stan and his wife Nai-Chu can cook their asses off! Last time I saw them, we all just got out of college, nobody knew shit about cooking, and now they are parents of two grown girls and one of them is a mother herself. Unbelievable! Last time I saw her (Stephanie), she was just a baby sound asleep in her crib.

Harry left 10 tickets at will-call for my family and he told me to make sure to come to the party in the hotel after the concert, because that was their very last gig of the whole tour and they were

having a big party afterwards. He wanted to surprise the rest of the guys by me showing up.
I made the party!

All the guys were screaming when they saw me, Dan Fernaro, Arturo Velasco, Nathen East and Andrew Woolfolk.

"Jesus! Gary, what the hell are you doing here?"

I said, "What do you mean what am I doing here? I live here!"

We had so much fun!!!

From L to R: Nathan East, Arturo Velasco, Harry Kim, Phil Collins, Me and Andrew Woolfolk at Jin-hua Hoel in Taipei

*****

Stan Lai

*To Dear Gary
For all the great times we had
Stan Lai
2014*

Stan and I grew up together in college, he was an English major and I was in business administration. He's probably one of the most creative and talented people that I've ever met in Taiwan. He always came up with some new ideas about what we should play or what kind of showcase we should put on just for the fun of it, and it worked beautifully most of the time.

I came to study Jazz in Boston and Stan went to UC Berkeley and got his doctorate in drama at age 27. Later, Stan went back to Taiwan to pursue his career. We never thought about the future when we were in college (at least I didn't), but look at us now. I'm here carrying on the Stein on Vine tradition and Stan turned out to be the most famous playwright and stage director in the Chinese-speaking world, meaning Taiwan, China, Hong Kong, Singapore and of course the Chinese in America.

We lost contact with each other after a brief get-together in 1980. I seldom watched any Chinese news or TV programs before cable was available. So I had no idea what Stan had been doing. But, Stan found me, and this is what he said:

'I was in LA touring my most famous work "Secret Love in Peach Blossom Land" in 1991. I hadn't seen Gary in years, and didn't know if the number I had was right. I actually looked up the yellow pages and saw the number hadn't changed. I called.

"Stein-on-Vine." I recognized Gary voice.

"Gary?"

"Yeah."

"It's Stan." (Long pause)

"Stan who?"

"Shit, man, it's Stan Lai."

Little did I know he would not expect a call from someone named Stan unless it was Stan Getz and I sure as hell didn't sound like Stan Getz.

Here are a couple of stories Stan told me:

1) 1994, my group was in LA touring a play called "Red Sky". I asked my actors to check out Stein-on-Vine, which was in my opinion (and I told them this frankly) the only place in LA where you were gonna find some culture! So they went, and Gary, you showed them the store, your collection of rare instruments, and your LA Riot guns. They had a great time. You know, some of those guys, Lee Li-chun and Chin Shi-chieh specifically, are two of the greatest actors on the Chinese language stage. I get a kick out of just what a fantastic place Stein-on-Vine is, a meeting place of everything! The same place the greatest

Chinese actors were standing in, is the same place all the greatest jazz musicians were standing.

After they went to the store, they went to have dinner at the newly opened Chuan-chu-de, the famous Beijing Peking Duck restaurant run by Chinese government people who decided to take their business to America. The waiter practically threw menus at them. Then they asked, in Chinese,

"What's good?"

You know what the guy said? "Nothing's good here."

They thought they heard wrong, so they asked, "What would you recommend?" and the guy said,

"Sirs, I urge you not to eat here. Everything's shitty here."

What would you do? They stood up, thanked him, and left. Strange!

(I'd actually been to that restaurant 3 times. The first time was great - best Peking duck I've ever had. The second time wasn't so good and the third time was terrible.)

2) Forgot what year, you took me to Catalina's (old place) to hear Cedar Walton. But you know who was playing with him as the headliner? Charles Lloyd. I had just started discovering what a great tenor player he was, and was collecting his CDs, and there he was. I hadn't listened to live jazz in years, so I wasn't sure if I was hearing right or if I was too excited or what, but it sounded so incredible and inspired what they played that night. I thought it was truly an amazing performance. It was good of you to reaffirm that it was great, so I could be sure. Then you introduced me to them. It was a great honor, and even a greater pleasure to see that when Cedar Walton shook hands with me, I could feel he took you as family, as a true

friend. For me, that evening also reaffirmed my faith in jazz, that there were practitioners who still shared the secret that is at the heart of this improvised art form.

(I remember that night, I remember well. It was one of the most incredible magical evenings that I've ever experienced - Cedar, Charles Lloyd, Billy Higgins, and Bob Hurst.

The magic started when they played Freddie Hubbard's tune "Little Sunflower". Suddenly, the band started to jell, the atmosphere changed and the audience began to respond to the groove, and then things just happened one after another. The guys were listening to each other and feeding ideas to one another. Everybody PLAYED! As a musician, there's nothing like you know you're sounding good and people are listening and digging it. What a night that was. I was so happy that Stan was able to be there and share that memorable evening with me.)

My Wife Michelle

XII: MY WIFE

A dear friend called one day from Taiwan and he wanted me to do him a favor.

He said, "Gary, a good friend of mine, Michelle, is coming to LA and she hates LA. I was wondering if you could take her out for me. Maybe take her to some good restaurants and maybe even some Jazz."

I told him, "Well, for you to call me knowing that I hate to entertain, this must be somebody special. Alright, I'll take care of her."

A few days passed and I totally forgot about it. Until one day at work I suddenly remembered that I needed to call and I did. She sounded very nice on the phone. I went to pick her up in Arcadia. She was nothing like what I expected even though I wasn't expecting anything if that makes any sense.

Instead of taking her to Lawry's roast beef like my friend had suggested, I took her to a little Italian joint on 3rd St. because she really didn't look like a heavy meat eater. We talked a lot. No, I talked a lot because this was the first Chinese girl that I could really talk to. She was born in Taiwan but grew up in New York. That's why she is so hip. She is a fashion designer and you can tell from the way she dressed.

Benny Green trio was playing at Catalina's that night. First time I saw Benny, he was with Blakey and I was very impressed by the way this young piano player Bennie Green swings. So, we went to see Benny. He had Christian McBride on bass and Carl Allen on drums. Those three kids were something else, they really played! I can tell that she was having a good time. Benny was so happy to see me because we hadn't seen each other for a while. Last time I saw him, he was using my back room to practice a couple of years ago.

Lynn once told me, "When you definitely know that you don't want to live the rest of your life without that person, that's when you know you are ready to get married."

My wife didn't really want to get married. She just wanted to shack together (pretty hip for a Chinese woman). But I told her, "Well, I am 46 years old. Say if I have another 30 years to live, I will have to spend about 10 years sleeping, give or take another 5 years for the times that we can't be together, that only leaves us maybe 15 years or so that we can actually be together. That's not really that much time left, is it?"

We dated a few more times. 3 months later, she gave up her designing career in Taiwan and became my wife.

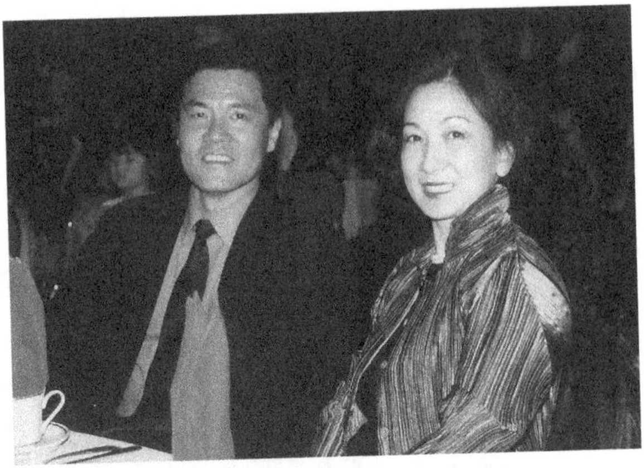

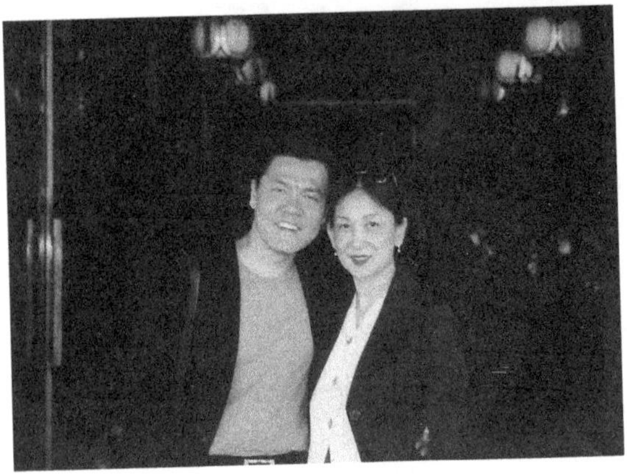

XIII: MOM'S DEATH

May 5th, 2009. Grace called around midnight last night from Taiwan. She told me Mom just died in her sleep at age 86.

Mom had diabetes for a long time. It wasn't all that bad until the last year or so.

Every year, for the past 30 some years Mom would make a trip to the US to visit us. She would start out from Tina's in San Jose then Vegas to visit Grace, then me. Mom actually loved visiting us. She loved the weather and the quietness here in the States. Taipei is a very noisy city. You can hear cars blowing their horns and motorcycles wailing by all night long.

My last visit with her was about five months ago. She looked so good considering she just came out of an angioplasty. Her one main vessel was opened up but the other two didn't even budge. She was ok living on one for a while. I remember she invited everybody to a big seafood restaurant for buffet. She looked so happy watching everybody pigging out and going back for more. You can't even imagine how much fresh seafood they had. Mom loved to treat. She loved to see people having a good time. I took a lot of pictures of her. She looked so good and so happy. Never thought that those were the last pictures I would ever take of her.

Later on, her toes started to bother her. It had gotten worse and worse and it became extremely painful. I never heard Mom complain about pain. She had the most incredible tolerance for pain. For her to occasionally scream out of pain, it had to be unbearable. It kills me when every time I'd call her she didn't want me to hear her suffer, and not want to talk to me. I just don't understand why such a wonderful human being like Mom had to suffer like that before her life ended. Even before I had a chance to tell her that I'm coming home to see her, she said it first,
"Don't come home to see me. Listen! Both of your brothers are standing right next to me crying, because they can't do anything to help. What can you do if you were here? You would be just like them standing here watching me suffer. What's the point? Promise me you're not coming home. I don't want you to see me like this. I know you are busy with your work. For you to come here is a total waste and meaningless!"

It was not a waste and meaningless for me but I wasn't about to argue. I said it all along: Mom was the most considerate person that I've ever known. Even now, she's still looking out for me. My only regret was I never made it home to be with her for Chinese New Years. 30 some years, I always thought I'd surprise her one-day by showing up at her doorway on Chinese New Years Eve. Well...

I couldn't stop crying every time I see Mom's picture which she had taken at a local photo shop. Grace found out by going to the same place to have Mom's pictures developed. The owner told Grace that Mom had a picture taken for the funeral. Grace found it with Mom's ID. So, Mom knew she was dying and went to have her picture taken and left the negative for Grace to find. That just killed me (Grace always said Mom was the smartest person). The picture has a purple background (Mom's favorite color) and she looked so beautiful and peaceful.

The funeral was beautiful. Fresh flowers that people sent covered the whole hall. All of Mom's dear friends were there. Mom's got a few "ma-gian" buddies who had been playing together for a long long time. Quite a few of them I hadn't seen for over 40 years, but I recognized them right away. Brother Charlie was a two star general in the Air Force before he retired, so all the chief commanders of the Air Force, Navy and Army showed and paid their respects to Mom. We didn't expect too many people to come because Charlie and Grace decided not to tell too many people about Mom's death. But somehow the word got out. So many people showed. The hall wasn't that big so people had to wait in line outside for their turn to come in. The MC kept getting notes from people and he just kept announcing people's titles and names. It seemed like it would never end.

It is so hard for all of us to accept Mom's death. Grace had been flying back and forth from the US to take care of Mom and so did Tina. Charlie purposely bought a condo right next to Mom. He used to go see her at least two, three times a day. Steve bought Mom a big electric massage chair. Charlie and Grace had done so much for Mom. I told Charlie I don't know how to thank him. He always said,

"Don't say that. I am right here. Of course I'd take care of Mom."

Grace told Mom that she wants to be her daughter again next life. Steve, Tina, and I just kept crying.

I have never met anybody as strong as Mom. She was the perfect example of a person with principle. She'd rather be poor than without principle. I can just hear her saying,

"If it's not yours, it will never be yours. If it is yours, it's always gonna be yours."

I remember a dear friend of mine Pam once asked me, "Gary, how did your Mom raise you?"

I said, "What do you mean?"

She said, "Well, I just want my son to treat me the way you treat your Mom."

That statement says it all.

I remember Mom spent 3 months in the US with me in 1989 and we celebrated Mother's Day together. I started the day by taking her for Chinese breakfast in Monterey Park early in the morning, then I took her shopping. Later we had lunch at Chan Dara (Thai restaurant in Hollywood). The waitress gave Mom a carnation for Mother's day and that made Mom so happy. Then I took her to visit Viola Stein which I did every Sunday. And after that I took her for dinner at Linda's.

What a wonderful place Linda's was. Linda Keegan had that place for over 4 years. It was a good restaurant with jazz on Melrose. She had different piano players every night with different bass players. Linda and Pinky Winters were the singers. Linda has an unusual style of singing and Pinky sings good ballads. There were always musicians and singers sitting in. It was a great hang!

Too bad Linda got herself in trouble with the IRS and she finally had to give it up. We had 4 years of good times. Lou Levy, Jimmy Rowles, Tom Garvin, Wig (Gerald Wiggins) and George Gaffney (all dead) were the regular piano players. And the bass players were: John Heard, Eric Von Essen, Putter Smith, Andy Simpkins, and whoever else was available.

Lou and Pinky were playing that night. Mom didn't know anything about Jazz, but she told me she liked the way Lou played. And after that, we went to The Loa (Ray Brown's jazz club in Santa Monica) to see Sweets Edison. Right after Sweets finished the first set, he came off the stage to give me a big hug, and I introduced him to Mom. Sweets said to me,

"Gary, tell your mom, she's a handsome lady, and she raised good children".

We had so much fun that day and Mom remembered every little thing we did till the day she died. I can just hear her saying,

"Remember that mother's day I spent with you in the States, and they gave me a carnation in that restaurant? And you took me to all those fun places? That was the best Mother's Day I'd ever had."

It brings tears to my eyes every time I think of that. That was the most precious 3 months I'd ever spent with her.

When Phil Collins was playing at the Great Western Forum, Harry Kim invited me to the concert. I took Mom along. I'm sure she was the oldest person in the whole joint. I think she was in her mid-70's. Anyway, Mom actually enjoyed it. She told me she liked the way Phil played the drums but she didn't mention anything about his singing. I told you, Mom's got great ears. But the next day she woke up with a terrible headache. It was way too loud for her.

Cedar Walton was playing at the old Catalina's one night. I took Mom to see him. They already met at the house when I had a dinner party earlier. When David Williams was taking a bass solo, Mom leaned over and said to me,

"He plays better than you, huh!"

I said, "Gee, thanks Mom!"

Brother Charlie gathered enough courage to ask Mom if she minded that we'd put her ashes right next to Dad's. Mom said,

"It's ok. After all he was my only man."

Can you imagine, one man for her whole life? It just don't work that way anymore.

I was the one who picked up Mom's remains after they cremated her and put them in a container. We took it all the way to the mountain where Dad was. I put Mom right next to Dad. I didn't know what to feel and felt kind of numb. But I do know one thing, Mom was such a strong woman, when she decided something, no one, I mean, NO ONE can change her mind! Years after the divorce, Dad was begging Mom to take him back. Well, you know the answer.

Don't really have much to say about my Dad except I feel deeply sorry for him. He did so much wrong to Mom and hurt her so. But, he did give her 5 wonderful children. The real sad thing is he never enjoyed any family love from any of his 5 children. None of us hates him, we just feel sorry for him.

XIV: CONCLUSION

Stan Lai brought the play "The Village" to LA in January 2011. He left 4 front seat tickets for me. I took my wife, her sister and her daughter to the Pasadena Civic Auditorium to check out the play. The play is about the lives of all the military families (Air Force, Navy and Army). When they first came to Taiwan with Chiang Kai-shek in 1949, they were supplied with over 100 so-called "Villages" to live in. I never lived in the real "Village" because Dad was working for the President so we were living in the "Presidential Village" (not the military ones). But at the Air Force Grade School I went to, almost every kid was from "The Village". So I was very familiar with the life style and the people of the Villages. I was hanging out in the Village almost every day.

Stan did a great job. The stories were so real, and the acting of every one was excellent. Every scene reminds me of what was going on in my childhood. Things that all the families had to deal with, the trouble that all the kids got themselves into, the music we were listening to, the slang we were using... a couple of times I was so touched I got a little misty.

Watching the play, remembering how I grew up, listening to the familiar songs of the late 50's and early 60's ('The End of The World', 'Que Sera Sera' ---- " some of them I hated as a child), all those late nights that I spent by myself woodshedding, trying to figure out tunes - melodies, chord changes and lyrics.

Look at me now, sitting in Stein on Vine listening to Hank Mobley's "Roll Call", looking at my Wall of Fame, all my dear friends who had made a mark for themselves in the world of Jazz. They are indeed American Treasures.

WOW, WHAT A TRIP!

Too bad I never kept a journal recording everything that happened in the store, but I pretty much covered most of what I can remember from the last 30 some years at Stein on Vine.

I consider myself one of the luckiest persons on this planet. I get to do what I like to do and I'm good at it. Every day is an adventure. I don't know who's coming in, who's gonna make my life a little different. I love the sign right behind me that says,

"Everyone brings joy to this room, some by entering, some by leaving".

And the other one that says,

"The only thing in life we have control of is our attitude."

Ain't that the truth?

The store keeps going like Jazz keeps going in this land of American Art. I'm doing my part trying to preserve this internationally recognized art form. Jazz really should be introduced to and learned by all Americans! It is the only American Art.

Come to think of it, had I gone back to Taiwan as I originally planned, I probably would have made a name for myself, and maybe a lot more money. But to exchange all the love and true friendship that I've earned from all my dear friends along with Maury, Stan Getz, Ray Brown, Al McKibbon, Lou Levy, Freddie Hubbard, Cedar, Wayne Shorter… and all the incredibly fun things that I have experienced through the last 30 some years?

HELL NO!!!

Gary Chen

May 2, 2013

Acknowledgements

Special thanks to:

My wife Michelle - My utmost gratitude to you for sacrificing your own career, putting up with me and supporting me every step of the way. Without you, everything is meaningless.

My family – My dearest Mom, you made me the way I am. Grace, Charlie, Steve and Tina, you guys are the most wonderful siblings that anybody could ever dream of. The qualities and values you inherited from Mom make me want to cry. I am so blessed!

Maury Stein – What can I say, Maury? You're the one who gave me this opportunity to enjoy this most incredible ride. I thank you and miss you.

Bob Danziger – My book draft would have been still in my folder if it weren't for you. Thank you for everything - your encouragement, your appreciation for the store, your hours and hours of work and support.

Richard Ratner – Your editing made me a better writer. I owe you one! Thank you for allowing me to sit on my ass for so long.

Also to:

Stan Lai, Larry Rott, Oliver Holmes for being part of completing this book.

INDEX

3
3 Deuces 229

7
77 Sunset Strip 22

A
A Funny Thing Happened on the way to Energy Independence 76
A Time for Love 101
Abel, David 164
Adachi, Dr. 163
Adderley, Cannonball 36, 242, 243
Afro American root 238
Afro Cuban music 238
Afro-Cubans, The 168
Akiyoshi, Toshiko 61, 201
Alaska 161
Aleppo, Syria 156
Alfonse's 96, 105, 117, 118, 131
All of You 177
Allen, Carl 285
Allen, Steve 97
Almario, Justo 254
Alter, Dr. 210
Ammons, Gene 197
Amsterdam Philharmonic Orchestra 175
Anchors Aweigh 193
Anka, Paul 22
Arlen, Harold 25
Arlette 165
Armstrong, Louis 24, 91
Astaire, Fred 25
Atlas, Jim 116, 138

B
Babasin, Harry 116
Bach 43, 166
Bacharach, Burt 20, 67
Baker, Chet 99
Banister, John 116
Barnet, Charlie 113
Barron, Kenny 190
Basie, Count 24, 44, 90, 115, 175, 208, 232
Battle Circle 177
Beatles 23, 35
Beatty, Warren 77
Bechet, Sidney 173
Bellson, Louie 103, 201, 209
Bengie 78, 125, 134
Bennett, Max 212, 228
Benson, George 92
Berghofer, Chuck 96, 153
Bergman, Alan 67
Berklee 42, 43, 44, 47, 192
Berklee School of Music 42
Berle, Milton 56
Berlin, Irving 25
Berry, Bill 78, 89, 103, 170, 171
Beverly Bistro 86
Beverly Hills 54, 56, 68, 76, 81, 83, 86, 89, 90, 114, 125
Beverly Hilton 226
Birdland 256
Birth of the Cool 36, 102, 107
Bitches Brew 36
Black and Blue 232
Blakey, Art 46, 107, 256, 263
Blazing Saddles 85
Blood Count 171
Bob Burns 83
Bock To Bock 203
Bolivia 264
Bonanza 76
BOSTON 42
Boston Pops 42, 188, 208
Boylston Street 46
Brashear, Oscar 198
Brecker Brothers' 262
Brecker, Michael 262
Brecker, Randy 262
Bregman, Buddy 113
Bridgewater, Dee Dee 262

Brookmeyer, Bob 179
Brooks, Mel 85
Brother to Brother by The Clayton
    Brothers 176
Brown, Clifford 83, 202, 205
Brown, Les 110
Brown, Ray 25, 46, 51, 78, 107, 145,
    154, 155, 156, 157, 158, 159, 163,
    165, 175, 208, 210, 213, 218, 229,
    235, 264, 293, 296
Brown's deli 236
Buddhism 136, 188, 206, 257, 271
Buddhist 127, 206
Budwig, Monty 57, 64, 165, 179
Buffet 79
Bull Camp 29
Burns, George 117
Burrell, Kenny 46
Burton, Gary 46
Bushkin, Joe 90, 91, 114, 131
Byers, Billy 110

C

Cachao, Israel Lopez 167
Campbell, Mike 179
Candoli 78, 93, 94, 215, 216
Candoli, Conte 94, 221
Candoli, Pete 169, 171, 239
Canters 213
Capitol Records 24, 109
Caravana Cubana 246
Carmelo's .. 64, 81, 108, 109, 118, 125
Carmen McRae, ... 165
Carter, Benny 173
Carter, Ron 46, 198, 259
Catalina's 107, 111, 118, 157, 163,
    191, 241, 242, 265, 282, 285, 293
Cedar-Sinai 76, 91, 128
Chambers, Paul 242, 243
Chan Dara 242, 292
Chan, Jackie 11
Chaney's, ... 118
Charles, Ray 208
Charlie Chaplin Studio" 102
Charlie Parker Quintet 64
Chasen's 56
Chavez, Julio Cesar 250
Chen, Charlie 15, 19, 20, 21, 294

Chen, Dad 9, 10, 11, 12, 13, 14, 15, 17,
    18, 20, 26, 37, 269, 270, 271, 272,
    273, 294, 295
Chen, Gary 2
Chen, Grace 15, 19, 269, 275, 276,
    277, 278, 289, 291
Chen, Michelle 285
Chen, Mom 9, 10, 11, 12, 13, 14, 15,
    16, 17, 19, 20, 26, 27, 28, 37, 42,
    45, 86, 160, 225, 235, 255, 269,
    270, 273, 275, 276, 277, 278, 289,
    290, 291, 293, 294
Chen, Steve 15, 21, 275, 291
Chen,Tina 9, 13, 15, 269, 276, 289,
    291
Chen-Stein 101, 123
Cherico, Gene 145
Chevere 246, 247, 278
Chez Paree 58
Chiang Kai-shek .. 9, 12, 13, 14, 15, 27,
    29, 217, 295
Chicago 23, 53, 55, 58, 96, 120, 125,
    138, 145, 197, 198, 211, 212, 213,
    218, 221, 224, 230, 232, 237
Chin Shi-chieh 281
China ... 10, 12, 13, 14, 16, 29, 90, 189,
    217, 272, 280
Chinaman 22, 67, 85, 135, 189, 222,
    225, 233, 235
Chinatown 45, 135, 199, 219, 220,
    225, 271
Chinese food ... 45, 122, 174, 212, 233,
    247, 264, 277
Chinese fortuneteller 135
Chinese New Year 41, 136
Ching Dynasty 16
Chivas 73
Christmas 45, 49, 55, 104, 160
Clare Fischer's Salsa Picante 108
Clarke, Kenny 229
Clatworthy, Benn 264
Claxton, William 149
Clayton, John 158, 164, 165, 175, 176,
    244
Clint .... See Clint Eastwood
Clinton, President Bill 173
Clooney, Rosemary 109
Close Enough for Love 101
Cobb, Jimmy 242
Cock and Bull 66
Cohn, Al 89, 95, 114, 184

Cole, Nat King, ... 109, 178, 263
Coleman, Ira 233
COLLEGE 29
Collins, John 178
Collins, Phil 278, 293
Coltrane, John 36
Coltrane, John .36, 46, 47, 87, 99, 134, 185, 193, 194, 198, 206, 222, 242, 243, 258
Concerts by The Sea 203
Cooper, Bob 113, 216
Count Basie Orchestra 201
Cremona 242
Crosby, Bing 91
Crosby, Israel 237
Cuba 238
Curtis, Tony 91
Czech Republic 112

D

Danziger, Bob 76, 131
Darin, Bobby 24
David Williams 265
Davis, Jr, Sammy 208, 232
Davis, Miles 35, 36, 47, 56, 99, 102, 107, 134, 174, 198, 223, 229, 232, 238, 242, 243, 256, 257, 259
De Julio, Jim 145
De La Hoya, Oscar 250
De Rosa, Vince 122
Debussy 109
DeFranco, Buddy 98
DeMonico, Chuck 99
Denis, Matt 223
Descarga 168
Desifinado 183
Desmond, Paul 38, 221
Diamonds Are A Girl's Best Friend .55
Diorio, Joe 64
Dodgers 210, 248
Dolphin 190
Dolphy, Eric 205, 206
Don't Let Me Be Lonely Tonight ... 262
Donaldson, Lou 260
Donte's 78, 117, 118, 230, 231
Dorsey, Jimmy 83
Dorsey, Tommy .83, 90, 109, 110, 211
Down Beat 35
Dr. Adachi 159

Dr. White 85
Duke .... See Ellington, Duke
Duke, George 201

E

E.S.P 256
East, Nathen 279
Eastwood, Clint 57
Eckstine, Billy 237
Edelman, Steve 174
Edison, Harry Sweets ... 117, 119, 215, 293
Edwards, Blake 78
Edwards, Teddy 182, 218
Einstein, Albert 133
El Chicano 246
El Rey theatre 236
Eldridge, Roy 178, 213
Ella in Rome .... See
Ellington, Duke 23, 24, 44, 89, 90, 134, 155, 173, 241, 265
Emily 101
Emperor Fu-yi 10
End of The World, The 295
Ernest (my Chinese buddy) 135
Evans, Bill 36, 46, 47, 48, 106, 179, 223, 226, 227, 242, 243
EWI 112

F

Fairfax Blvd 132
Feldman, Victor 99
Ferguson, Maynard 61, 89, 99, 103, 139, 140, 169, 256
Ferguson, Sherman 46, 83
Fernaro, Dan 279
Fiddmont, Keith 118
Findley, Chuck 83, 139, 170
Fishelson, Stan 71
Fitzgerald, Ella 24, 36, 98, 109, 110, 163, 164, 211, 212, 213, 217, 218, 235
Fontana, Carl 150
Footprints 256, 259
For Musicians Only 229
Forever Funeral Home 131
Forum 248, 250, 293
Fournier, Vernell 237

French horn players, The 122
Fu Jen 28, 29, 49
Fu Jen University 28, 49
Fugitive, The 22
Fuller, Curtis 206, 264

G

Gaffney, George 292
Garcia, Andy 168
Garland, Judy 109
Garner, Errol 263
Garvin, Tom 292
Gary Chen .. 2, 94, 296, *See* Chen, Gary
Gelbart, Larry 84
Gelson's 126
Gender problem 210
Gershwin, George and Ira 25
Getz, Stan 36, 53, 54, 67, 76, 80, 89, 97, 102, 106, 108, 111, 115, 117, 131, 170, 181, 182, 183, 184, 188, 192, 208, 213, 223, 225, 257, 258, 259, 261, 281, 296
Giant Steps 77, 133, 134
Gibson Super-400 46
Gillespie, Dizzy 64, 91, 93, 94, 117, 155, 208, 213, 218, 229, 232, 259, 263
Girl from Ibanema, The 35, 191
Giuffre, Jimmy 138
God Bless America 133
Gohonzon 188
Gongyo 206
Gonzalves, Paul 90
Goodman, Benny ... 53, 90, 96, 97, 110, 114, 213
Gordon, Dexter 46, 47
Gornisht Helfin 189
Gottlieb, William P. 218, 229
Grammy 112, 168, 176, 177, 232, 247
Grandfather of Mambo 167
Granz, Norman 115, 184, 213
Green, Benny 163, 285
Guan, Ernest 49
Guerin, Johnny 98, 99
Guerrero, Pedro 250
Gunsmoke 22

H

Haggart, Bobby 160
Hall, Jim 36, 138, 221
Hamilton, Jeff 163, 176, 177
Hamilton, Scott 165
Hancock, Herbie 198
Hanna, Jake 61
Happy Birthday' 133
Harrell, Tom 262
Harris, Eddie 197, 198, 208
Harrison, George 98
Hawaii 65, 98, 162
Hawkins, Coleman 119, 205, 232, 240
Heard, John 51, 77, 137, 178, 200, 233, 293
Heath, Percy 242
Heaven Can Wait 77
Heavy Weather 257
Heifetz, Jascha 133
Hendrickson, Al 116
Herman, Woody 61, 71, 83, 89, 93, 95, 99, 105, 110, 114, 115, 165, 173, 184, 193, 209, 211, 224, *See* Woody Herman
Higgins, Billy 206, 217, 265, 283
High Anxiety 85
Highway Patrol 76
Hillside Cemetery 131
Hillside Mortuary 131
Hines, Earl 263
Hines, Earl "fatha" 173
Ho, Don 65
Holiday, Billie 102, 110, 115, 173, 178, 240
Holloway, Red 262
Hollywood ... 51, 56, 79, 109, 121, 131, 140, 146, 164, 168, 173, 176, 202, 216, 222, 236, 247, 292
Holocaust 189
Hop Singh's 118, 182
Horne, Lena 237
House of Blues 168
Hovic 49
How High the Moon 25
Hubbard, Freddie 51, 77, 122, 202, 203, 256, 263, 283, 296
Huffstetter, Steve 170
Humphries, Roger 262
Hurst, Bob 283
Hutcherson, Bobby 206

I

I guess I'll Hang My Tears Out to Dry 55
I Stand Corrected 210
I'm Gonna Live Till I Die 176
Idea House, The 34
In A Little Spanish Town 80
Indiana University's School of Music 175
Inglewood, California 114
Ironside 22
It's a Great life 75
It's Been a Long Long Time 55

J

Jackson, Milt 241
Jacquet, Illionois 119
Jamaica Plain 44
Jamal, Ahmad 191, 201, 237
James, Harry 120, 158, 193
Japan 78, 156, 159, 161, 164, 208, 215, 217, 218
Japanese .. 12, 17, 26, 73, 78, 160, 164, 219, 276
Jazz 7, 11, 22, 24, 35, 36, 38, 46, 48, 54, 77, 83, 90, 101, 103, 106, 115, 116, 119, 121, 150, 164, 173, 174, 176, 177, 179, 184, 187, 197, 213, 235, 256, 259, 260, 261, 267, 280, 285, 293, 295, 296
Jazz Messengers 263
Jewish settlers 189
Jews ... 55, 85, 131, 162, 189, 211, 212
Jobim, Antonio Carlos 67
Johnson, J.J. 110
Johnson, Keith 141
Johnson, Plas 171, 224
Jolly, Pete 57
Jones, Elvin 103
Jones, Hank 111, 155, 213, 263
Jones, Philly Joe 119
Jones, Quincy 246
Jones, Shirley 126
Jones, Tom 23
Just In Time 55

K

Kahn, Sammy 67
Kamuka, Richie 99
Kansas City, Missouri 179
Karlo 185, 186, 271, 272
Katrina 37
Katzman, Lee 220
Keegan, Linda 292
Keezer, Geoff 107
Kelly, Gene 25, 193
Kenton, Stan 99, 103, 114
Kern, Jerome 25
Kessel, Barney 121, 165
Keystone Korner, San Francisco ... 190
Kim, Harry 278, 293
Kind of Blue 35, 36
King, BB 35
Kolstein, Samuel & Barrie 106
Konitz, Lee 230
Kramer, Hal 134, 189, 203

L

LA Coliseum 251
LA Phil 122, 247
Lady .... See Billie Holiday
Lai, Stan 33, 35, 36, 106, 278, 280, 281, 295
LaFaro, Scott 106
Land, Harold 205
Lang, Mike 57
Langer's deli 229
Last Emperor, The 10
Last Samurai, The 113
Laughlin 232
Laurel Canyon 81
Lawry's 285
Le Café 118
Leary, James 207
Lee Chee 277
Lee Li-chun 281
Lee, Bruce 30, 250
Lee, Peggy 25, 98, 109, 209
Leitham, Jennifer 209, 210
Leitham, John 121
Lennie Tristano 230
Leonard, Herman 149
Let It Snow, Let It Snow, Let It Snow 55

Lettermen, The 116
Levant, Oscar 25
Levey, Stan 229
Levy, Lou ...... 47, 51, 56, 57, 61, 77, 83, 92, 95, 96, 110, 115, 116, 131, 171, 172, 179, 184, 190, 192, 196, 211, 214, 215, 216, 217, 218, 219, 220, 221, 223, 225, 226, 227, 228, 233, 235, 239, 264, 292, 296, *See* Lou Levy
Liam-Mu 277
Light House all Stars 99
Lin, Keith 33
Linda's 292
Little House on the Prairie 75
Little Sunflower 283
Liu Rong-shen 10
Live in Berlin 36
Lloyd, Charles 282
Loa, The 118, 156, 174, 293
loch in kop 189
London 119, 184, 216
Long-En 277
Los Angeles Philharmonic 122, 176
Lovano, Joe 262
Lynn 63, 64, 65, 66, 67, 68, 69, 75, 85, 86, 104, 125, 126, 127, 129, 130, 131, 225, 286

M

M. K. Stein .... *See* Stein, Maury
Machito 168, 255
Maebe, Art 122
Maestro Galee 168
Magnusson, Bob 83
Malibu ... 185, 186, 188, 194, 234, 236
Mancini, Henry 57, 67
Mandel, Johnny 67, 101, 110, 193
Manne, Shelly 99, 103, 165
Mao 10, 12, 13, 217
Marquez, Sal 170, 196
Marsh, Warne 230
Martin D-35 38
Martin, Dean 109
Martinas, Nick 96
Mathis, Johnny 109
Maupin, Bennie 262
Maury .... *See* Stein, Maury
McBride, Christian 165, 262, 285

McCartney, Paul 209
McKibbon, Al 115, 155, 161, 231, 239, 247, 251, 296
Mcneely, Jim 182
McRae, Carmen 25, 165
Mehta, Zubin 122
Mel Brook's 85
Mel Lewis band 216
Menza, Don 102
Mercer, Johnny 23, 25
Mesa, Oscar 247
Meyer, Edgar 165
Mickman, Herb 105
Milan, Mike 145
Miller, Glenn 110
Miller, Mulgrew 233
Mingus, Charlie 243
Minton's Playhouse 237
Mission Impossible 22, 57
Mitchell, Blue 206
Mitchell, Joni 98
Mitchell, Red 105, 206
Mobley, Hank 295
Moisha .... *See* Maury Stein
Money tree 118
Mongolian BBQ 165
Monk, Thelonius ... 170, 208, 217, 218, 232, 237, 238, 260
Monk's "Straight no Chaser" 170
Monroe, Louisiana. 150
Monterey Park 122, 233, 292
Montgomery Brothers 203
Montgomery, Alabama 178
Montgomery, Wes 36
Monty Alexander Trio 175
Moore, Ralph 217
Morgan, Frank 179
Most, Abe 142
Motian, Paul 106
Mouzon, Alphonse 246
Mozart 109
Mr. Sheng 137
Mr. Stein 53
Mraz, George 111, 182
Mulligan, Gerry 107, 114, 209
Musicians' Union 76
Musso and Frank 222

N

Nai-Chu 278
Nash, Dick 218
National Medal of Arts 173
NCSB (North Country Street Band)
.... 33, 35
Nefertiti 256
New Orleans 37
New York .. 47, 49, 83, 89, 90, 95, 101,
   103, 106, 107, 109, 116, 145, 155,
   168, 173, 193, 195, 211, 216, 218,
   220, 229, 232, 235, 256, 257, 260,
   263, 266, 285
Newark Arts High School 256
Nica's Dream 260
Nichiren Buddhism 127
Nimitz 217, 230
Nixon 14, 218
nudist camp 51

O

Oh Look At Me Now 91
Orquesta Filarmonica de La Habana
.... 168

P

Pacific Ocean 194, 196
Palm Springs 68
Palo Alto 185
Paper Moon 35
Paris 147, 156, 179, 216
Parker, Charlie (Bird) 36, 64, 117,
   122, 155, 202, 212, 229, 276, 291
Party's Over, The 55
Pasadena Civic Auditorium 295
Pastorius, Jaco 256, 257
Paul Whiteman clarinet award 53
Pavarotti, Luciano 104
Pell, Dave 113
Pena, Ralph 138
People 55, 57, 190, 215, 223
Peppi 125, 134
Peter Gunn 171
Peterson, Oscar 201, 213, 263
Petrucciani, Michel 166
Pettiford, Oscar 193, 229
Phillips, Flip 211, 213
Pink Panther 171
Piscatello, Chuck 108
Poco Royal 248
Porter, Cole 20, 25
Porter, Nat King Cole 177
Powell, Bud 212
Professional Drum Shop 246
Puente, Tito 246

Q

Que Sera Sera' 295
Queen Latifah 176
Quemoy and Matsu 217

R

Rabbath, Francois 156
Ramano, Joe 217
Raney, Jimmy 182
Rat Race, The 91
Red Skelton Show 75, 76
Red Sky 281
Redondo Beach 203
Regalado, Rudy 210, 238, 239, 246,
   278
Rich, Buddy 68, 83, 103, 208, 213
Riddle, Nelson 98, 109, 110
Roach, Max 205, 229
Robins' Nest 119
Robinson, Smokey 126
Rodney, Red 64
Rogers and Hart 25
Rogers, Shorty 99, 196, 216
Rollins, Sonny 46, 201, 208
Ronstadt, Linda 109
Rose, David 75, 76
Rosolino, Frank 103, 150
Ross, Barney 53
Rowles, Jimmy 110, 116, 179, 218,
   292
Roy Hargrove Quintet 177
Rubinstein, Arthur 133
Ruggeri 242
Russian Ballet 174
Russian Revolution 189

S

Saint, The 22

Sanchez, Michito 254
Santa Barbara 91, 131, 227
Santa Monica and Doheny 130
Sassy .... *See* Sarah Vaughan
Satchmo 24
Saunders, Carl 170
Schifrin, Lalo 57
Schubert Theater 71
Schwarzenegger 259
Scott, Tom 99
Secret Love in Peach Blossom Land
.... 281
Segovia, Andres 36
Selden, Fred 112
Selmer 79, 113, 114, 208
Severinsen, Doc 209
Shadow of Your Smile, The 101
Shanghai Diamond Garden 85
Shank, Bud 113
Shearing, George ... 122, 209, 232, 237
Sheldon, Jack 103, 169, 171
Shelly's Manne-Hole 226
Sherman's cigarettes 73
Shew, Bobby 83
Shorter, Wayne 117, 198, 256, 257, 258, 259, 296
Shrine Auditorium 67
Shulman, Alan 109
Sigismonti, Henry 122, 202
Silver, Horace 107, 256, 260
Simpkins, Andy 145, 293
Simpkins, Kay 230
Sims, Zoot 89, 114, 115, 116, 184
Sinatra and Basie at the Sands 24
Sinatra, Frank 24, 25, 55, 56, 57, 98, 109, 110, 117, 145, 193, 208, 213, 214, 220, 232, 235
Sinatra, Nancy 153
Sister Sadie 260
Skip 68, 69
Smith, Keely 109
Smith. Putter 293
Some Skunk Funk 262
Song for My Father 260
Spivak, Charlie 109
Spokane 110
Sportsman's Lodge 170
Stainer, Jacob 233
Stan .... *See* Getz, Stan
Star Trek 112

Stein on Vine 7, 50, 52, 54, 71, 94, 129, 137, 154, 171, 223, 224, 278, 280, 295, 296
Stein, Maury ... 6, 51, 53, 60, 75, 78, 91, 121, 128, 161, 182, 183, 224
Stein, Mike 54, 96, 132
Stein, Viola .. 53, 65, 87, 125, 128, 130, 132, 134, 292
Stein-on-Vine 89, 281
Stern, Mike 46
Stevens, Connie .. 116, 117, *See* Connie Stevens
Stevens, Connie 116
Stewart, Slam 46
Stitt, Sonny 117
Stradivarius 146
Stratocaster 73
Stravinsky, Igor 168, 257
Strayhorn, Billy 171
Streisand, Barbara 57
Strollin 260
Styne, Jule 25, 55, 56, 59, 60, 96
Suicide is Painless (theme for M*A*S*H*) 101
Sullivan, Ed 23
Sullivan, Ira 64
Summers, Bob 170
Sunset Boulevard 147
Super sax 220

T

Tae Kuan Do 30
Tai Chong 29
TAIWAN .. 9, 10, 11, 12, 13, 14, 15, 21, 26, 27, 33, 35, 37, 38, 41, 42, 45, 49, 56, 76, 90, 95, 97, 116, 117, 134, 173, 212, 217, 256, 269, 273, 275, 277, 278, 280, 285, 286, 289, 295, 296
Take 5 .... 38, 44, 221
Tatum, Art 155, 178, 211, 240
Taylor, James 262
Teagarden, Jack 53, 182
Terminator 2 258
Thad Jones-Mel Lewis orchestra 89
Thomas, David Clayton 23
Thompson, Charles Phillip 119
Thompson, Don 201
Thompson, Lucky 205, 261

Thompson, Sir Charles............... 119
Three Coins In The Fountain 55
Time After Time..55
Tjader, Cal 201, 232
Tommy's Hamburger 222
Tonight Show, The.....................................92
Tormé, Mel........................ 25, 120, 209
Toshiko Akiyoshi.....................................61
Tumbao Para Los Congueros De Mi
  Vida... 232
Twilight Zone, The...................................22
Tyner, McCoy 46

U

Ugetsu 264
Universal Amphitheater............67, 168
Unkill him 59

V

Vanguard 47, 106, 220
Vaughan, Sarah 25, 211, 212, 230
Vegas 69, 150, 160, 221, 250, 251,
  255, 269, 289
Velasco, Arturo................................... 279
Velvet Fog, The 121
Venezuela 210, 246
Venice, California 175
Victor Hills 29
Village, The 295
Villa-Lobos, Heitor............................... 168
Vinegar, Leroy 116
Viola.............................. *See* Viola Stein
Von Essen, Eric........................... 179, 293
Von Karajan, Herbert 168

W

Waller, Fats 173
Walt Disney Concert Hall................... 262
Walton, Cedar 164, 206, 207, 217,
  233, 239, 256, 262, 263, 264, 265,
  266, 267, 282, 283, 293, 296
Wang, Leo 49
Warwick, Dionne 20
Watrous, Bill... 209

Watts, Ernie 150
Weather Report...................................256
Webster, Ben 110
Welk, Lawrence 23
Wells, Buck...53
Wendy and Me.....................................117
WGN Symphony Orchestra 53
When the Saints Go Marching In..... 76
Whopper 43
Wiggins, Gerald 292
Williams, Andy...................................... 23
Williams, Buster..................................206
Williams, David 217, 293
Williams, Joe 201
Williams, John B. 204
Williams, Paul 67
Williams, Tony......................... 198, 259
Williams. Joe 67
Willie "The Lion" Smith.....................173
Willophant..161
Wilmington, Delaware 83
Wilson, Nancy 201, 208
Winters, Pinky 292
With Every Breath I Take.................243
Wong Tong soup 276
Wood, Jimmy 119
Woolfolk, Andrew 279

Y

Yang Shiao-lo.. 11
Yeager, Bob 246
Year of Dragon 9
Yi Jing..135
Yiddish..189
Young Musicians Foundation Debut
  Orchestra..179
Young, Lester (Pres)..... 110, 115, 119,
  178, 213, 260, 263
Yugoslavia................................... 145, 148

Z

Zabo, Frank 170
Zappa, Frank... 98
Zawinul, Joe............. 246, 255, 256, 257